STUDENT MANUAL

Microsoft® Office Excel® 2010: Part 2 (Second Edition)

Microsoft® Office Excel® 2010: Part 2 (Second Edition)

Microsoft® Office Excel® 2010: Part 2 (Second Edition)

Part Number: 091019
Course Edition: 1.0

Acknowledgements

PROJECT TEAM

Author	Media Designer	Content Editor
Tim Barnosky	Alex Tong	Catherine M. Albano

Notices

DISCLAIMER

While Logical Operations, Inc. takes care to ensure the accuracy and quality of these materials, we cannot guarantee their accuracy, and all materials are provided without any warranty whatsoever, including, but not limited to, the implied warranties of merchantability or fitness for a particular purpose. The name used in the data files for this course is that of a fictitious company. Any resemblance to current or future companies is purely coincidental. We do not believe we have used anyone's name in creating this course, but if we have, please notify us and we will change the name in the next revision of the course. Logical Operations is an independent provider of integrated training solutions for individuals, businesses, educational institutions, and government agencies. Use of screenshots, photographs of another entity's products, or another entity's product name or service in this book is for editorial purposes only. No such use should be construed to imply sponsorship or endorsement of the book by, nor any affiliation of such entity with Logical Operations. This courseware may contain links to sites on the internet that are owned and operated by third parties (the "External Sites"). Logical Operations is not responsible for the availability of, or the content located on or through, any External Site. Please contact Logical Operations if you have any concerns regarding such links or External Sites.

TRADEMARK NOTICES

Microsoft® Office Excel® 2010: Part 2 (Second Edition)

About This Course

Whether you need to crunch numbers for sales, inventory, information technology, human resources, or other organizational purposes and departments, the ability to get the right information to the right people at the right time can create a powerful competitive advantage. After all, the world runs on data more than ever before and that's a trend not likely to change, or even slow down, any time soon. But with so much data available and being created on a nearly constant basis, the ability to make sense of that data becomes more critical and challenging with every passing day. You already know how to get Excel to perform simple calculations and how to modify your workbooks and worksheets to make them easier to read, interpret, and present to others. But Excel is capable of doing so much more. In order to gain a truly competitive edge, you need to be able to extract actionable organizational intelligence from your raw data. In other words, when you have questions about your data, you need to know how to get Excel to provide the answers for you. And that's exactly what this course aims to help you do.

This course builds upon the foundational knowledge presented in the *Microsoft® Office Excel® 2010: Part 1 (Second Edition)* course and will help start you down the road to creating advanced workbooks and worksheets that can help deepen your organizational intelligence. The ability to analyze massive amounts of data, extract actionable intelligence from it, and present that information to decision makers is the cornerstone of driving a successful organization that is able to compete at a high level.

This course covers Microsoft Office Specialist exam objectives to help students prepare for the Excel 2010 Exam and the Excel 2010 Expert Exam.

Course Description

Target Student

This course is designed for students who already have foundational knowledge and skills in Excel 2010 and who wish to begin taking advantage of some of the higher-level functionality in Excel to analyze and present data.

Course Prerequisites

To ensure success, students should have completed Logical Operations' *Microsoft® Office Excel® 2010: Part 1 (Second Edition)* or have the equivalent knowledge and experience.

Course Objectives

Upon successful completion of this course, you will be able to leverage the power of data analysis and presentation in order to make informed, intelligent organizational decisions.

You will:

- Customize the Excel environment.

- Create advanced formulas.
- Analyze data by using functions and conditional formatting.
- Organize and analyze datasets and tables.
- Visualize data by using basic charts.
- Analyze data by using PivotTables, slicers, and PivotCharts.

The LogicalCHOICE Home Screen

The LogicalCHOICE Home screen is your entry point to the LogicalCHOICE learning experience, of which this course manual is only one part. Visit the LogicalCHOICE Course screen both during and after class to make use of the world of support and instructional resources that make up the LogicalCHOICE experience.

Log-on and access information for your LogicalCHOICE environment will be provided with your class experience. On the LogicalCHOICE Home screen, you can access the LogicalCHOICE Course screens for your specific courses.

Each LogicalCHOICE Course screen will give you access to the following resources:

- eBook: an interactive electronic version of the printed book for your course.
- LearnTOs: brief animated components that enhance and extend the classroom learning experience.

Depending on the nature of your course and the choices of your learning provider, the LogicalCHOICE Course screen may also include access to elements such as:

- The interactive eBook.
- Social media resources that enable you to collaborate with others in the learning community using professional communications sites such as LinkedIn or microblogging tools such as Twitter.
- Checklists with useful post-class reference information.
- Any course files you will download.
- The course assessment.
- Notices from the LogicalCHOICE administrator.
- Virtual labs, for remote access to the technical environment for your course.
- Your personal whiteboard for sketches and notes.
- Newsletters and other communications from your learning provider.
- Mentoring services.
- A link to the website of your training provider.
- The LogicalCHOICE store.

Visit your LogicalCHOICE Home screen often to connect, communicate, and extend your learning experience!

How to Use This Book

As You Learn

This book is divided into lessons and topics, covering a subject or a set of related subjects. In most cases, lessons are arranged in order of increasing proficiency.

The results-oriented topics include relevant and supporting information you need to master the content. Each topic has various types of activities designed to enable you to practice the guidelines and procedures as well as to solidify your understanding of the informational material presented in the course. Procedures and guidelines are presented in a concise fashion along with activities and discussions. Information is provided for reference and reflection in such a way as to facilitate understanding and practice.

Data files for various activities as well as other supporting files for the course are available by download from the LogicalCHOICE Course screen. In addition to sample data for the course exercises, the course files may contain media components to enhance your learning and additional reference materials for use both during and after the course.

At the back of the book, you will find a glossary of the definitions of the terms and concepts used throughout the course. You will also find an index to assist in locating information within the instructional components of the book.

As You Review

Any method of instruction is only as effective as the time and effort you, the student, are willing to invest in it. In addition, some of the information that you learn in class may not be important to you immediately, but it may become important later. For this reason, we encourage you to spend some time reviewing the content of the course after your time in the classroom.

As a Reference

The organization and layout of this book make it an easy-to-use resource for future reference. Taking advantage of the glossary, index, and table of contents, you can use this book as a first source of definitions, background information, and summaries.

Course Icons

Watch throughout the material for these visual cues:

Icon	Description
	A **Note** provides additional information, guidance, or hints about a topic or task.
	A **Caution** helps make you aware of places where you need to be particularly careful with your actions, settings, or decisions so that you can be sure to get the desired results of an activity or task.
	LearnTO notes show you where an associated LearnTO is particularly relevant to the content. Access LearnTOs from your LogicalCHOICE Course screen.
	Checklists provide job aids you can use after class as a reference to performing skills back on the job. Access checklists from your LogicalCHOICE Course screen.
	Social notes remind you to check your LogicalCHOICE Course screen for opportunities to interact with the LogicalCHOICE community using social media.
	Notes Pages are intentionally left blank for you to write on.

1 | Customizing the Excel Environment

Lesson Time: 45 minutes

Lesson Objectives

In this lesson, you will customize the Excel environment. You will:

- Configure Excel options.
- Customize the ribbon and the **Quick Access Toolbar**.
- Enable Excel add-ins.

Lesson Introduction

As you are already familiar with Excel 2010, you are, no doubt, able to navigate your way around the Excel environment and locate the basic commands you frequently use. But not everyone uses Excel in the same way and, depending on what you use Excel for, you may use whole sets of commands regularly that other users barely touch. Wouldn't it be nice if you could configure the Excel environment to better suit your regular daily work flow? Or perhaps there are default settings within Excel that don't quite mesh with your needs, such as the default number of worksheets in a workbook or the default location for saving files. In addition, there are a number of supplemental applications and features that not everyone uses, so they don't automatically come activated. What if you're one of the users who has a need for these features?

Like the other Microsoft Office 2010 applications, Excel 2010 provides you with a wide variety of options when it comes to customizing your Excel experience. Knowing where to find these options and what they do will not only save you time and effort, but it can also help you craft an Excel environment that meshes with your preferred work flow.

TOPIC A

Configure Excel Options

Some of Excel's default settings and options have an easily observable effect on your overall Excel experience. Consider, for example, the number of worksheets included in a new workbook. Other settings, such as where Excel automatically saves files, are less obvious. Global system settings in Excel have a direct impact on your experience as a user. As so many people use Excel, and for vastly different purposes, it makes sense that configuring and changing these options and settings can have a significant impact on how efficiently Excel works for you.

Excel 2010 provides you with a vast array of options for tweaking the behind the scenes behavior of the application to suit nearly any organizational or specific user need. Knowing where to find these options, and what each of them do, will make it easy for you to quickly adjust Excel's default behavior whenever the need arises. This means that when you need to react to changes in your work environment, you can quickly configure Excel to work the way you need it to, when you need it.

The Excel Options Dialog Box

You can adjust and configure global Excel 2010 system settings by using the **Excel Options** dialog box. It is divided into a series of 10 tabs, each of which contains a set of related system settings options. You can access the **Excel Options** dialog box by selecting **File→Options**.

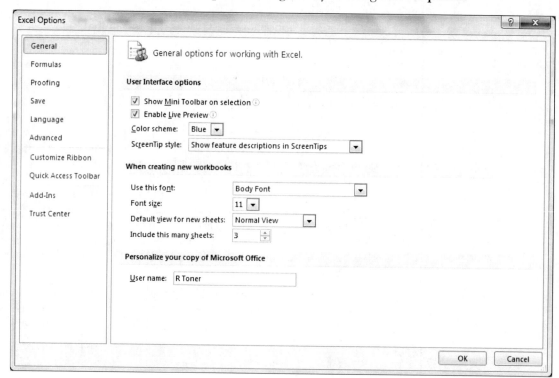

Figure 1-1: The Excel Options dialog box organizes Excel system settings into categories of related options.

The following table lists the types of system settings you will find on the various **Excel Options** dialog box tabs.

Excel Options Dialog Box Tab	Contains Options For
General	Adjusting the display of certain on-screen elements and toolbars, configuring the default settings for new workbooks, and personalizing Excel for a particular user.
Formulas	Configuring formula and error checking settings.
Proofing	Configuring AutoCorrect settings, configuring spelling check settings, and selecting the desired dictionary and language to use for proofing features.
Save	Selecting how often and to which directory Excel automatically saves workbook files, configuring offline editing settings, and preserving visual aspects of workbooks when opening workbook files in previous versions of Excel.
Language	Selecting the desired language for Excel editing features, for worksheet content, and for ScreenTips.
Advanced	Adjusting settings that directly affect many common Excel tasks.
Customize Ribbon	Customizing the tabs, groups, and commands on the ribbon.
Quick Access Toolbar	Customizing the **Quick Access Toolbar**.
Add-Ins	Installing, activating, and deactivating supplemental Excel features and functionality.
Trust Center	Configuring privacy and security settings that affect all Office 2010 applications.

General Options

The **General** tab in the **Excel Options** dialog box contains settings that affect some common Excel functionality.

General Tab Section	Contains Options For
User Interface options	Managing the display of the **Mini Toolbar**, the Live Preview feature, and ScreenTips, and for selecting the color scheme for the Excel application window.
When creating new workbooks	Managing default workbook settings, such as the font and font size, the view to which workbooks open, and the number of worksheets in a new blank workbook.
Personalize your copy of Microsoft Office	Modifying the default user name for all Office 2010 applications. This is the name that will be displayed as the author in Office file properties and in comments you add to documents.

Formulas Options

The **Formulas** tab in the **Excel Options** dialog box contains settings that affect how Excel works with and displays formulas and functions, and how error checking features behave.

Formulas Tab Section	Contains Options For
Calculation options	Configuring how Excel executes calculations in functions and formulas.

Formulas Tab Section	Contains Options For
Working with formulas	Toggling formula features on or off.
Error Checking	Toggling automatic error checking on or off, and changing the display of discovered errors.
Error checking rules	Toggling particular error-checking rules on or off.

Proofing Options

The **Proofing** tab in the **Excel Options** dialog box contains settings that affect how Excel performs AutoCorrect and spelling check functions.

Proofing Tab Section	Description
AutoCorrect options	Displays the **AutoCorrect Options** button, which opens the **AutoCorrect** dialog box.
When correcting spelling in Microsoft Office programs	Contains options for managing how Excel, and other Office applications, check for misspellings, for selecting the dictionary against which Excel checks word spellings, and for configuring particular language-specific options.

The AutoCorrect Dialog Box

The **AutoCorrect** dialog box contains options settings for managing how Excel automatically corrects spelling and other data entry issues as you type. It is divided into a series of four tabs that contain related settings options.

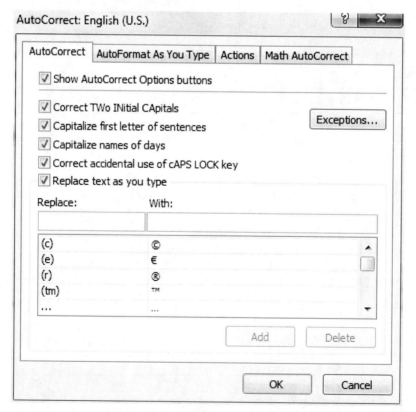

Figure 1-2: Use the AutoCorrect dialog box to configure how Excel corrects common misspellings.

AutoCorrect Dialog Box Tab	Contains Options For
AutoCorrect	Toggling specific AutoCorrect functionality on and off, such as whether or not Excel automatically capitalizes the first word of a sentence if you forget to. From here you can also manage how Excel automatically corrects common typing errors such as replacing "teh" with "the."
AutoFormat As You Type	Toggling particular AutoFormatting options on or off, such as whether or not Excel automatically formats URLs as hyperlinks.
Actions	Enabling or disabling additional automatic actions in context menus.
Math AutoCorrect	Managing how Excel automatically enters mathematical symbols based on keyboard input. For example, by default, if you type \pi, Excel replaces the text with the mathematical symbol π.

Save Options

The **Save** tab in the **Excel Options** dialog box contains settings that affect how and to which directory Excel saves workbook files.

Save Tab Section	Contains Options For
Save workbooks	Selecting the default file format that Excel saves workbooks in, for determining how often Excel automatically saves unsaved workbooks and for selecting the default directories for saving workbooks and for the AutoRecover feature.
AutoRecover Exceptions for	Enabling or disabling the AutoRecover feature for particular workbooks.
Offline editing options for document management server files	Selecting where Excel saves draft copies of workbook files that you check out of a Microsoft SharePoint site.
Preserve visual appearance of the workbook	Selecting or modifying the color palette that Excel will use when opening a workbook in a previous version of Excel.

Language Options

The **Language** tab in the **Excel Options** dialog box contains settings that affect which languages and dictionaries Excel references for a variety of purposes.

Language Tab Section	Contains Options For
Choose Editing Languages	Adding or removing languages Excel will use to check for spelling, grammar, and other language-related issues.
Choose Display and Help Languages	Selecting which language to use for the display of command and tab names, and within the Excel Help system.
Choose ScreenTip Language	Selecting the language Excel uses to display ScreenTips.

 Note: If you want to know more about adding languages in Excel, view the LearnTO **Add Languages to Microsoft Excel** presentation from the **LearnTO** tile on the LogicalCHOICE Course screen.

Advanced Options

The **Advanced** tab in the **Excel Options** dialog box contains settings that affect a wide array of commonly used Excel functionality. The options on the **Advanced** tab will likely have the greatest overall effect on your Excel user experience. The following table identifies the types of option settings you will find in some of the more commonly used sections of the **Advanced** tab.

Advanced Tab Section	Contains Options For
Editing options	Configuring navigation functionality, configuring data entry and editing settings, and toggling features such as AutoFill and AutoComplete on or off.
Cut, copy, and paste	Toggling various cut, copy, and paste functionality on or off.
Image Size and Quality	Determining whether or not Excel compresses graphical objects saved in workbooks, and for setting the default graphics resolution level.
Print	Enabling or disabling high quality mode, which determines the overall print quality of objects in worksheets.
Chart	Toggling the display of particular chart elements on or off.
Display	Managing the overall display of the Excel application window. From here you can set the number of recent documents that are displayed in the Backstage view, set the default unit of measurement for rulers, and toggle on or off the display of screen elements such as the **Formula Bar** and comment indicators.
Display options for this workbook	Managing the display of particular workbooks. From here you can toggle the display of user interface (UI) elements, such as scroll bars and worksheet tabs, on or off.
Display options for this worksheet	Managing the display of particular worksheets. From here you can toggle the view of column and row headers on or off, decide whether to display formulas or values in cells, toggle the view of gridlines on or off, and change the color of worksheet gridlines.
When calculating this workbook	Managing how Excel deals with links to other documents and how the display of numeric values affects the accuracy of calculations.
General	Managing a wide array of application-wide settings, such as whether or not sounds play when you make a mistake, and whether or not Excel prompts you to update links to external documents.

The Trust Center

The **Trust Center** tab provides you with access to information about Excel privacy and security policies along with commands for changing privacy and security settings. From here, you can follow a number of links to published security and privacy policies or open the **Trust Center** dialog box, which is where you can configure privacy and security settings. You can access the **Trust Center** dialog box by selecting the **Trust Center Settings** button.

 Note: Microsoft recommends consulting with your system administrator before changing **Trust Center** settings, as these may greatly increase or decrease your computer and network security.

The Trust Center Dialog Box

The **Trust Center** dialog box is divided into 11 tabs that provide you with access to groups of related security and privacy options.

Trust Center Tab	Allows You To
Trusted Publishers	Generate a list of publishers you trust. Outside content from trusted publishers is not subject to the same validation process as content from non-trusted publishers.
Trusted Locations	Specify folders on your computer in which you would like to store files from trusted publishers. Content from these folders is not subject to the same security and validation process as content from other folders.
Trusted Documents	Manage how Excel treats trusted documents. Once you've trusted a document, Excel no longer subjects it to the same security validation process. You should trust documents only if you truly trust the source of the documents.
Add-ins	Enable or disable the use of Excel add-ins and specify whether or not add-ins require security certificates.
ActiveX Settings	Manage how Excel interacts with files containing active content. Active content can contain malicious code.
Macro Settings	Enable or disable the use of macros and manage how Excel interacts with workbook files containing macros.
Protected View	Specify whether or not files from particular sources, such as the Internet or email attachments, will cause Excel to open them in the Protected view.
Message Bar	Specify whether or not Excel displays a warning whenever files containing active content are opened.
External Content	Manage security settings for dealing with external data sources and workbooks.
File Block Settings	Specify which file formats prompt Excel to open in Protected view.
Privacy Options	Toggle various privacy settings on or off and access the **Document Inspector**, which allows you to remove personal information, such as the author's name, from files before you share them with other users.

 Access the Checklist tile on your LogicalCHOICE course screen for reference information and job aids on **How to Configure Excel Options.**

ACTIVITY 1–1
Configuring Excel Options

Before You Begin

Excel 2010 is installed on your computer with the default settings and the Excel 2010 icon is pinned to the taskbar. Your computer is powered on and you are logged in, but Excel 2010 is not open.

Scenario

You are the Authors and Publications manager for Fuller and Ackerman Publishing, a mid-sized book publishing company headquartered in Greene City, Richland (RL). Fuller and Ackerman owns and operates offices and presses in several locations throughout the Unites States and around the world. Your company publishes books from a variety of genres, in a number of different languages, and has authors from around the world under contract.

As the Authors and Publications manager, your duties include tracking and managing the work that all authors produce for Fuller and Ackerman. Additionally, you are responsible for ensuring that royalties, advances, and bonuses are calculated accurately and paid in a timely manner. You use Microsoft Excel 2010 to keep track of authors, publications, and payments, and have a number of worksheets that you use for this purpose.

Although you generally like Excel's functionality and are comfortable with using many of its commands and features, there are a few changes you feel would help you work more efficiently and effectively. First, as you often find yourself removing at least one worksheet from each of your new workbooks, you decide to change the default number of worksheets for a new workbook from three to two. Also, as you have been working closely with a manager in one of Fuller and Ackerman's Canadian offices, you decide to add English (Canada) as an editing language. Finally, as you often use the same few workbooks frequently, you would like to not have to search through a lot of recently used workbooks to reopen the one you're looking for, so you decide to change how many recently used Excel workbooks are displayed in the Backstage view.

 Note: Activities may vary slightly if the software vendor has issued digital updates. Your instructor will notify you of any changes.

1. Open Excel 2010.

2. Set the default number of worksheets for a new, blank workbook to 2.
   a) Select **File→Options**.
   b) In the **Excel Options** dialog box, ensure that the **General** tab is selected.
   c) In the **When creating new workbooks** section, change the **Include this many sheets** setting from **3** to **2**.

3. Add English (Canada) as an editing language.
   a) Select the **Language** tab.
   b) In the **Choose Editing Languages** section, from the **[Add additional editing languages]** drop-down menu, select **English (Canada)**.
   c) Select **Add**.
   d) Verify that **English (Canada)** appears in the list of editing languages.

4. Change the number of recently used workbooks that are displayed in the Backstage view.
   a) Select the **Advanced** tab.

b) Scroll down to the **Display** section.

c) Set the value in the **Show this number of Recent Documents** spin box to **10**.

5. In the **Excel Options** dialog box, select **OK**.

6. In the **Microsoft Office 2010 Language Preferences Change** dialog box, select **OK**.

7. Close Excel 2010 so the new language preferences take effect, and then reopen Excel.

TOPIC B

Customize the Ribbon and the Quick Access Toolbar

As people in vastly different organizations use Excel for a wide range of purposes, it should come as no surprise that one of the biggest differences in the way people use Excel lies in which commands each person uses. If you work in the finance department for a large company, you likely use the commands on the **Formulas** tab more than someone who uses Excel as a project management tool. Or perhaps you're an engineer who uses the engineering and statistical functions more than math or LOOKUP functions. In this case, you may not like the fact that many of the functions you use are buried in secondary menus. In any case, regardless of why or how you use Excel, you want ready access to the commands you use most.

Fortunately, Excel 2010 provides you with a number of options for customizing the Excel user interface (UI), so the tools you use most are where you need them. Taking the time to understand what changes you can make and where to make them will provide you with the ability to craft the perfect Excel environment for your needs, even if those needs frequently change.

The Customize Ribbon Tab

One of the best ways to improve your overall Excel work flow is to customize the ribbon. The commands on the **Customize Ribbon** tab of the **Excel Options** dialog box allow you to modify the Excel ribbon so that all of the commands you use are right where you need them. You can rearrange the existing ribbon tabs and the groups within each tab. You can even move a group from one tab to another. Additionally, you can rename any tab or group, and you can remove any tab from the ribbon and any group from a tab.

Excel 2010 also allows you to create new custom tabs and groups if modifying the existing ones doesn't suit your needs. When you create a new custom tab, Excel automatically creates a group within that tab. You can add groups to existing tabs; custom groups enable you to add *or* remove commands.

Customizing the ribbon does have some limitations. You cannot rearrange the default commands on any of the existing groups and you cannot remove the default commands. And, although you can rename tabs and groups, you cannot rename any of the commands, whether they are in custom or existing groups.

Once you have customized the ribbon, you can export your modified ribbon as a file and import it on another computer that has Excel 2010 installed on it. In this way, you can enjoy the same custom environment regardless of where you work.

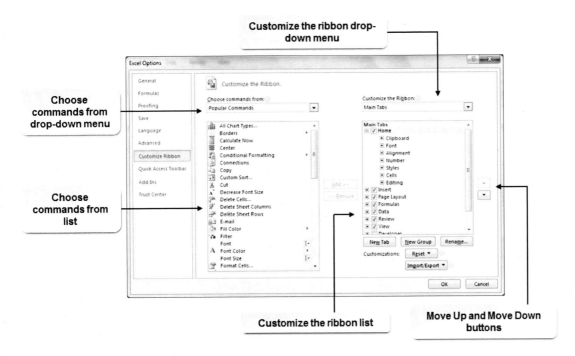

Figure 1-3: The Customize Ribbon tab on the Excel Options dialog box.

The following table describes the various elements of the **Customize Ribbon** tab.

Customize Ribbon Tab Element	Description
Choose commands from drop-down menu	Selects which commands are displayed in the **Choose commands from** list.
Choose commands from list	Displays the commands you can add to custom ribbon groups.
Customize the Ribbon drop-down menu	Selects which tabs display in the **Customize the Ribbon** list. You can select all tabs, just the main tabs, or just the tool (contextual) tabs.
Customize the Ribbon list	Displays the tabs, groups, and commands in their current organizational structure.
Add button	Adds commands selected in the **Choose commands from** list to the currently selected custom group.
Remove button	Removes the currently selected command, group, or tab from the ribbon. You cannot remove any of the default commands from their groups.
Move Up button	Moves the currently selected tab, group, or command up one place in the hierarchy. You cannot move default ribbon commands.
Move Down button	Moves the currently selected tab, group, or command down in the hierarchy. You cannot move default ribbon commands.
New Tab button	Adds a new custom tab after the currently selected tab. Excel automatically includes a new custom group on all new custom tabs.
New Group button	Add a new custom group after the currently selected group.

Customize Ribbon Tab Element	Description
Rename button	Opens the **Rename** dialog box, enabling you to rename the currently selected tab or group. You cannot rename commands.
Reset button	Enables you to reset either the currently selected tab to its default state or the entire ribbon to its default state.
Import/Export button	Enables you to export your current ribbon customization configuration for use on other computers, or import a ribbon customization from another computer.

The Customize the Ribbon List Hierarchy

The **Customize the Ribbon** list is arranged in a tree hierarchy. The top level of the tree represents the ribbon tabs. The groups are contained within the tabs, one level down in the hierarchy. The commands are contained within the groups. Commands with a drop-down menu contain another sub-level, which displays the commands that are contained within the drop-down menu.

 Note: Custom tabs and groups appear with the text *(Custom)* next to their names.

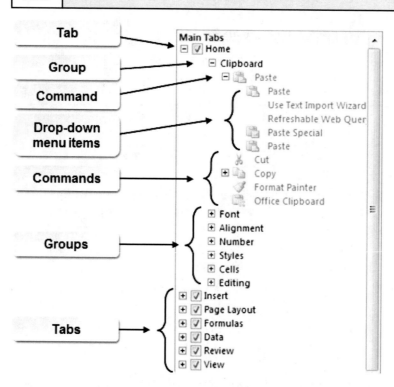

Figure 1–4: The tree hierarchy within the Customize the Ribbon list.

The Quick Access Toolbar Tab

You can use the commands and other elements of the **Quick Access Toolbar** tab to customize the **Quick Access Toolbar**. This works in much the same fashion as the **Customize Ribbon** tab with a few minor differences. As there is much less of an organizational structure to the **Quick Access Toolbar**, your options here are mainly limited simply to adding or removing commands and rearranging the order of commands. But you can add sections to the **Quick Access Toolbar** for the purpose of organizing commands by using visual borders called *separators*.

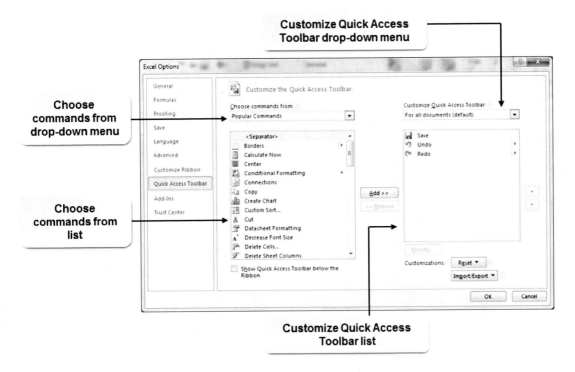

Figure 1-5: The Quick Access Toolbar tab.

The following table describes the various elements of the Quick Access Toolbar tab.

Quick Access Toolbar Tab Element	Description
Choose commands from drop-down menu	Selects which commands are displayed in the **Choose commands from list**.
Choose commands from list	Displays the commands you can add to the **Quick Access Toolbar**.
Customize Quick Access Toolbar drop-down menu	Selects whether **Quick Access Toolbar** customizations apply to all workbooks or just the current workbook.
Customize Quick Access Toolbar list	Displays the current **Quick Access Toolbar** configuration.
Add button	Adds commands selected in the **Choose commands from** list to the **Quick Access Toolbar**.
Remove button	Removes the currently selected command from the **Quick Access Toolbar**.
Move Up button	Moves the currently selected command up one place in the **Customize Quick Access Toolbar** list.
Move Down button	Moves the currently selected command down one place in the **Customize Quick Access Toolbar** list.
Reset button	Enables you to reset either the **Quick Access Toolbar** or the **Quick Access Toolbar** and the ribbon to the default configuration.

Quick Access Toolbar Tab Element	Description
Import/Export button	Enables you to export your current **Quick Access Toolbar** customization configuration for use on other computers or import a **Quick Access Toolbar** customization from another computer.

The Customize Quick Access Toolbar Menu

You can also add or remove commands from the **Quick Access Toolbar**, or **QAT**, by using the **Customize Quick Access Toolbar** menu, but your options here are a bit more limited. From the **Customize Quick Access Toolbar** menu, you can add or remove commands from a limited set of some of the most commonly used Excel commands. You cannot rearrange commands or add **separators** to the **QAT** from here.

The **Customize Quick Access Toolbar** menu also provides you with the ability to move the **QAT** so it is positioned below the ribbon. To access the **Customize Quick Access Toolbar** menu, select the **Customize Quick Access Toolbar** button ⧩ to the right of the **QAT**.

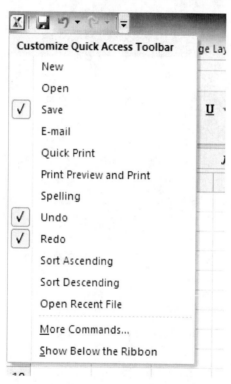

Figure 1-6: Check or uncheck the command options in the Customize Quick Access Toolbar menu to add them to or remove them from the QAT.

 Access the Checklist tile on your **LogicalCHOICE** course screen for reference information and job aids on How to Customize the Ribbon and the **Quick Access Toolbar.**

ACTIVITY 1-2
Customizing the Ribbon and the Quick Access Toolbar

Before You Begin
Excel 2010 is open.

Scenario
There are a few other modifications you would like to make to the Excel environment to help you work more efficiently. Because you create and reopen a number of workbook files daily, you would like to have access to the **New** and **Open** commands on the **Quick Access Toolbar**. And, as you most frequently use the commands on the **Home** tab and the **Formulas** tab, you want to place them next to each other on the ribbon. Finally, there is a command you know you will be using a lot in the future, so you decide to add it to both the ribbon and the **Quick Access Toolbar**.

---

1. Add the **New** and **Open** commands to the **Quick Access Toolbar**.
   a) On the right side of the **Quick Access Toolbar**, select the **Customize Quick Access Toolbar** button.

   `|⇩`

   b) From the **Customize Quick Access Toolbar** menu, verify the **New** command is selected.
   c) Add the **Open** command to the **Quick Access Toolbar**.

2. Move the **Formulas** tab so that it is to the right of the **Home** tab on the ribbon.
   a) Select **File→Options**.
   b) In the **Excel Options** dialog box, select the **Customize Ribbon** tab.
   c) In the **Customize the Ribbon** drop-down menu, ensure that **Main Tabs** is selected.
   d) In the **Customize the Ribbon** list, select **Formulas**.

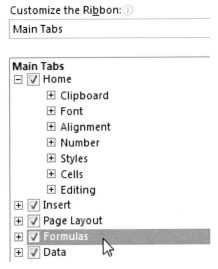

e) Select the **Move Up** button twice, so that the **Formulas** tab appears just below the displayed groups of the **Home** tab.

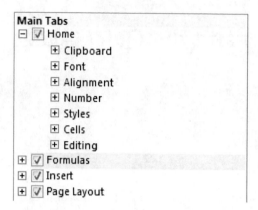

```
Main Tabs
☐ ✓ Home
        ⊞ Clipboard
        ⊞ Font
        ⊞ Alignment
        ⊞ Number
        ⊞ Styles
        ⊞ Cells
        ⊞ Editing
  ⊞ ✓ Formulas
  ⊞ ✓ Insert
  ⊞ ✓ Page Layout
```

f) Select **OK** and then verify that the **Home** tab and the **Formulas** tab appear next to each other on the ribbon.

3. Add the **Insert PivotTable** command to the **Quick Access Toolbar**.

a) Select **File→Options**.
b) In the **Excel Options** dialog box, select the **Quick Access Toolbar** tab.
c) From the **Choose commands from** drop-down menu, select **All Commands**.
d) In the **Choose commands from** list, scroll down and select **Insert PivotTable**.
e) Select **Add**.

 Note: It is okay to leave the **Excel Options** dialog box open here.

4. Add the **PivotTable** and **Insert Slicer** commands to the ribbon in a custom group.

a) In the **Excel Options** dialog box, select the **Customize Ribbon** tab.
b) In the **Customize the Ribbon** drop-down menu, ensure that **Main Tabs** is selected.
c) In the **Customize the Ribbon** list, in the **Home** tab hierarchy, select **Editing** and then, below this list, select **New Group**.

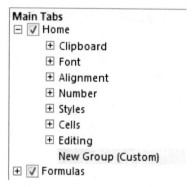

```
Main Tabs
☐ ✓ Home
        ⊞ Clipboard
        ⊞ Font
        ⊞ Alignment
        ⊞ Number
        ⊞ Styles
        ⊞ Cells
        ⊞ Editing
           New Group (Custom)
  ⊞ ✓ Formulas
```

d) Select **Rename**.
e) In the **Rename** dialog box, in the **Display name** field, type *PivotTable* and then select **OK**.
f) In the **Choose commands from** drop-down menu, ensure that **Popular Commands** is selected.
g) In the **Choose commands from** list, scroll down, select **PivotTable**, and then select **Add**.

h) Ensure that the **PivotTable** command now appears in the newly created **PivotTable (Custom)** group.

> ⊞ Cells
> ⊞ Editing
> ⊟ PivotTable (Custom)
>   🔲 PivotTable
> ⊞ ☑ Formulas

i) In the **Choose commands from** drop-down menu, select **All Commands**.
j) In the **Choose commands from** list, scroll down, select **Insert Slicer**, and then select **Add**.
k) In the **Excel Options** dialog box, select **OK**.

5. Verify that the **Insert PivotTable** command now appears on the **Quick Access Toolbar** and the **PivotTable** and **Insert Slicer** commands now appear in the **PivotTable** group on the **Home** tab.

TOPIC C

Enable Excel Add-Ins

Excel 2010 is loaded with a robust set of tools and features meant to help you get the most out of your data. If the default functionality suits all of your needs, you may not need to customize Excel beyond the option or UI changes you have already made. But there are entire sets of additional functionality available to Excel users who need a little more power in their Excel installations. If you're one of these users, you'll need to know how to access the available additional functionality.

Fortunately, Excel 2010 makes it easy to activate only the additional tools and features you need to perform your job. Taking a few moments now to understand how to find and activate these additional tools and features means you'll be able to call upon Excel's additional capabilities whenever the need arises.

Add-Ins

Add-ins are supplemental programs for Microsoft Office applications that provide additional features and functionality not available in a standard installation. Some add-ins, such as the Analysis ToolPak and the Solver add-in, come installed with Excel but are simply not activated by default. Other add-ins can be downloaded from Microsoft Office Online and then activated. You can also develop custom add-ins to enhance Excel's functionality, if you have the programming acumen to do so. Add-ins must be enabled for you to have access to their features and functionality.

The Add-Ins Tab

You can view and manage your Excel add-ins from the **Add-Ins** tab on the **Excel Options** dialog box. From here you can view all add-ins that are installed on your computer, and all add-ins that are both installed and enabled. This is also where you can access dialog boxes for the various add-in types, which allow you to enable and disable add-ins as needed.

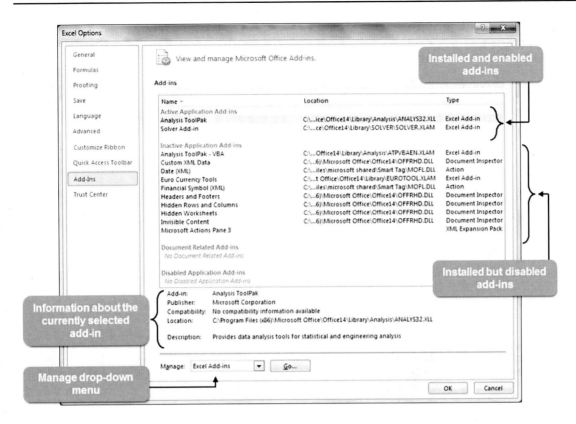

Figure 1-7: The Add-Ins tab.

The following table describes some of the key elements of the **Add-Ins** tab.

Add-Ins Tab Element	Allows You To
Active Application Add-ins section	View a list of all add-ins currently installed and enabled on your computer.
Inactive Application Add-ins section	View a list of all add-ins that are currently installed on your computer but that are disabled.
Type column	View add-in types. These typically give you a clue to the general functionality or features the add-in provides for Excel.
Add-in information	View additional information about the currently selected add-in.
Manage drop-down menu	Access the dialog boxes for the various add-in types. From these dialog boxes, you can enable or disable add-ins as needed.

 Note: For more information on adding further capabilities to Excel, watch the LearnTO **Expand Excel's Capabilities Using Add-Ins** presentation from the **LearnTO** tile on the LogicalCHOICE Course screen.

 Access the Checklist tile on your LogicalCHOICE course screen for reference information and job aids on How to Enable Add-Ins.

ACTIVITY 1-3
Enabling Excel Add-Ins

Before You Begin

Excel 2010 is open.

Scenario

There is one final Excel customization you wish to make. As you frequently work with currency figures for European offices and authors, you would like to add the ability to work with currency figures in terms of the Euro. You decide to activate the **Euro Currency Tools** add-in.

---

1. Select **File→Options**.

2. In the **Excel Options** dialog box, select the **Add-Ins** tab.

3. At the bottom of the **Add-ins** section, in the **Manage** drop-down menu, ensure that **Excel Add-ins** is selected and then select **Go**.

4. In the **Add-Ins** dialog box, check the **Euro Currency Tools** check box and then select **OK**.

5. Ensure that the **Euro Currency Tools** add-in is now enabled.
   a) Open the **Excel Options** dialog box and select the **Add-Ins** tab.
   b) In the **Add-ins** section, ensure that the **Euro Currency Tools** add-in appears in the **Active Application Add-ins** list.

Add-ins

Name ▲	Location	Type
Active Application Add-ins		
Euro Currency Tools	C:\...t Office\Office14\Library\EUROTOOL.XLAM	Excel Add-in
Inactive Application Add-ins		
Analysis ToolPak	C:\...ice\Office14\Library\Analysis\ANALYS32.XLL	Excel Add-in
Analysis ToolPak - VBA	C:\...Office14\Library\Analysis\ATPVBAEN.XLAM	Excel Add-in

6. Close the **Excel Options** dialog box.

Summary

In this lesson, you customized the Excel environment by configuring options and settings, customizing the ribbon and the **QAT**, and by managing add-ins. As you develop your Excel skills and experience, you will almost certainly find that you like some of Excel's default functionality, while, at other times, it will seem to hold you back. With the ability to tailor the Excel environment to suit your needs and your personal work flow, you'll have Excel working harder for you, which will make you more efficient and productive.

What changes do you anticipate making to the Excel environment to help you work more efficiently?

Do you think you'll most likely add customizations to the QAT or the ribbon? Why?

 Note: Check your LogicalCHOICE Course screen for opportunities to interact with your classmates, peers, and the larger LogicalCHOICE online community about the topics covered in this course or other topics you are interested in. From the Course screen you can also access available resources for a more continuous learning experience.

2 Creating Advanced Formulas

Lesson Time: 1 hour, 45 minutes

Lesson Objectives

In this lesson, you will create advanced formulas. You will:

- Use range names in formulas.

- Use specialized functions.

- Use array formulas.

Lesson Introduction

You already know how to get Excel to perform simple calculations to make your job easier. However, manually entering formulas will take you only so far. The commonly used functions in Excel may not be enough to handle more complex data analysis needs. As you progress with Excel, and as you are called upon to provide a deeper understanding of your organizational data to organizational decision makers, you'll need to know how to ask Excel more complex questions about your data and to get the answers you expect.

Of course, the more complex your data analysis tasks are, the more complexity you're likely to need in your formulas and functions. This means that you'll need to know how to talk to Excel at a higher level to get the most out of your data. As with mathematics in general, and all forms of computer programming, understating the language Excel speaks is the key to having conversations with Excel and getting the answers you need.

TOPIC A

Use Range Names in Formulas

It is a rare individual who works in a bubble with little to no contact with other people. As such, it is highly likely that you will not be the only person working with and analyzing data with your workbooks. This means it's essential that everyone working in the same workbook understands precisely what the formulas and functions are calculating. Although cell and range references make including figures in calculations and reusing those figures in multiple calculations easy, it's not always apparent at first glance what the formula is calculating. Manually typing or selecting cell and range references in large workbooks with many formulas can become tedious and potentially lead to errors. Wouldn't it be nice if there were a clearer, simpler way to include cell and range references in Excel?

Excel 2010 allows you to name ranges for use in functions and formulas. Mastering this key trick to creating formulas and functions is an easy way to use the same ranges over and over in your worksheets and to make those formulas and functions clearer to others who view and work in your workbook files. This is truly one of the most powerful features of Excel. Once you know how to name ranges and refer to those ranges by name in your formulas, you'll be developing complex, interconnected worksheets in no time.

Cell and Range Names

Cell names and *range names* are exactly what they sound like. They are meaningful names you assign to a given cell or range to make it easier to both understand what calculations are being performed in a formula and reuse the references for a number of purposes. Take a look at the following image, which shows two versions of the same formula, one using cell references and one using named cells.

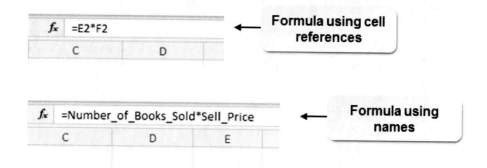

Figure 2-1: The same formula using cell references and names.

Now, imagine that you open this workbook months, or even years, after you created it. At first glance, which formula is easier to interpret? And, if you share this workbook with a colleague, which would make it clearer to the workbook recipient what her or she is looking at? It's pretty clear how powerful a feature this is.

 Note: Cell and range references aren't the only items you can name in Excel. You can name other objects, such as tables and even formulas themselves. Collectively, the names you assign to all of these items are known as *defined names*.

In short, cell and range names are concise, descriptive names you can assign to cells or ranges for the purpose of making formulas easier to read and maintain. You can assign a name to both contiguous ranges and noncontiguous ranges. Names refer to absolute references by default but you can change those to relative references to facilitate the reuse of formulas.

> **Note:** It may be a good idea to indicate in a name whether the reference is absolute or relative, as the name will be displayed precisely as you created it regardless of which type of reference it contains.

Although you can come up with an incredible array of different names, there are some rules you must follow:

- Names must begin with a letter, an underscore, or a backslash.
- After the first character, names can contain letters, numbers, periods, and underscores.
- Names cannot contain spaces.
- Names cannot be the same as a cell or a range reference. For example, you cannot use *$A$1* as a name.
- Names have a defined scope, either to a worksheet or a workbook, and must be unique within that scope.
- Names can contain up to 255 total characters.
- Excel does not recognize casing differences for names. So, within the same scope, you cannot, for example, create both *SalesTotals* and *salestotals* as names.
- You can use a single letter as a name, you cannot do so by using either *C* or *R*, either uppercase or lowercase, as these are used as shorthand for selecting an entire row or an entire column in other Excel features.

Names and the Name Box

There are several methods you can use to create names in Excel 2010. The most direct of these is to use the **Name Box**. To name a cell or a range, you can simply select the desired cell or range and then type the desired name in the **Name Box**. Once you've created named cells and ranges, you can access those cells and ranges from the **Name Box** drop-down menu. This is a quick way to select a cell or range that you've already named. Additionally, if you manually select a named cell or range on a worksheet, the name, not the cell reference, is displayed in the **Name Box**. Names created in the **Name Box**, by default, have "Workbook" as their scope.

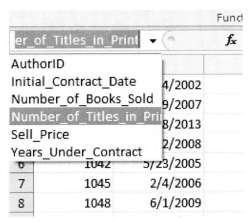

Figure 2-2: Named ranges in the Name Box.

The New Name Dialog Box

You can also name cells or ranges by using the **New Name** dialog box. The advantage here is that you have greater control over configuring precisely what the name refers to. You can access the **New Name** dialog box by selecting **Formulas→Defined Names→Define Name**.

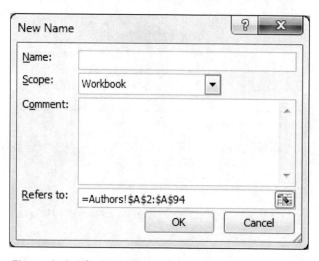

Figure 2–3: The New Name dialog box gives you greater control over naming cells and ranges.

The following table describes the various elements of the **New Name** dialog box.

New Name Dialog Box Element	Allows You To
Name field	Enter a name for the cell or range.
Scope drop-down menu	Assign a scope to the name. This can be either the entire workbook or a particular worksheet. You cannot create two identical names within the same scope. You can, however, create identical names for both a worksheet and the workbook containing that worksheet. On the worksheet, the name that has the worksheet as its scope will take precedence. On all other worksheets, the name that has the workbook as its scope will take precedence.
Comment field	Enter a brief description of the named cell or range to help clarify its purpose.
Refers to field	View or edit the name's reference. Whatever cell or range is selected when you open the **New Name** dialog box will be displayed as an absolute reference in the **Refers to** field by default.

The Create from Selection Command

Another method you can use to name ranges is the **Create from Selection** command. This command enables you to quickly and easily create a single range name or multiple range names at once, based on the range you currently have selected. The **Create from Selection** command does not work for naming individual cells. By default, named ranges you create by using this command have "Workbook" as their scope.

When you select a range and then select the **Create from Selection** command, Excel opens the **Create Names from Selection** dialog box, which allows you to select the cells from which Excel will create the names. This feature works best for ranges with clearly defined content types and appropriately labeled row and column headers. You may get unexpected results or error messages if headers don't align with Excel's naming conventions. If you use the **Create from Selection** command when a range in a single row or column in selected, Excel will create a single named range. If a range that covers multiple rows and columns is selected, Excel will create a series of named ranges based on the cell selection and the option you check in the **Create Names from Selection** dialog box. The cells from which Excel creates the names are not included in the range reference for the named ranges. The **Create from Selection** command is available in the **Defined**

Names group on the **Formulas** tab. You can also use the **Ctrl+Shift+F3** keyboard shortcut to open the **Create Names from Selection** dialog box.

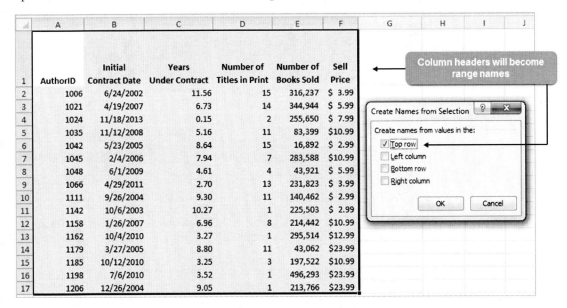

Figure 2-4: Use the Create from Selection command to quickly create multiple named ranges.

The Name Manager Dialog Box 7◁ Add new data rows ✗

As most workbooks are dynamic, changing documents, it stands to reason that you will likely have to edit named cells and ranges from time to time. For example, if you need to add rows to a range of data, you will likely want named column ranges within that range of data to include the new rows. Excel 2010 provides the **Name Manager** dialog box, a tool you can use to view and manage all of the named objects in your workbooks. From here, you can rename, edit, and delete existing named objects, and access the **New Name** dialog box to create new named cells or ranges. You cannot, however, change the scope of an existing cell or range name by using the **Name Manager** dialog box. To do this, you can delete the existing name and create a new one with the desired scope. The **Name Manager** dialog box also displays a **Filter** command, which you can use to filter the display of existing names. Use the **Filter** command, for example, to view only those names that have the entire workbook as their scope, names that have a particular worksheet as their scope, or names containing errors. You can access the **Name Manager** dialog box by selecting **Formulas→Defined Names→Name Manager**.

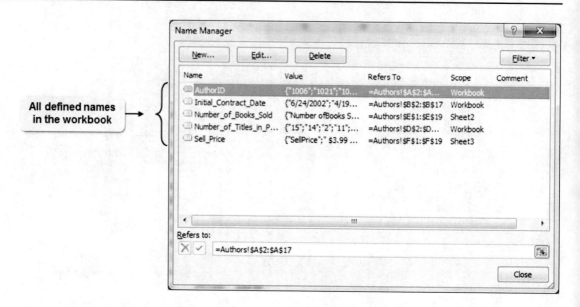

All defined names in the workbook

Figure 2-5: The Name Manager dialog box.

 Access the Checklist tile on your LogicalCHOICE course screen for reference information and job aids on How to Name and Edit Ranges.

ACTIVITY 2-1
Naming and Editing Ranges

Data File

C:\091019Data\Creating Advanced Formulas\author_data.xlsx

Before You Begin

Excel 2010 is open.

Scenario

Your supervisor has asked you to provide her with information about total income by author. You have raw data for Fuller's authors tracked in a worksheet that contains information about how long each author has been with the company, how many titles each currently has published through Fuller and Ackerman, how many total books each author has sold, and the price at which each author's books sell. Before you perform the calculations to determine how much each author has contributed to Fuller's income, you decide to name the various ranges for use in formulas to make the worksheet easier for your supervisor, and anyone else who may end up using it, to interpret.

1. Open the **author_data.xlsx** workbook.

2. Use the **Name Box** to create a named range in the **AuthorID** column.

   a) Select cell **A2** and press **Ctrl+Shift+down arrow**.
   b) Select the **Name Box**, type *Author_ID* and press **Enter**.

3. Use the **New Name** dialog box to create a named range in the **Initial Contract Date** column.

   a) Select cell **B2** and press **Ctrl+Shift+down arrow**.
   b) Select **Formulas→Defined Names→Define Name**.
   c) In the **New Name** dialog box, in the **Name** field, type *Initial_Contract_Date*
   d) Ensure that **Workbook** is selected in the **Scope** drop-down menu.
   e) Ensure that the **Refers to** field displays the following range reference: **=Authors!$B$2:$B$94**.
   f) Select **OK**.

4. Use the **Create from Selection** command to create a named range in the **Years Under Contract** column.

   a) Select the range **C1:C94** and then select **Formulas→Defined Names→Create from Selection**.
   b) In the **Create Names from Selection** dialog box, ensure that the **Top row** check box is checked and then select **OK**.

5. Verify that the three named ranges exist by selecting the **Name Box** down arrow and confirming that the names appear as expected.

6. Use the **Create from Selection** command to create named ranges for the final three columns simultaneously.

   a) Select cell **D1** and press **Ctrl+Shift+right arrow**.
   b) Press **Ctrl+Shift+down arrow**.
   c) Select **Formulas→Defined Names→Create from Selection**.
   d) In the **Create Names from Selection** dialog box, ensure that the **Top row** check box is checked and then select **OK**.
   e) Verify that Excel created three unique named ranges for the final three columns.

7. Edit the range names for the **Number of Titles in Print** and **Number of Books Sold** columns to make them a bit shorter.
   a) Select **Formulas→Defined Names→Name Manager**.
   b) In the **Name Manager** dialog box, select the **Number_of_Books_Sold** range name and then select **Edit**.
   c) In the **Edit Name** dialog box, in the **Name** field, type *No_of_Books_Sold* and select **OK**.
   d) Change the range name **Number_of_Titles_in_Print** to *No_of_Titles_in_Print*
   e) Close the **Name Manager** dialog box.
   f) Verify that the names have changed as expected.

8. Save the workbook to the **C:\091019Data\Creating Advanced Formulas** folder as *my_author_data.xlsx*

Cell and Range Names in Formulas

Although it's certainly helpful to be able to name a range or a cell for easy navigation, the real power of this feature lies in the ability to easily identify references in formulas and to quickly and accurately insert references into multiple formulas. Once you've defined a name, you can simply use the name in place of a standard cell or range reference in any formula or function.

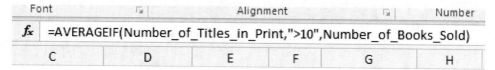

Figure 2–6: Named cells and ranges make it easier to identify the purpose of formulas and to enter cell and range references more accurately.

As with many of the features and functions in Office applications, Excel provides several ways to perform a task. Such a task, in Excel, is inserting cell and range names in formulas and functions. The most common of these many methods are manually typing the name in a formula or function, using the **Use in Formula** command, and using the **Formula AutoComplete** feature. Let's look at each of these in some detail.

Manually Entering Cell or Range Names

The most direct method for including cell or range names instead of references in formulas or functions is to simply type them. Wherever you would normally enter a cell or range reference, you can type a defined name instead. The formula will reference the cell or range by name just as it would if you typed the cell or range reference, and your calculation results will be the same.

 Note: It is important to note that you can still type the cell or range references for a named cell or range in a formula, and they will still appear as cell or range references.

You can also manually select a cell or range that you've applied a name to directly on a worksheet to enter it into a formula just as you would with any unnamed range or cell. When you do this, Excel automatically displays the name, not the reference, though.

The Use in Formula Command Method

Excel 2010 includes a ribbon command you can use to insert cell and range names into formulas and functions: the **Use in Formula** command. As with manually typing a cell or a range name, you can use this method anywhere you would normally enter a range or cell reference in a formula. Instead of typing the name, you simply select the **Use in Formula** command, and then select the desired defined name from the drop-down menu. You can access the **Use in Formula** command by selecting **Formulas→Defined Names→Use in Formula**.

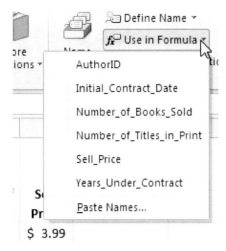

Figure 2-7: The Use in Formula command displays all valid defined names for use in formulas and functions.

From the **Use in Formula** drop-down menu, you can also select **Paste Names**, which opens the **Paste Name** dialog box. This provides you with yet another option for selecting a named cell or range. The added benefit here is that there is a keyboard shortcut, **F3**, that you can use to quickly open the **Paste Name** dialog box.

The Formula AutoComplete Method

You already know the Formula AutoComplete feature can help you enter functions into worksheet cells without having to type the full function name. Well, the Formula AutoComplete feature can also help you enter range and cell names into formulas and functions, and it works in the exact same way. As you type a formula or a function into a cell, whether directly into the cell or by using the **Formula Bar**, and you begin to type a cell or range name, the Formula AutoComplete feature automatically opens the same pop-up menu that appears when you type a function name. You can select any valid named cells or ranges from the pop-up menu to enter into the formula or function. The pop-up menu automatically filters the available defined names just as it would Excel functions. You can differentiate between functions and defined names in the Formula AutoComplete feature by viewing the icon next to each option. Functions will display the **Insert Function** icon $\textit{f}_x$, whereas defined names will display an icon that looks like a paper tag ▯ . Once you've entered the cell or range name, you simply continue entering the rest of the formula or function as you normally would.

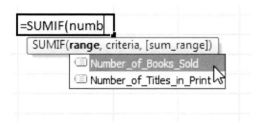

Figure 2-8: Adding a range name by using the Formula AutoComplete feature.

▦ | **Access the Checklist tile on your LogicalCHOICE course screen for reference information and job aids on How to Use Defined Names in Formulas and Functions.**

ACTIVITY 2–2
Using Defined Names in a Formula

Before You Begin

The my_author_data.xlsx workbook is open.

Scenario

Now that you have created named ranges for the various columns, you will use them to enter functions to provide your supervisor with the income-per-author data she has asked for. For the purposes of this worksheet, Fuller and Ackerman defines income earned as the number of books sold multiplied by the sell price. To maintain consistency and to facilitate using the income earned data in future calculations, you decide to name the range for the calculation results as well.

1. Add a column label for the income earned data.
    a) Select cell **G1**.
    b) Type *Income Earned* and press **Enter**.

2. Use range names to enter a formula that will calculate the income earned.
    a) Ensure that cell **G2** is selected.
    b) Type *=no*
    c) From the Formula AutoComplete pop-up menu, double-click **No_of_Books_Sold**.

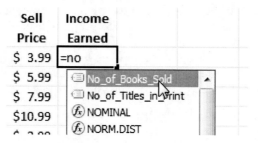

    d) Type an asterisk (*) and select **Formulas→Defined Names→Use in Formula→Sell_Price**.

    e) Press **Ctrl+Enter**.

f) Verify that the formula behaves as expected, and that it displays defined names instead of cell references.

f_x	=No_of_Books_Sold*Sell_Price			
C	D	E	F	G
Years Under Contract	**Number of Titles in Print**	**Number of Books Sold**	**Sell Price**	**Income Earned**
11.56	15	316,237	$ 3.99	1261786
6.73	14	344.944	$ 5.99	

3. With cell **G2** selected, select the **Home** tab and, from the **Number Format** drop-down menu in the **Number** group, select **Currency**.

4. Adjust the width of column **G** to accommodate the new formatting.

5. Copy the formula for all authors on the worksheet.
   a) Ensure that cell **G2** is still selected.
   b) Double-click the **fill handle** in the bottom-right corner of the cell.

Sell Price	**Income Earned**
$ 3.99	$1,261,785.63
$ 5.99	

   c) Press **Ctrl+.** (the period key) to invert the active cell in the range and verify that Excel copied the formula in the entire range **G2:G94**.
   d) Press **Ctrl+.** again to return the active cell back to the top of column **G**.
   e) If necessary, re-adjust the width of column **G** to accommodate all of the entries.

6. Assign the name *Income_Earned* to the range **G2:G94**.

7. Save the file.

TOPIC B

Use Specialized Functions

You are already familiar with the most basic functions and formulas in Excel. You're also likely aware that there are far more complex tasks you can perform in Excel beyond adding up rows and columns and multiplying the sum by some other figure. As you progress in your knowledge of Excel, and in your career, you are likely to be called upon to perform more and more complex number crunching and data analysis tasks. As such, you'll need to have a much better handle on Excel functions than you did previously.

Excel contains an incredibly vast array of built-in functions that you can use to perform a staggering number of calculations. You'll need to know how to locate specific functions when performing specific tasks. You'll need to know a great deal about the syntax of these functions if you expect Excel to provide answers to your questions. Taking the time now to build a foundational understanding of how some of the more specialized and complex functions work, will give you the tools you need to ask Excel more and more complex questions related to your data.

Function Categories

You will find every built-in Excel function in the **Function Library** group on the **Formulas** tab. Here, the vast collection of available functions is organized into task-related categories. There are 11 standard categories of included functions and this can be expanded by installing certain Excel add-ins.

 Note: You have to access several of these categories from the **More Functions** drop-down menu in the **Function Library** group.

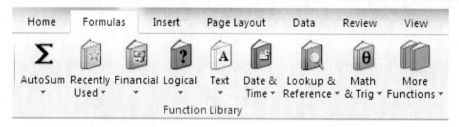

Figure 2-9: The Function Library group on the Formulas tab.

Function Library Category	Contains Functions For
Financial	Calculating financial figures such as accrued interest, rates of return, monthly payments, and asset depreciation.
Logical	Returning a value of either TRUE or FALSE for a given set of criteria. Use these in conjunction with other functions or formulas to perform calculations based on certain conditions. Basically, this adds a decision-making dimension to Excel functions and formulas.
Text	Manipulating text. For example, you can use these functions to convert text to all uppercase or all lowercase, or to join text strings from multiple cells.
Date & Time	Working with dates and times. For example, you can use these functions to simply return the current date, or to calculate the number of working days in a given period.
Lookup & Reference	Finding specific values in a table or a given range.

Function Library Category	Contains Functions For
Math & Trig	Performing a variety of common mathematical calculations.
Statistical	Performing common statistical analysis tasks, such as calculating the mean, median, or mode of a dataset, or the standard deviation of a population or a sample.
Engineering	Performing engineering calculations and conversions. Many of these functions deal with Bessel functions and complex numbers.
Cube	Performing complex, multidimensional data analysis by fetching data from Online Analytical Processing (OLAP) cubes.
Information	Providing information about your data and worksheets. For example, you can use these functions to identify the directory in which a workbook is saved, or to determine if the data in a cell is text, a number, or a reference to another cell.
Compatibility	Working with workbook files in multiple versions of Excel. The compatibility functions are older versions of functions that are still available in Excel 2010 but that have been changed or improved in various ways. Compatibility functions are compatible with previous versions of Excel, but the newer versions of the same functions may not be.

Note: For more information on the types of changes made to functions in the **Compatibility** category, open the **Excel Help** window and, in the **Table of Contents** pane, expand the **Function Reference** section and select the **What's New: Changes made to Excel functions** link.

The Excel Function Reference

While it is certainly advantageous to be familiar with the purpose and syntax of functions you regularly work with, you will likely run into situations in which you need to use functions you are unfamiliar with or in which you need to identify which function serves a given purpose. In these cases, you'll want a fast, easy way to look up such information. Fortunately, Excel 2010 provides you with a powerful resource to do so: the *Excel function reference*. The function reference is not a separate, discrete tool; it is a Help resource available whether you search Excel Help on your computer or online. The function reference is basically a Help article that lists all Excel functions by category and describes each in detail. Each entry for functions includes a general description of the function's task, any special considerations you should keep in mind regarding its use, a description of the function's syntax and arguments, and examples of the function in use. You can access the function reference by simply typing *Excel functions by category* into either search field in the **Excel Help** window and then selecting either the **List of worksheet functions (by category)** or the **Excel functions (by category)** link.

Note: You can also expand the **Function reference** section in the **Excel Help** window's **Table of Contents** pane to access function references by function category.

Note: The **Insert Function** dialog box also provides some assistance for identifying the correct function to use for particular tasks, although it is much less detailed than what is available in the function reference. Because of this, you may find it helpful to use the **Insert Function** dialog box to identify the correct function and then look up that function in the function reference to see detailed information about it.

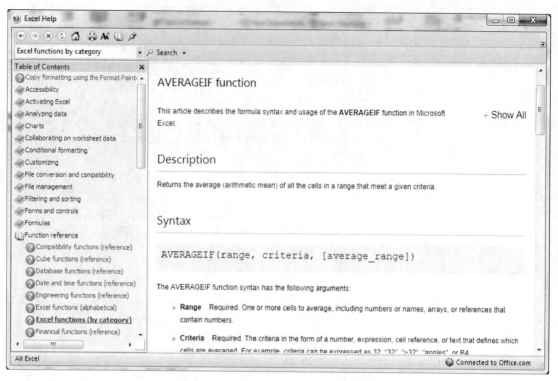

Figure 2-10: Use the function reference to examine any function in detail.

 Access the Checklist tile on your LogicalCHOICE course screen for reference information and job aids on How to Locate Functions by Using the Excel Function Reference.

Logical Operator Basics

Before you examine the syntax of more Excel functions, there is a group of operators you may not yet be familiar with in terms of Excel: logical operators. You might, however, remember these as the mathematical symbols that indicate conditions such as one figure being greater than or less than another. As you advance in your understanding of Excel functions, you will find that these logical operators form the basis for using many of Excel's functions and taking advantage of many of its features. For now, it will be enough to simply understand what these logical operators mean. The following table describes what each of the operators means in Excel functions.

Logical Operator	Meaning
=	Equal to
<	Less than
>	Greater than
<=	Less than or equal to
>=	Greater than or equal to
<>	Not equal to

Function Syntax

By now, you have likely familiarized yourself with the syntax for a number of basic Excel functions and have had some opportunity to use them regularly. You'll remember that a function's syntax defines the structure of the function and identifies the required and optional arguments you can use to complete it. As you advance in your Excel proficiency, you'll want to add to your lexicon of familiar functions so you don't have to look up functions frequently as you develop your workbooks. Here is an overview of some of the commonly used Excel functions you may not already be familiar with.

The SUMIF Function

Syntax: =SUMIF(range, criteria, [sum_range])

 Note: Remember that, in Excel function syntax, arguments within square brackets ([ ]) are optional.

Description: This function adds the values in a given range that meet some specific criteria. Use this function, for example, if you'd like to add all sales figures greater than a particular value in a column. In the function's syntax, **range** is the range of cells to which the criteria is applied, **criteria** is the condition that must be met, and **sum_range** is the range of cells from which to add values if you want that range to differ from the one specified in the **range** argument. If you do not specify a range for the optional **sum_range** argument, the function sums the qualifying values from the cells specified in the **range** argument.

 Note: The **criteria** argument must be enclosed in quotation marks (" ") if it contains text, mathematical operators, or logical operators. This is common among the various functions that contain the **criteria** argument.

Examples of values that can be added to the SUMIF function are included in the following table.

To Add These Values	Enter This Function
All numbers greater than 10 in the range A1:A10.	=SUMIF(A1:A10, ">10")
All numbers in the range B1:B10 that correspond to the text entry "Bill" in the range A1:A10. In other words, if you have a list of names in column A, and corresponding sales values in column B, this function would add all figures for people named Bill.	=SUMIF(A1:A10, "Bill", B1:B10)
Every instance of the value 5 in the range A1:A10.	=SUMIF(A1:A10, 5)

The AVERAGEIF Function

Syntax: =AVERAGEIF(range, criteria, [average_range])

Description: This function returns the arithmetic mean of every cell in a range that meets the specified criteria. You would use this formula, for example, if you wanted to find the average value of all sales figures that are less than or equal to some specified amount. In the function's syntax, **range** is the range of cells to which the criteria is applied, **criteria** is the condition that must be met, and **average_range** is the range of cells from which the mean is calculated if you want that range to differ from the one specified in the **range** argument. If you do not specify a range in the optional **average_range** argument, the function finds the average of the qualifying values from the cells specified in the **range** argument.

Examples of values that can be added to the AVERAGEIF function are included in the following table.

To Find the Average of These Values	Enter This Function
All numbers less than or equal to 20 in the range A1:A10.	=AVERAGEIF(A1:A10, "<=20")
All numbers in the range C1:C10 that correspond to a value that is greater than or equal to 100,000 in the range B1:B10. For example, if the range A1:A10 contains authors' names, the range B1:B10 displays total sales per author, and the range C1:C10 contains the authors' sales commissions, then this function would return the average sales commission for authors who sold $100,000 or more worth of books.	=AVERAGEIF(B1:B10, ">=100000", C1:C10)

 Note: When including numeric values in function arguments, do not use commas to separate the numerals at each magnitude of 1,000. Excel will read this as the end of one argument and the beginning of the next argument.

The COUNTIF Function

Syntax: =COUNTIF(range, criteria)

Description: This function counts the number of cells in the specified range that contain data matching the specified criteria. You could use this function, for example, to count the number of sales reps who have met or exceeded a particular sales target or the number of people in your organization named "Betty." In the function's syntax, **range** is the range of cells to which the criteria is applied and from which the qualifying entries are counted, and **criteria** is the condition that must be met for an entry to be counted. The COUNTIF function counts values from within the **range** argument only.

Examples of values that can be added to the COUNTIF function are included in the following table.

To Count the Number of Cells Containing	Enter This Function
Values greater than or equal to 1,000 in the range A1:A10.	=COUNTIF(A1:A10, ">=1000")
An instance of the value 13 in the range B1:C20.	=COUNTIF(B1:C20, 13)
The name "Fred" in the range A1:A350	=COUNTIF(A1:A350, "Fred")

IFS Functions

The AVERAGEIF, COUNTIF, and SUMIF functions all have an equivalent function that enables you to perform the respective calculations on a dataset that meets more than one specified criterion. These are the AVERAGEIFS, COUNTIFS, and SUMIFS functions, respectively. The main differences in the function syntaxes for the "IFS" functions are that the arguments are in a different order and that there are additional, optional arguments for the additional criteria. Otherwise, they function essentially the same as their counterparts. Here is the function syntax for each of these "IFS" functions:

=AVERAGEIFS(average_range, criteria_range1, criteria1, [criteria_range2], [criteria2], ...)

=COUNTIFS(criteria_range1, criteria1, [criteria_range2], [criteria2], ...)

=SUMIFS(sum_range, criteria_range1, criteria1, [criteria_range2], [criteria2], ...)

COUNTA

Syntax: =COUNTA(value1, [value2], ...)

Description: This function counts the number of cells specified by the arguments that are not empty. This function does not distinguish between the various content types, such as formulas, values, and text. The arguments can be either cell or range references or both.

Examples of values that can be added to the COUNTA function are included in the following table.

To Count the Number of Non-Empty Cells	Enter This Function
In the range A1:A50	=COUNTA(A1:A50)
In the range A1:B30	=COUNTA(A1:B30)
In the range A1:A10 and in cells B3 and C9	=COUNTA(A1:A10, B3, C9)

The PMT function

Syntax: =PMT(rate, nper, pv, [fv], [type])

Description: This function calculates the payments for a loan with a fixed interest rate and fixed payment periods. You can use this function, for example, to calculate your payments for a fixed-rate mortgage, auto loan, or student loan. In the function's syntax, here are the required arguments: **rate** is the loan's fixed interest rate, **nper** is the total number of payments for the loan (for example, monthly payments for a three-year loan occur 36 times), **pv** is the present value (principal) of the loan. There are two optional arguments for the function: **fv** (future value of the loan) and **type**. The **fv** argument is used to indicate the remaining balance on the loan at the end of the specified period. Typically this will be zero (meaning the loan is fully paid off), which is the value if you omit this argument. If you want to calculate the payments to partially pay off the loan, use the **fv** argument to indicate how much should be left over once all of the payments are made. The **type** argument indicates whether the payment is due at the end of each payment period (indicated by a zero or by omitting the argument), or at the beginning of each pay period (indicated by a 1).

 Note: When using the **PMT** function, you must account for how often you plan to make payments when you enter the values for the **rate** and **nper** arguments. So, if the interest rate is 9 percent and you're making monthly payments for three years, the value for **rate** should be **.09/12**, and the value for **nper** should be **36**. If you make annual payments on the same loan, **rate** would be **.09** and **nper** would be **3**.

Examples of values that can be added to the PMT function are included in the following table.

To Calculate	Enter This Function
Monthly payments to fully pay off a five-year loan for $50,000, with a fixed 5-percent interest rate, and payments due at the end of each month.	=PMT(.05/12, 60, 50000)
Annual payments to pay off half of a $60,000 loan in five years, with a fixed 7-percent interest rate, and payments due at the beginning of the year.	=PMT(.07, 5, 60000, 30000, 1)

The STDEV.P function

Syntax: =STDEV.P(number1, [number2], ...)

Description: This function calculates the standard deviation of an entire population of related values. This is a common statistical calculation that indicates how far away from the average value of the population each individual value is. The arguments for this function can be cell or range references or both; they can also be fixed values. This function ignores all text and logical values in the cells indicated by the arguments.

Examples of values that can be added to the STDEV.P function are included in the following table.

To Calculate the Standard Deviation of the Values in These Cells	Enter This Function
A1:A100	=STDEV.P(A1:A100)
A1:B20 and C10	=STDEV.P(A1:B20, C10)

Automatic Workbook Calculation Considerations

By default, Excel 2010 automatically recalculates the values returned by a formula or function if the data feeding the formula or function changes. In numerous cases, this functionality is preferred by many users. However, in large workbooks, with thousands of rows or columns of data and a large number of interdependent formulas, automatic recalculation can take anywhere from a few seconds to more than a minute. If you need to update multiple values in such a workbook, the automatic calculation functionality can actually hinder your efforts; while Excel is recalculating you are unable to work in your worksheets. In these cases, you may want to temporarily disable automatic workbook calculations, revise the necessary data, and then update the workbook calculations. You can also choose to keep automatic workbook calculations turned off and manually update calculations by using the **Calculate Now** command when updates are necessary.

 Access the Checklist tile on your LogicalCHOICE course screen for reference information and job aids on **How to Use Specialized Functions.**

ACTIVITY 2-3
Locating and Using Specialized Functions

Before You Begin
The my_author_data.xlsx file is open.

Scenario
Your supervisor is pleased with the income earned information you provided her for the list of authors. Now she is asking for more specific information from the raw data regarding authors and their sales. Specifically, she would like to know the following:

How many authors have been with the company for five or fewer years?

What is the average sales total for authors whose books sell for more than $5.99?

You're fairly certain you know which function to use to answer your supervisor's second question (the AVERAGEIF function), but you are unsure of which function to use to answer the first question. You decide to use the **Insert Function** dialog box to help you determine the best function to use before making the calculations. Once you've determined which functions you need to use, you will add labels on the worksheet to identify the new values the functions will return.

1. Determine which function will help answer your supervisor's first question.
   a) On the **Formula Bar**, select the **Insert Function** button. *fx*
   b) In the **Insert Function** dialog box, in the **Search for a function** field, type *Count entries at or below a certain value* and select **Go**.
   c) Beneath the **Select a function** section, review the description of the COUNT function.
   d) In the **Select a function** section, select **COUNTIF** and review its description.

2. **Which of these functions would best answer the question: How many authors have been with the company for five or fewer years?**

3. Close the **Insert Function** dialog box.

4. Add labels for the cells that will contain the functions.
   a) Select cell **J2** and type *Authors Five or Fewer Years*
   b) Press **Enter**.
   c) Adjust the width of column **J** to accommodate the new text.
   d) Ensure that cell **J3** is selected, type *Average Sales Over $5.99* and press **Enter**.

5. Use the COUNTIF function to answer your supervisor's first question.
   a) Select cell **K2** and select the **Insert Function** button.
   b) In the **Insert Function** dialog box, if the COUNTIF function does not appear in the **Select a function** list, in the **Search for a function** field, type *countif* and select **Go**.
   c) In the **Select a function** list, ensure that **COUNTIF** is selected and select **OK**.
   d) In the **Function Arguments** dialog box, select the **Range** field's **Collapse Dialog** button.
   e) Select cell **C2**, press **Ctrl+Shift+down arrow**, and press **Enter**.

    f) Ensure that **Years_Under_Contract** appears in the **Range** field.

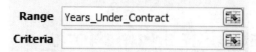

    g) In the **Criteria** field, type *<=5* and select **OK**.

6. Use the AVERAGEIF function to answer your supervisor's second question.
    a) Select cell **K3** and type *=aver*
    b) From the **Formula AutoComplete** pop-up menu, double-click **AVERAGEIF**.
    c) Type *se*
    d) From the **Formula AutoComplete** pop-up menu, double-click **Sell_Price** and type a comma (,).

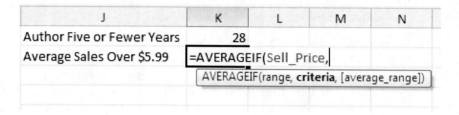

    e) Type *">5.99"* and type a comma.

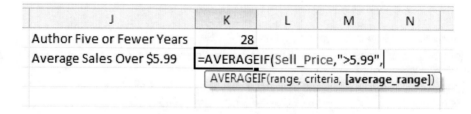

    f) Type *inc* and double-click **Income_Earned** in the pop-up window.
    g) Press **Ctrl+Enter**.
    h) Apply the **Currency** formatting to cell **K3**.

7. Save the workbook.

TOPIC C

Use Array Formulas

As you have used Excel for some time, you're well aware of the advantages of reusing formulas in worksheets. By copying a formula down a column or across a row, you save yourself the effort of manually typing the formula in each cell or pasting the formula over an over again. This works well in smaller worksheets, but what if you had to drag a formula down a column with 10,000 rows? Although that would be much easier than manually typing a formula 10,000 times, this can still be awkward and time consuming. It seems there should be an easier way to perform a calculation on a large number of cells simultaneously.

Excel 2010 contains array formulas, a powerful feature, that is largely underused. Array formulas allow you to perform a calculation on a large number of cells simultaneously, as well as a number of other seemingly complex computations, quickly, easily, and accurately. Gaining a foundational understanding of how to use these powerful Excel formulas will open whole new doors to you, help protect the integrity of your data, and, generally, make your Excel working life much easier.

Arrays

In order to understand how array formulas work, you'll need to know what an *array* is. An array, in the most basic sense, is simply a group of items. In Excel, an array is a group of cells. An array can be made up of cells in a single row or a single column, which are referred to as one-dimensional horizontal arrays and one-dimensional vertical arrays, respectively. An array can also include cells in multiple rows or columns, in which case it is known as a two-dimensional array. You may be thinking that arrays sound exactly like ranges, and that would be correct. The key difference between an array and a range is that an array is the representation of the location of the range in a computer's memory. Put another way, when an array formula acts upon a range, the range becomes an array. It is the range stored in the machine's memory so that the machine can perform calculations on it.

 Note: You can store arrays by using defined names just as you can create named cells and ranges.

Array Formulas

Array formulas allow you to perform multiple calculations on cells in an array simultaneously. To illustrate the power and effectiveness of array formulas consider the following image.

	A	B	C	D	E
1	**Author**	**Sales**	**Rate**	**Commission**	
2	Fred	$25,000.00	7.00%	$1,750.00	
3	Sally	$32,700.00	9.00%	$2,943.00	
4	Amy	$48,325.00	9.00%	$4,349.25	
5	Lauren	$75,456.00	9.00%	$6,791.04	
6	Bill	$103,210.00	12.00%	$12,385.20	
7	John	$5,978.00	7.00%	$418.46	
8					
9			**Total**	$28,636.95	
10					

Here, a formula has been entered in cell **D2** to multiply the author's sales by his or her commission rate. The formula was copied down the column from cell **D2** to cell **D7** and then the SUM function was used in cell **D9** to total the commission payments for all authors. This is likely the method you would have used in the same situation. However, imagine that you were trying to do the same for a publishing company with 5,000 authors. It's easy to see how this could become quite a chore. Now, consider this example.

	A	B	C	D	E
1	**Author**	**Sales**	**Rate**		
2	Fred	$25,000.00	7.00%		
3	Sally	$32,700.00	9.00%		
4	Amy	$48,325.00	9.00%		
5	Lauren	$75,456.00	9.00%		
6	Bill	$103,210.00	12.00%		
7	John	$5,978.00	7.00%		
8					
9		**Total Commissions Paid**		$28,636.95	
10					

Here, the same total has been reached, but without taking all the extra steps as in the first example. So, how does one do this? By using array formulas. Here, Excel has been directed to multiply the figures in column **B** by the figures in column **C**, and then add the products together and display the total in cell **D9**. And it was done by using a single formula. Let's take a closer look at how this works.

There are actually two general types of array formulas: *single-cell array formulas* and *multi-cell array formulas*. The illustrated example utilizes a single-cell array formula, but let's first look at multi-cell array formulas, as they may illustrate how array formulas work a little bit better.

Multi-Cell Array Formulas

As you may have guessed, you enter multi-cell array formulas in multiple cells, which yields multiple results for the calculation. Look back at the first example and consider the steps it took to calculate the commission payment for all authors. First, a simple multiplication formula was entered, and then it was dragged down to paste it in the remaining cells in the column. What if this didn't need to be done? Using multi-cell array formulas, you can calculate the commission payment for all authors at once, but you have to know how to tell Excel to do this.

Because array formulas work on arrays (ranges) instead of just single cells, you can enter a single array formula into all of the cells in the range **D2:D7** at once, and Excel will calculate the commission payment for all authors simultaneously. To do this, you would select the entire range **D2:D7** and then enter the following formula in the **Formula Bar**:

=B2:B7*C2:C7

Here, we're telling Excel to multiply the corresponding set of cells from each row together and place the associated results in the corresponding cells in the range **D2:D7**. But there's a catch: If you simply press **Enter** or **Tab** to enter the formula, Excel will calculate the result for the active cell only, leaving the others blank. In order to enter an array formula in worksheet cells, you must press **Ctrl+Shift+Enter**. For this reason, array formulas are often referred to as *Ctrl-Shift-Enter*, or CSE, formulas. When you enter this array formula properly, the worksheet will look like this.

	D2			f_x {=B2:B7*C2:C7}	
	A	B	C	D	E
1	**Author**	**Sales**	**Rate**	**Commission**	
2	Fred	$25,000.00	7.00%	$1,750.00	
3	Sally	$32,700.00	9.00%	$2,943.00	
4	Amy	$48,325.00	9.00%	$4,349.25	
5	Lauren	$75,456.00	9.00%	$6,791.04	
6	Bill	$103,210.00	12.00%	$12,385.20	
7	John	$5,978.00	7.00%	$418.46	
8					

There are a couple of key points to mention here. First, notice the curly brackets Excel automatically placed around the formula when it was entered. Those designate an array in Excel (more on that later). Second, Excel entered the exact same formula in each cell in the range **D2:D7**. You cannot change any of the array formulas without changing all of them, and you must press **Ctrl+Shift +Enter** if you wish to modify the array formula. This adds a level of protection for the formulas in your worksheets. Again, there will be more on this later.

Single-Cell Array Formulas

Single-cell array formulas perform multiple calculations on arrays and display the result in a single cell. In the second example mentioned previously, a single-cell array formula was used to both multiply the sales figures by the rates for each author and to add those results together to get the total payment figure, all with a single formula in cell **D9**.

	D9			f_x {=SUM(B2:B7*C2:C7)}	
	A	B	C	D	E
1	**Author**	**Sales**	**Rate**		
2	Fred	$25,000.00	7.00%		
3	Sally	$32,700.00	9.00%		
4	Amy	$48,325.00	9.00%		
5	Lauren	$75,456.00	9.00%		
6	Bill	$103,210.00	12.00%		
7	John	$5,978.00	7.00%		
8					
9		**Total Commissions Paid**		$28,636.95	
10					

Notice here that Excel automatically added the curly brackets around the formula, indicating it is an array formula. Also take note that the SUM function was used with the range references as arguments to complete the calculation. The array formula performed the first part of the calculation just as the multi-cell array formula example did, and then it used the SUM function to add all of the results together. This illustrates the true power of the array formula.

You can use array formulas to save time, ensure formula accuracy, create leaner workbooks that take up less storage space and refresh calculations more quickly, use less real estate on your worksheets, and add a level of protection to your workbook calculations.

Array Formula Syntax

As is the case with any formula or function in Excel, understanding array and array formula syntax lies at the core of mastering array formulas. We'll first look at array syntax and examine how that applies to array formula syntax.

Array Syntax

As previously mentioned, arrays are similar to ranges but they exist in a computer's memory as opposed to existing in a series of worksheet cells. Although you can reference cell ranges in array formulas, you can also create arrays that exist only in memory. These arrays are known as *array constants*. An array constant is simply a series of values, logical values, or text entries stored in memory (as defined names) or entered directly into array formulas, as opposed to being entered in cells. Once created, array constants can be used in array formulas just as a constant can be used in a standard formula. There are four key points of array constant syntax:

- As with array formulas, array constants must be enclosed in curly brackets. There is an important difference between the two, though: You manually type the curly brackets to create an array constant.
- To separate entries into columns in an array constant, use commas.
- To separate entries into rows in an array constant, use semi-colons.
- If you include text entries in an array constant, they must be enclosed in double quotation marks (" ").

Consider the following example:

10	15	20
12	56	32
11	98	78

The array constant equivalent of this range is {**10, 15, 20; 12, 56, 32; 11, 98, 78**}.

 Note: Keep in mind that array constants don't exist in actual, "physical" cells, so cell and range references do not apply.

So, rather than taking up worksheet space by populating the numeric values, you can simply use the array constant. Remember that you can also save an array by using a defined name so you can reuse it in multiple array formulas.

Arrays in Array Formula Syntax

You create array formulas by using any formula operators or existing functions you would use to create standard formulas and functions in Excel. The key difference in the syntax of array formulas, as opposed to standard formulas and functions, is the set of curly brackets that enclose the formula. Excel automatically places brackets around a formula or function when you enter it by pressing **Ctrl+Shift+Enter**.

The other main difference is that you can include ranges and array constants as arguments in array formulas in order to perform multiple calculations by using formula and function operators simultaneously, without having to copy formulas in multiple cells. Let's look at one more example to illustrate this point.

D8	▼	f_x {=SUM(B2:B6*C2:C6*D2:D6)}

	A	B	C	D	E	F
1	Rep	Units Sold	Price	Rate		
2	Fred	12	$1,500.00	9.0%		
3	Amy	87	$1,700.00	8.0%		
4	Josephine	15	$3,265.00	12.0%		
5	Terri	65	$1,578.00	7.0%		
6	Joe	38	$9,874.00	9.0%		
7						
8			Total Commissions	$60,277.98		
9						

This example is slightly more complex than the first one. Here, the number of units each sales rep sold is being multiplied by the cost of the product each rep sells and then multiplying that number by each sales rep's commission rate. This is all enclosed in a SUM function, so in one step, the total sales commissions the organization will have to pay out was calculated. Let's break down the syntax:

- The curly brackets tell Excel that this is an array formula, so it can perform operations on related values from a series of arrays (in this case, ranges).
- The SUM function tells Excel to add a series of values.
- The set of parentheses enclose the arguments for the SUM function as they would for a standard SUM function.
- The arguments for the SUM function, as this is an array formula, are telling Excel to multiply the corresponding values in the various columns for each rep. For example, for Fred, the formula multiplies 12 by 1,500 and then multiplies the product of that calculation by 9 percent. For Amy, the formula multiplies 87 by 1,700, and then multiplies the product by 8 percent. This carries on for each rep, and then Excel sums all of those values to give us the total commissions paid of $67,277.98.

It is also important to remember that you can simply include array constants in array formulas, and these can be used in place of or in conjunction with range references. Let's say you need to present the information from the previous example at a sales meeting, and you don't want to advertise commission rates for sales reps to the other people in the room. By using array constants, you can create the same array formula without the need to display the commission rate data in cells.

D8	▼	f_x {=SUM(B2:B6*C2:C6*{0.09;0.08;0.12;0.07;0.09})}

	A	B	C	D	E	F	G
1	Rep	Units Sold	Price				
2	Fred	12	$1,500.00				
3	Amy	87	$1,700.00				
4	Josephine	15	$3,265.00				
5	Terri	65	$1,578.00				
6	Joe	38	$9,874.00				
7							
8			Total Commissions	$60,277.98			
9							

Notice here, the range reference **D2:D6** was simple replaced with the array constant **{0.09;0.08;0.12;0.07;0.09}**. This way, the data doesn't need to appear in the worksheet but the array formula performs the same calculation. Remember that you must manually type the curly brackets around array constants in array formulas. You must also press **Ctrl+Shift+Enter** to enter the formula as an array formula; again, Excel automatically places the outside curly brackets around the entire array formula.

Let's look at one more simple example of how array formulas can work on entire ranges (arrays) of data. Let's say you want to multiply one range of values by another range of values, but the values are contained in multiple rows and columns as in this worksheet:

	A5		▼	f_x	{=A1:C3*E1:G3}		
	A	**B**	**C**	**D**	**E**	**F**	**G**
1	10	20	30		2	3	4
2	15	25	35		2	3	4
3	20	40	60		2	3	4
4							
5	20	60	120				
6	30	75	140				
7	40	120	240				
8							

Here, the array formula is multiplying the corresponding values from the range A1:C3 and the range E1:G3 and returning the products in the cells in A5:C7. The formula systematically multiplies the value in A1 by the value in E1 and places the result in cell A5. Then it does the same for B1 and F1 and places the result in B5. This carries on until all nine values are calculated and the results are returned in the associated cells. And it's all done with a single array formula.

Array Formula Rules

You must follow some pretty specific rules when working with arrays and array formulas. While some of these have been touched upon in the previous sections, here is a recap of the rules we've already covered and a few rules that have not been mentioned.

Array Formula Rules

- You must press **Ctrl+Shift+Enter** to enter an array formula. This is perhaps the most important rule you should remember about array formulas.
- Excel automatically places the curly brackets around an array formula when you press **Ctrl-Shift-Enter**. If you type them in the formula yourself, Excel treats the formula like text. Remember that all formulas must begin with an equal sign. If you begin a formula with an open curly bracket, Excel won't know you want to enter a formula.
- You can use any of the built-in functions in Excel as array formulas.

Multi-Cell Array Formula Rules

- You must select all cells into which you wish to place a multi-cell array formula first, and then enter the formula.
- You cannot edit or delete a multi-cell array formula in just one or only some of the cells containing it. You must delete or change it in all cells at once.
- You can move an entire multi-cell array formula, but you cannot move only some of the cells included in the formula.
- You cannot insert or delete rows, columns, or cells in a multi-cell array formula, but you can add rows or columns to the end of one.

Array Rules

- You must manually enter the curly brackets around array constants.
- In arrays, commas separate entries into columns and semi-colons separate entries into rows.
- Arrays can contain numeric values, text, or logical values.
- In arrays, text must be enclosed in double quotation marks (" ").
- Array constants cannot contain other arrays, formulas, or functions.
- You can save array constants as defined names, and use those defined names in formulas and functions just as you would a named cell or range.

 Access the Checklist tile on your LogicalCHOICE course screen for reference information and job aids on How to Use Array Formulas.

ACTIVITY 2-4
Using Array Formulas

Before You Begin
The my_author_data.xlsx file is open.

Scenario
Company leadership is interested in knowing more about how much value they're receiving from the company's relationships with its authors. In addition to the information you've already provided, your supervisor is now asking for detailed information about income based on the number of titles each of the authors has published through Fuller and Ackerman and the average income the company has earned per contract year. Specifically, she wants to know:

- How much income has the company generated from each author per title?
- What is the average income per year under contract for all authors?

You'd like anyone viewing your workbook to be able to easily tell how you arrived at these figures, so you decide not to use the calculated totals in the **Income Earned** column to perform the calculations to answer the first question. You also decide to use array formulas to answer both questions to avoid unnecessary copying of formulas.

---

1. Label a column for income per title and add a new label for average income per contract year.
   a) Select cell **H1**, type *Income Per Title* and press **Enter**.
   b) Select cell **J4**, type *Average Income/Contract Year* and press **Enter**.
   c) If necessary, adjust the width of column **J** to accommodate the new label.

2. Use a multi-cell array formula to determine the income per title for each author.
   a) In the **Name Box**, type *h2:h94* and press **Enter**.

    Note: Please follow these steps precisely as written. After you type the range and press **Enter**, you can simply begin typing the text in the following step. You do not need to select anything on-screen first.

   b) Type *=(n*
   c) From the pop-up menu, double-click **No_of_Books_Sold**.
   d) Type **se*
   e) From the pop-up menu, double-click **Sell_Price**.
   f) Type *)/no* and, from the pop-up menu, select **No_of_Titles_in_Print**.

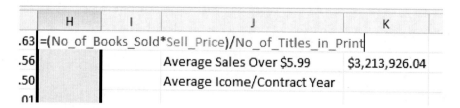

   g) Press **Ctrl+Shift+Enter**.

h) Verify that Excel placed curly brackets around the formula and entered it into all of the selected cells.

> *fx* {=(No_of_Books_Sold*Sell_Price)/No_of_Titles_in_Print}

i) Apply the **Currency** number format to the cells in column **H**.

3. Use a single-cell array formula to determine the overall average of income per contract year.
   a) Select cell **K4**.
   b) Enter the following formula: *=average(Income_Earned/Years_Under_Contract)*
   c) Press **Ctrl+Shift+Enter**.
   d) Verify that Excel placed curly brackets around the function and then entered it into cell **K4**.

> *fx* {=AVERAGE(Income_Earned/Years_Under_Contract)}

	H	I	J	K
	Income Per			
:arned	**Title**			
785.63	$84,119.04		Author Five or Fewer Years	28
214.56	$147,586.75		Average Sales Over $5.99	$3,213,926.04
643.50	$1,021,321.75		Average Icome/Contract Year	602911.8288
555.01	$83,323.18			

e) Apply the **Currency** number format to cell **K4**.

4. Save and close the workbook.

Summary

In this lesson, you created advanced formulas by using range and cell names instead of references, by examining the syntax of commonly used specialized functions, and by writing array formulas to perform multiple calculations simultaneously. You are just beginning to unlock Excel's potential as a data analysis tool, which will take you beyond using Excel as a mere calculator and data storage tool. By building this foundational knowledge of Excel formula syntax, you are taking the first steps to true Excel mastery.

How do you think using defined names will benefit you as you create future workbooks?

How do you plan to incorporate the use of array formulas in your workbooks?

 Note: Check your LogicalCHOICE Course screen for opportunities to interact with your classmates, peers, and the larger LogicalCHOICE online community about the topics covered in this course or other topics you are interested in. From the Course screen you can also access available resources for a more continuous learning experience.

3 | Analyzing Data with Functions and Conditional Formatting

Lesson Time: 45 minutes

Lesson Objectives

In this lesson, you will analyze data with functions and formulas. You will:

*   Analyze data by using text and logical functions.

*   Apply advanced conditional formatting.

Lesson Introduction

So far, you have started creating some of the more advanced functions and formulas possible within Excel. In that process, you have begun to see how Excel can be used for much more than simple calculations and is, in fact, a powerful data analysis tool. Now that you have had a glimpse of some of Excel's more powerful functions, it's time to start asking Excel some more difficult questions.

Data analysis, at its core, is about asking questions of your data and getting the answers you need to ensure your organization's decision makers are taking action based on sound organizational intelligence. In order to do that, you'll need to take a deeper dive into the world of Excel functions and formulas. Analyzing data in Excel essentially boils down to two tasks: manipulating your data to ask questions of it and displaying the answers in a way that people can understand them. In this lesson, you'll begin to do just that.

TOPIC A

Analyze Data by Using Text and Logical Functions

You're already familiar with some of the most basic and most commonly used Excel functions. As your data analysis tasks become more and more complex or if you simply work in a specialized field and require specific functions more than other users might, you'll want to keep adding to your lexicon of familiar functions. The more comfortable and knowledgeable you become with a wide variety of Excel functions, the more able you will be to ask Excel questions of your data and get the answers you need.

Text Functions

Text functions in Excel, as you may have guessed, allow you to manipulate, piece together, or analyze textual content in your worksheets. Although you can use text functions to perform some data analysis, a better way to think of them is as a way to prepare your data for analysis or transfer. Essentially, text functions can help you format textual data in a particular way to suit your needs. For example, you may need to incorporate data from an external source, say a database or a website, into an existing worksheet. Or, you may need to upload your existing data from Excel workbooks into a database. In such cases, there is a good chance the formatting requirements for data entries do not match. If this is the case, re-entering all of the data could be time-consuming and lead to errors. You'll want to take advantage of the text functions in Excel to clean up your data to better align with the given requirements.

Let's take a look at the purpose and syntax for some of the more commonly used Excel text functions.

The LEFT and RIGHT Functions

Syntax: =LEFT(text, [num_chars]), or =RIGHT(text, [num_chars])

Description: The LEFT and RIGHT functions return a specified number of characters from either the left or the right side of a text string, including spaces. You would use these functions, for example, if you needed to enter all organizational employee names into a database table, but the table supports only, say, the first five letters of someone's last name. In that case, you would need to truncate all entries in the last name column to only contain five characters. For both of these functions, the syntax is the same. The required **text** argument tells the function where to reference the text, if you enter a cell reference, or states the text to be examined (although this would likely be used far less frequently). If you enter a text string in the **text** argument manually in these functions, you must surround the text with double quotation marks (" "). The optional **num_chars** argument specifies the number of characters you want Excel to return. Remember that this includes blank spaces. If you don't specify a value for the **num_chars** argument, Excel returns only the first character.

In the following examples, assume the text string *Amy Hall* is entered in cell **A1**.

To Return These Characters	Enter This Function
A	=LEFT(A1)
Amy H	=LEFT(A1, 5)
Hall	=RIGHT(A1, 4)
Fred	=LEFT("Freddy", 4)

The MID Function

Syntax: =MID(text, start_num, num_chars)

Description: This function is similar to the LEFT and RIGHT functions with the exception that it returns characters from the middle of a text string. In the function's syntax, the required **text** argument tells the function where to reference the text, if you enter a cell reference, or states the text to be examined. As with the LEFT and RIGHT functions, if you manually enter a text string in the **text** argument in the MID function, you must surround it with double quotation marks (" "). The required **start_num** argument tells the function which character to start with, and the required **num_chars** argument tells it how many characters to return; empty spaces count for each of these arguments. Unlike the LEFT and RIGHT functions, you must enter a value for the **num_chars** argument.

In the following examples, assume that the text string *Frederick Thomas Rose* is entered in cell **D4**.

To Return These Characters	Enter This Function
Thomas	=MID(D4, 11, 6)
Thom	=MID(D4, 11, 4)
Thomas R	=MID(D4, 11, 8)
rick Thomas R	=MID("Frederick Thomas Rose", 6, 13)

The LEN Function

Syntax: =LEN(text)

Description: This function simply returns the number of characters present in a text string, including spaces. The name, LEN, is a shortened version of the word "length," which could help you remember its purpose. You could use this function, for example, to check a column of data to ensure that all entries are within the allowed number of characters to enter into a database. Another useful application of this function is to determine if entries will fit within cells you have formatted to only allow a particular number of characters. This lets you know whether or not you can copy and paste the text to the new cells without encountering errors. In the function's syntax, the **text** argument tells the function where to reference the text string, if you enter a cell reference, or states the text to be examined. If you manually enter a text string in the **text** argument, you must surround it with double quotation marks (" ").

In the following examples, assume that the text string *Amy Hall* is entered in cell **A1** and the text string *Frederick Thomas Rose* is entered in cell **D4**.

If You Enter This Function	Excel Returns This Value
=LEN(A1)	8
=LEN(D4)	21

The TRIM Function

Syntax: =TRIM(text)

Description: This function removes all empty spaces from cells containing text strings except for single spaces between words. This function can solve a number of data compatibility issues, such as leading empty spaces at the beginning of text strings, extra spaces between words, and trailing empty spaces entered following text strings (which can be especially problematic, as they are more difficult to notice by simply looking at your data). In the function's syntax, the **text** argument tells the function where to reference the text string; overwhelmingly, this will be a cell reference. Although the TRIM function works if you manually type the text string into the **text** argument enclosed in double quotes, there is little reason to ever do this.

In the following examples, assume that each text string is entered in cell **A1** without the quotation marks, which are included for your spacing reference.

For This Original Text String	This Function	Returns This Value
"Amy Hall"	=TRIM(A1)	"Amy Hall"
"Frederick Rose"	=TRIM(A1)	"Frederick Rose"
"Robert Toner "	=TRIM(A1)	"Robert Toner"

The UPPER, LOWER, and PROPER Functions

Syntax: =UPPER(text), =LOWER(text), or =PROPER(text)

Description: Use these functions to correct casing issues that may make textual data invalid for particular applications. The UPPER function converts all lowercase characters in a text string to uppercase characters; the LOWER function does the opposite. The PROPER function capitalizes the first character of each word in a text string and ensures that all other characters are lowercase. The **text** argument for all three functions tells Excel where to reference the text strings. Typically, you will use cell references for the **text** argument, although, as in other Excel text functions, you can manually enter the text string, surrounded by double quotation marks, in the argument.

In the following examples, assume each text string is entered in cell **B2** without the quotation marks.

For This Original Text String	This Function	Returns This Value
"Amy Hall"	=UPPER(B2)	"AMY HALL"
"Freddy ROSE"	=LOWER(B2)	"freddy rose"
"robert toner"	=PROPER(B2)	"Robert Toner"
"jERRY aPPLETon"	=PROPER(B2)	"Jerry Appleton"

The CONCATENATE Function

One of the most powerful text functions available in Excel 2010 is the CONCATENATE function. This function allows you to concatenate, or join together, text strings from multiple cells into a single cell. This function can save you massive amounts of time when you need to pull together data from multiple cells that already exists in your worksheets. Say you've been placed in charge of updating your organizations' personnel records, which the human resources department saves in Excel workbooks. You've been asked by HR to change the format that names are entered in. Previously, first and last names were entered into separate columns within the worksheets, but now they want full names entered into a single column. The CONCATENATE function is perfect for tasks such as this.

Here is the syntax for the CONCATENATE function: =CONCATENATE(text1, [text2], ...)

In the function's syntax, **text1** is the only required argument, which represents the first string of text you wish to include in the new cell. You can add up to 254 other arguments, for a total of 255 joined text strings. You can manually type text or numerical values as arguments and you can use cell references to include text entered into cells. The CONCATENATE function will include empty spaces (leading spaces, trailing spaces, and spaces between words and values in cells) when it joins text strings together. If you wish to include spaces where none are present in the original data, you can use an empty space enclosed in double quotation marks (" ") as an argument.

Let's take a look at a few examples.

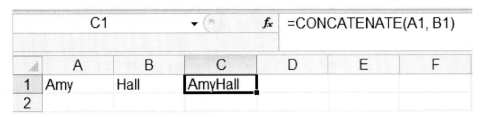

In this first example, notice the CONCATENATE function joined the text strings from cells A1 and B1 together in cell C1, and that there is no space between the first and the last name. This is because there are no leading or trailing spaces in either cell A1 or B1, and because one was not included in the function. Now let's modify this function to include a space between the names.

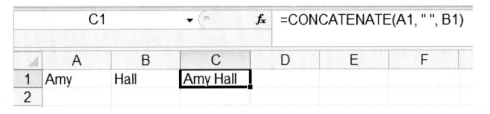

Here, the CONCATENATE function placed a space between the first and the last name because the empty space was included as an argument. In this last example, you see the CONCATENATE function used to join text from more than two cells, to change the order the text strings display in, and to add a character manually.

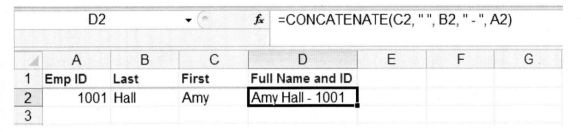

Text Concatenation with the Ampersand

There is an easier way, one that many Excel users prefer, to concatenate text strings and numeric values from worksheet cells: the ampersand (&) operator in formulas. By using this method, you can still include either cell references or text and values entered in double quotation marks to join text strings. This is how the first and the third examples would work if you used the ampersand operator in formulas instead of the CONCATENATE function.

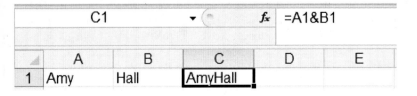

	D2	▼		*fx*	=B2&" "&C2&" - "&A2	

	A	B	C	D	E
1	Emp ID	Last	First	Full Name and ID	
2	1001	Hall	Amy	Hall Amy - 1001	
3					

Logical Functions

As previously mentioned, one of the keys to data analysis is the ability to ask Excel questions about your data and get the answers you need. Perhaps the most foundational set of tools to do this is the collection of logical functions available in Excel. Logical functions enable you to ask questions of your data, for which Excel can return one of two values: TRUE or FALSE. Logical functions also enable you to perform calculations when certain conditions are met or to perform different calculations based on a variety of criteria.

By adding simple logical decision making to your formulas and functions, you can begin to gain a whole new perspective on the information available in your raw data. For example, logical functions can help answer questions such as:

- Did my sales reps reach or beat their sales targets for the quarter?
- Is revenue up from last year?
- Does this applicant meet all of the requirements to be approved for a loan?
- Which products are for sale in Mexico and were produced in India?
- If this sales rep met her goal for the quarter, what is her commission payment?

It's clear to see from this small sample of questions how the use of Logical functions can be a powerful and useful method for extracting intelligence from your data. Before you dive in to the operators and syntax associated with logical functions, you need to take a look at a new type of cell data: *logical values.*

Logical Values

You are already familiar with the four basic types of data that can be entered into Excel cells: numeric values, text/labels, formulas/functions, and dates and times. When working with logical functions and operators in Excel, you will encounter a new type of data: logical values. The only values that Excel can return when you apply a logical test to your data are TRUE or FALSE. This actually forms the basis for all logic used in computer programming and why the binary numbering system is so critical to how computers operate. In Excel, these logical values serve the same purpose as they do for programmers, establishing whether or not given criteria have been met.

Logical values may look like text, but they are quite different in both appearance (for the most part) and behavior. First, logical values are always displayed in all capital letters, which distinguishes them from standard text strings. In fact, if you simply enter "true," "false," "True," or "False" in a cell, Excel automatically converts the text to logical values and displays them in all caps. In order to even be able to enter these as stand-alone text strings, you must format the cell for text only or use text functions/formulas to enter the text.

Second, logical values behave similarly to numeric values in functions and formulas, and in some cases are treated as either a 1 or a 0. And, logical values can be used as arguments in certain functions as well as being returned by Excel as the result of a function performing a logical test.

*f*ₓ =(E2*F2)>1000000

	C	D	E	F	G	
	Years Under Contract	Number of Titles in Print	Number of Books Sold	Sell Price	Sales Greater Than $1 Million?	
	11.56	15	316,237	$ 3.99	TRUE	
	6.73	14	344,944	$ 5.99	TRUE	
	0.15	2	255,650	$ 7.99	TRUE	} Logical values
	5.16	11	83,399	$10.99	FALSE	
	8.64	15	16,892	$ 2.99	FALSE	
	7.94	7	283,588	$10.99	TRUE	

Figure 3-1: Logical values appear to be simple text, but behave much differently. Excel displays logical values in all capital letters to help distinguish them from simple text.

Logical Operators

One other key component of working with Logical functions that you need to examine before diving into specific logical functions and their syntax is *logical operators*. Logical operators behave similarly to mathematical and reference operators in that they tell Excel which specific task to perform. You use logical operators, also known as *comparison operators*, to examine two values to see if they meet a specific logical condition. If the values meet the logical condition, the operation returns a logical value of TRUE; if the values do not meet the logical condition, the operation returns a logical value of FALSE. For example, say you have the value **10** in cell **A1**, and the value **15** in cell **B1**. If you use logical operators to ask Excel if the value in cell A1 is greater than the value in cell B1, Excel will return the logical value FALSE.

The following table describes the syntax and purpose of the logical operators in Excel.

Name	Comparison Operator	This Logical Operator Determines Whether or Not
Equal to	=	The specified values are the same.
Greater than	>	The first value is greater than the second value.
Less than	<	The first value is less than the second value.
Greater than or equal to	>=	The first value is greater than or equal to the second value.
Less than or equal to	<=	The first value is less than or equal to the second value.
Not equal to	<>	The specified values are different.

 Note: Remember that Excel is not a "what you see is what you get" type of environment. It may not always be immediately clear whether two values are equal to each other, or whether or not one is greater than the other simply by looking at them. For example, if you format cells to display only one decimal place but the values entered in those cells contain two or more decimal places, they may appear to be equal when they are not.

Logical Function Syntax

Now that you have some background on logical functions and their associated logical values and operators, it's time to start examining exactly what they can do for you. As with any other type of Excel function, the key to understanding logical functions is understanding their syntax. Let's take a close look at the syntax for the three most important and commonly used logical functions.

The AND Function

Syntax: =AND(logical1, [logical2], ..., [logical30])

Description: The AND function returns the logical value TRUE when all arguments entered in the function are true and returns the logical value FALSE if any one of the arguments is not true. You would use this function, for example, to determine if a sales rep has fulfilled all requirements to receive a commission bonus or to determine if an applicant has met all requirements to qualify for a loan.

In the function's syntax, **logical1** is the first logical test you wish to apply. Technically, only one argument is required in the AND function, but typically more than one is used; if you only wish to perform a single logical test, you could simply enter a formula with the single logical test. The AND function can contain up to 30 arguments, all of which must either return a logical value, or be a cell or range reference or an array containing logical values. In addition to using logical operators to return a logical value, you can also use mathematical statements as arguments. For example, 1+1=2 would return a logical value of TRUE.

For the following examples, assume cell **A1** contains the value 10, the cell **B1** contains the value 15, and the cell **C1** contains the value 20. Also, assume cell **D1** contains the logical value FALSE.

If You Enter This Function	Excel Will Return This Logical Value
=AND(A1<B1, B1<C1)	TRUE
=AND(A1<B1, A1>C1)	FALSE
=AND(A1<>B1, 1+1=2)	TRUE
=AND(C1>B1, D1)	FALSE
=AND(TRUE, A1<50)	TRUE

The OR Function

Syntax: =OR(logical1, [logical2], ..., [logical30])

Description: The only difference between the OR function and the AND function is that the OR function will return a logical value of TRUE if any one of the arguments evaluates to TRUE. It contains the same arguments, can support the same number of arguments, and the arguments can be the same items as with the AND function. If all of the arguments in an OR function are not true, the function will return the logical value FALSE. You would use this function, for example, if you wanted to identify sales reps who achieved at least one out of a set of multiple sales targets.

For the following examples, assume cell **A1** contains the value 10, cell **B1** contains the value 15, and cell **C1** contains the value 20. Also, assume cell **D1** contains the logical value TRUE.

If You Enter This Function	Excel Will Return This Logical Value
=OR(A1<B1, B1>C1)	TRUE
=OR(A1>B1, B1>C1)	FALSE
=OR(A1=B1, 1+1=2)	TRUE
=OR(A1>=B1, D1)	TRUE
=OR(FALSE, A1<5)	FALSE

The IF Function

Syntax: =IF(logical_test, value_if_true, value_if_false)

Description: The IF function returns one value if the logical test you enter as an argument is true, and it returns a different value if the logical test is not true. You would use this function, for example, to determine a sales rep's commission if, and only if, he or she met a particular sales goal.

In the function's syntax, **logical_test** is the condition you would like test, for example, are employee X's sales more than $1 million? You can use any item that returns a logical value for this argument: cells, ranges, or arrays populated with logical values, simple logical statements, or even other logical functions. Excel returns the result of the **value_if_true** argument if the logical condition is met. It returns the result of the **value_if_false** argument if the logical condition is not met. Either of these arguments can contain numeric values, references, text, or even formulas and functions. Text strings in either the **value_if_true** or the **value_if_false** arguments must be enclosed in double quotation marks. (" "). If you do not enter a value in these arguments, they return the numeric value zero (0).

Let's take a look at a couple of examples of the IF function in worksheets. In this first example, sales reps will receive a 9-percent commission on their annual sales if those sales meet or exceed the $1,000 threshold. Otherwise, they will not receive a commission.

	G2			*fx*	=IF(F2>=1000, F2*$B$6, "No commission")	

	A	B	C	D	E	F	G
1	Sales Rep	Q1	Q2	Q3	Q4	Total	Commission
2	Amy	$100.00	$125.00	$300.00	$250.00	$775.00	No commission
3	Fred	$225.00	$400.00	$750.00	$325.00	$1,700.00	
4	Bill	$400.00	$350.00	$200.00	$400.00	$1,350.00	
5							
6	**Rate**	9.0%					

In this example, the **logical_test** argument asks Excel to examine the value in cell **F2** to determine if it is greater than or equal to 1,000. If it is, Excel should multiply the value in cell **F2** by the commission rate in cell **B6**. If it is not, Excel should display the text "No commission." As the logical test returns a value of FALSE, Excel displays the text. Now let's see what happens when the formula is dragged down to the next rep's row.

	G3			*fx*	=IF(F3>=1000, F3*$B$6, "No commission")	

	A	B	C	D	E	F	G
1	Sales Rep	Q1	Q2	Q3	Q4	Total	Commission
2	Amy	$100.00	$125.00	$300.00	$250.00	$775.00	No commission
3	Fred	$225.00	$400.00	$750.00	$325.00	$1,700.00	$153.00
4	Bill	$400.00	$350.00	$200.00	$400.00	$1,350.00	
5							
6	**Rate**	9.0%					

In this case, as the value in cell **F3** is greater than 1,000, meaning the logical test returns a value of TRUE, Excel performs the calculation in the **value_if_true** argument and returns the result in the cell.

Keep in mind that you don't always need an IF function to perform a calculation. You could simply use it to answer the question "Does each sales rep get a commission?" Here's what you would enter:

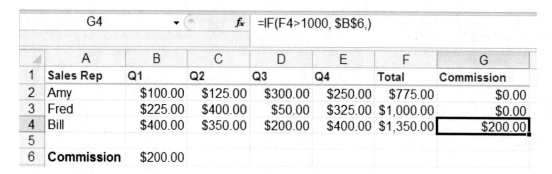

Or, you can simply ask the IF function to return the value in a particular cell if the condition is met. In this last example, assume the sales reps get a flat $200 commission only if their sales exceed $1,000.

	A	B	C	D	E	F	G
1	Sales Rep	Q1	Q2	Q3	Q4	Total	Commission
2	Amy	$100.00	$125.00	$300.00	$250.00	$775.00	$0.00
3	Fred	$225.00	$400.00	$50.00	$325.00	$1,000.00	$0.00
4	Bill	$400.00	$350.00	$200.00	$400.00	$1,350.00	$200.00
5							
6	Commission	$200.00					

G4 ▾ fx =IF(F4>1000, $B$6,)

Here, because the **value_if_true** argument contains a cell reference, the function returns the value in cell **B6** when the logical test returns the value TRUE. Also, as the **value_if_false** argument was left off, the function returns a value of zero (0) in cases where the logical condition was not met.

 Note: You must include the second comma in the IF function arguments if you want the function to return 0 when the logical condition isn't met. Otherwise, it will return a value of FALSE.

Start with Questions, End with Testing

As you begin to use Excel to analyze data, it's important to keep in mind one of the central tenants of data analysis: It's all about asking the right questions to get the answers you need. We've already looked at a few of the types of questions Excel's logical functions can answer. You have an entire arsenal of functions, in a number of categories, at your disposal that can help you answer any number of questions. To get the answers you need, you simply need to know which functions to use. Take a look at the following questions and think about which functions would help you find the answers you seek.

- What was the highest sales total for all stores in the company?
- How many sales reps met or beat the sales goal?
- What are the total sales for sales reps who didn't reach $100,000 in sales?
- On average, how many bikes were shipped each month last year?

Let's consider the first question. You're trying to determine which store had the highest sales total. Imagine you have sales data for all of the store locations in a company in a single worksheet, and total sales are listed in a single column. Given this scenario, you just need to find the largest figure in that column. This tells us to use the MAX function, which will return the largest value in the column if that's where you ask it to look.

For the second question, you'd like to know the number of sales reps who achieved a certain goal. This tells us to use the COUNTIF function, which returns the total number of entries that meet a specified criteria.

The third question is asking for the total amount of sales for reps who didn't reach a particular level. We would use the SUMIF function to total all figures below the 100,000 mark.

The final question seeks to find the average number of units shipped per month of a particular product. If you have the number of units of bikes shipped each month in one column, you would use the AVERAGE function to get the answer.

Remember that you can use the function reference to help you determine which function to use if you're ever unsure. Once you've determined which is the appropriate function to use to answer your question, it's a best practice to test the function in a separate workbook or on a separate worksheet to ensure it returns the answer you're expecting. You can enter simple values in the function arguments and compare the answer to what you calculate manually. Or you can copy a small sample of your data, run the function against it, and examine the returned value to determine if Excel is giving you the answers you expect.

So, determine what it is, exactly, that you want Excel to answer, identify the proper function to use, and then test your formulas or functions to ensure they do what you expect. Following this simple practice can save you countless hours of troubleshooting down the road.

 Access the Checklist tile on your LogicalCHOICE course screen for reference information and job aids on How to Analyze Data by Using Functions.

ACTIVITY 3-1
Using Text Functions

Data File

C:\091019Data\Analyzing Data with Functions and Conditional Formatting
\author_master_roster.xlsx

Before You Begin

Excel 2010 is open.

Scenario

Within the past year, Fuller and Ackerman acquired two smaller publishing houses, bringing the total number of contracted authors to near 1,000. The company has been working to integrate the author rosters for the other two companies into its existing lists. With the increase in people to keep track of, the human resources and IT departments have recommended tracking the information in a newly designed database. There is, however, one issue with this: The format you've been using to keep track of authors doesn't match the requirements of the new database design or other HR workbooks. You decide to use Excel's text functions to reformat your master list of authors to accommodate the new requirements.

Your current master roster, which includes the newly added authors, lists the authors' last names, first names, and middle initials in separate columns. The new requirement is for the first names and the middle initials to appear in the same cell. You decide to use the CONCATENATE function to join the entries into single cells. Your database administrator has also informed you that the last name column for the authors has a limit of 10 characters. After a quick scan of your roster, you realize several last name entries go beyond this limit. So, you decide to use the LEFT function to include only the first 10 characters of all last names. Once you reformat the data, you will be able to copy and paste it to a clean worksheet to hand off to the IT department and Human Resources. And, once this process is approved and finalized, you can begin integrating the full author roster into the workbooks you use to track author performance.

---

1. Open the **author_master_roster.xlsx** file.

2. Create two new columns to accommodate the newly formatted author information.
   a) Select cell **G1**, type *Last Name 10 Char* and press **Tab**.
   b) In cell **H1**, type *First, MI* and press **Enter**.
   c) Adjust the width of the columns to accommodate the new labels and then use the **Format Painter** to match the formating of the new column labels to the existing column labels.

3. Use the LEFT function to return only the first 10 characters of the author last names.
   a) Select cell **G2**.
   b) Select **Formulas→Function Library→Text→LEFT**.
   c) In the **Function Arguments** dialog box, in the **Text** field, select the **Collapse Dialog** button.
   d) Select cell **B2** and press **Enter**.
   e) In the **Num_chars** field, type *10* and select **OK**.
   f) Double-click the **fill handle** to copy the function down column **G**.

4. Use the CONCATENATE function to return the authors' first names and middle initials in the correct format.

a) Select cell **H2** and then select **Formulas→Function Library→Text→CONCATENATE**.
b) In the **Function Arguments** dialog box, in the **Text1** field, select the **Collapse Dialog** button.
c) Select cell **C2** and press **Enter**.
d) In the **Text2** field, type **", "**

 Note: Be sure to include the space after the comma before typing the closing double quotation mark (").

e) In the **Text3** field, select the **Collapse Dialog** button, select cell **D2**, and press **Enter**.
f) Select **OK**.
g) Ensure that Excel returned the text values as expected.

Function Library				Defined Names	

*f*ₓ =CONCATENATE(C2,", ",D2)

C	D	E	F	G	H
First Name	M.I.	Initial Contract Date	Royalty Rate	Last Name 10 Char	First, MI
Idella	S	8/18/2004	9%	Balasubram	Idella, S

h) Double-click the **fill handle** to copy the function down column **H**.
i) Adjust the width of column **H** to accommodate the new text.

5. Save the workbook to the **C:\091019Data\Analyzing Data with Functions and Conditional Formatting** folder as *my_author_master_roster.xlsx* and close the workbook.

ACTIVITY 3-2
Analyzing Data by Using Logical Functions

Data File

C:\091019Data\Analyzing Data with Functions and Conditional Formatting\author_data_03.xlsx

Before You Begin

Excel 2010 is open.

Scenario

Your supervisor has asked for more information regarding the performance and value of Fuller and Ackerman's authors. The company is considering offering more publication opportunities for authors they consider "early producers," authors who have been under contract for fewer than two years and who have published more than four books. Fuller and Ackerman (F&A) leaders are also considering offering bonuses to "high producers" or "long-time authors." F&A considers authors to be "high producers" if they have published 10 or more books and "long-term" if they have been under contract for more than five years.

You realize you'll need to add more columns to the author data workbook you've been developing, so you moved some of the data you previously calculated onto another worksheet and named it "Statistics." You are now ready to add the new columns to identify the authors who meet the given criteria. You plan to use Excel's logical functions to identify the authors who are eligible for further opportunities or bonuses.

---

1. Open the **author_data_03.xlsx** workbook file.

2. Add the column labels for "early producers" and for authors who may be bonus-eligible.
    a) Select cell I1, type *Early Producer?* and press **Tab**.
    b) Add the label *5+ Years or High Producer?* to column J.

3. Use range names to enter a logical function to answer the following question: Which authors have been under contract for fewer than two years and have published more than four books?
    a) Select cell I2.
    b) Type *=and*
    c) From the pop-up menu, double-click **AND**.
    d) Type *years* and, from the pop-up menu, double-click **Years_Under_Contract**.
    e) Type *<2,*

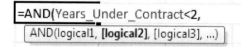

    f) Type *no* and double-click **No_of_Titles_in_Print**.

g) Type *>4* and press **Ctrl+Enter**.

Function Library				Defined Na
fx	=AND(Years_Under_Contract<2,No_of_Titles_in_Print>4)			
C	D	E	F	G

h) Verify that Excel returned the logical value **FALSE** in cell I2.
i) Double-click the fill handle to copy the AND function down the column.

4. Use range names to enter a logical function to answer the following question: Which authors have published 10 or more books or have been under contract for more than five years?

a) Select cell **J2**.
b) Type *=or* and, in the pop-up menu, double-click **OR**.
c) Type *no* and double-click **No_of_Titles_in_Print**.
d) Type *>=10,*

```
=OR(No_of_Titles_in_Print>=10,
   OR(logical1, [logical2], [logical3], ...)
```

e) Type *years* and double-click **Years_Under_Contract**.
f) Type *>5* and press **Ctrl+Enter**.

Function Library				Defined Names
fx	=OR(No_of_Titles_in_Print>=10,Years_Under_Contract>5)			
C	D	E	F	G

g) Verify that Excel returned the logical value **TRUE** in cell J2.
h) Double-click the **fill handle** to copy the OR function down the column.

5. Save the workbook to the **C:\091019Data\Analyzing Data with Functions and Conditional Formatting** folder as *my_author_data_03.xlsx*

TOPIC B

Apply Advanced Conditional Formatting

Nearly every organization needs people who can ask Excel questions about its data to get the information leaders need to make important decision. But often, workbooks and worksheets contain massive amounts of data that can take up thousands of rows and columns. It can be intimidating and confusing to scan across such large worksheets to identify overall patterns in your data or to quickly determine what areas personnel need to direct their attention to. Anyone who's ever examined a large worksheet knows this to be true. Although you've likely applied some basic conditional formatting to highlight particular values in your worksheets, this doesn't necessarily reveal the patterns or trends present in your data. You need a way to format your worksheets so that these patterns or trends stand out immediately. Excel's conditional formatting capabilities go far beyond simple highlighting.

Once you've gotten the answers you need about your data to enable leaders to make informed decisions, you'll need to present that data to them in a way they can use. You'll need to be able to capitalize on Excel's more advanced conditional formatting capabilities to help reveal nuanced patterns in your worksheets that would otherwise be difficult, if not impossible, to discern. Developing these skills will allow you and your organizational leaders to leverage all of the hard work that went into analyzing your raw data in the first place.

Data Bars

Although it's helpful to identify and highlight values that fall above or below a certain threshold, or that fall within some particular range near the top or the bottom of a set of numbers, there is a lot going on in your data at all levels, from top to bottom. Excel includes a number of more advanced and more detailed conditional formatting options than those available in the **Highlight Cells Rules** and the **Top/Bottom Rules** menus. One of these is data bars.

Data bars are graphical representations of the relative value of data in a range of cells compared to the rest of the data in the same range. Data bars appear in worksheet cells behind displayed values, giving worksheet viewers an instant picture of where particular cell values lie when compared to other cell data. The larger the value is in a particular cell, the longer the data bar. Excel includes a variety of pre-formatted data-bar styles and provides you with several options for customizing their appearance and behavior. You can access the data bars commands and options by selecting **Home→Styles→Conditional Formatting→Data Bars**.

Number of Titles in Print	Number of Books Sold	Sell Price	Total Sales
15	316,237	$ 3.99	$ 1,261,785.63
14	344,944	$ 5.99	$ 2,066,214.56
2	255,650	$ 7.99	$ 2,042,643.50
11	83,399	$10.99	$ 916,555.01
15	16,892	$ 2.99	$ 50,507.08
7	283,588	$10.99	$ 3,116,632.12
4	43,921	$ 5.99	$ 263,086.79
13	231,823	$ 3.99	$ 924,973.77
11	140,462	$ 2.99	$ 419,981.38
1	225,503	$ 2.99	$ 674,253.97
8	214,442	$10.99	$ 2,356,717.58
1	295,514	$12.99	$ 3,838,726.86
11	43,062	$23.99	$ 1,033,057.38
3	197,522	$10.99	$ 2,170,766.78
1	496,293	$23.99	$ 11,906,069.07
1	213,766	$23.99	$ 5,128,246.34
12	365,614	$ 9.99	$ 3,652,483.86
4	307,741	$ 5.99	$ 1,843,368.59

Figure 3-2: Data bars give worksheet viewers an instant snapshot of relative values.

Color Scales

Like data bars, *color scales* give worksheet viewers a graphical representation of the relative values of cell data. Instead of appearing as bars of various lengths, however, color scales use various shades of either two or three colors to represent relative values. In a two-color scale, Excel displays high and low values in various shades of the two colors; the darker the color, the closer the value is to either the very highest or the very lowest values. You can use a three-color scale to represent low, middle, and high-range values. Excel includes a number of pre-formatted color scales and provides you with various options for customizing these to suit your needs. You can access the color scales commands and options by selecting **Home→Styles→Conditional Formatting→Color Scales**.

 Note: It is possible to apply more than one type of conditional formatting to the same range of cells.

Number of Titles in Print	Number of Books Sold	Sell Price	Total Sales
7	283,588	$10.99	$ 3,116,632.12
4	43,921	$ 5.99	$ 263,086.79
13	231,823	$ 3.99	$ 924,973.77
11	140,462	$ 2.99	$ 419,981.38
1	225,503	$ 2.99	$ 674,253.97
8	214,442	$10.99	$ 2,356,717.58
1	295,514	$12.99	$ 3,838,726.86
11	43,062	$23.99	$ 1,033,057.38
3	197,522	$10.99	$ 2,170,766.78
1	496,293	$23.99	$ 11,906,069.07
1	213,766	$23.99	$ 5,128,246.34
12	365,614	$ 9.99	$ 3,652,483.86
4	307,741	$ 5.99	$ 1,843,368.59
5	380,640	$ 7.99	$ 3,041,313.60
12	159,593	$ 3.99	$ 636,776.07
1	269,278	$ 3.99	$ 1,074,419.22
2	491,853	$12.99	$ 6,389,170.47
4	188,565	$ 2.99	$ 563,809.35

Figure 3–3: Color scales use two or three colors of various shades to represent relative cell values.

Icon Sets

Icon sets function in much the same way as data bars and color scales, but they use sets of icons to represent relative values. For example, you can use icon sets to identify relative values using a star-rating system: one star could represent very low values, three stars could represent mid-range values, and five stars could represent the highest values. Or, you might want to use a downward-facing red arrow to represent low values and an upward-facing green arrow to represent high values. Excel includes an extensive set of pre-formatted icon sets and provides you with further customization options. You can access the icon sets commands and options by selecting **Home→Styles→Conditional Formatting→Icon Sets**.

> **Note:** Data bars, color scales, and icon sets appear only in cells that contain some type of numeric data such as values or dates. They do not work with data types such as text and logical values.

Number of Titles in Print	Number of Books Sold	Sell Price		Total Sales
11	43,062	$23.99	⬇	$ 1,033,057.38
3	197,522	$10.99	⬇	$ 2,170,766.78
1	496,293	$23.99	⬆	$11,906,069.07
1	213,766	$23.99	➡	$ 5,128,246.34
12	365,614	$ 9.99	⬇	$ 3,652,483.86
4	307,741	$ 5.99	⬇	$ 1,843,368.59
5	380,640	$ 7.99	⬇	$ 3,041,313.60
12	159,593	$ 3.99	⬇	$ 636,776.07
1	269,278	$ 3.99	⬇	$ 1,074,419.22
2	491,853	$12.99	➡	$ 6,389,170.47
4	188,565	$ 2.99	⬇	$ 563,809.35
8	366,628	$23.99	⬆	$ 8,795,405.72

Figure 3–4: Use icon sets to graphically represent relative values with a variety of symbols or pictures.

Custom Conditional Formats

In addition to the pre-configured conditional formatting options available in Excel 2010, you have the option of creating completely custom conditional formats to suit your needs. The tools available in Excel enable you to create specific rules by which to apply conditional formatting and to tailor the display of conditionally formatted cells in a incredible array of options. You can start with one of Excel's pre-formatted options and then adjust it to better suit your needs. Or, you can create completely from scratch sets of rules and formatting options. In addition to the built-in cell formatting options and the data bars, color scales, and icon sets, you can use nearly any of Excel's cell formatting options, such as number, font, and border formatting, to format cells that meet the conditions you set. The cell formatting options not available for use as conditional formats are those on the **Protection** and **Alignment** tabs in the **Format Cells** dialog box.

The New Formatting Rule Dialog Box

The **New Formatting Rule** dialog box enables you to create fully customized conditional formatting rules and to customize the display of cells that meet the given criteria. The **New Formatting Rule** dialog box is divided into two sections: the **Select a Rule Type** list and the **Edit the Rule Description** section.

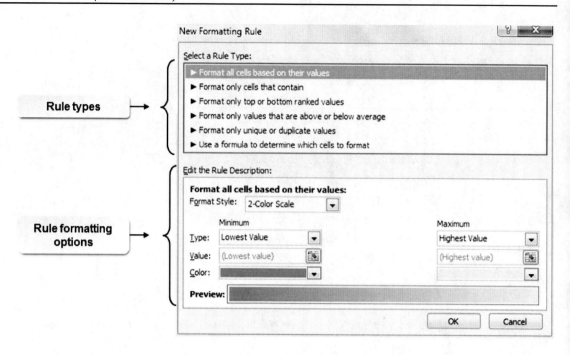

Figure 3-5: Add new conditional formatting rules by using the New Formatting Rule dialog box.

The **Select a Rule Type** list displays six categories of rule types from which you can select the general kind of rule you wish to use to apply conditional formatting. The following table provides some detail on what these categories represent.

Rule Type	Will Apply Formatting to Cells
Format all cells based on their values	Based on the relative values of the data in a range. This is the same rule type used by data bar, color scale, and icon set conditional formatting.
Format only cells that contain	Based on the type of data contained in a specified range. You can use this rule type to format cells based on criteria such as numerical values, specific text entries, particular dates, or cell errors.
Format only top or bottom ranked values	Containing values that fall within a specified percentage of the top or bottom range of values. For example, you can apply formatting to the top 5 percent of values or the bottom 22 percent of values.
Format only values that are above or below average	Containing values that are either above or below the average value of all data in the selected range. You can also use this rule type to apply formatting to values that fall either above or below the 1st, 2nd, or 3rd standard deviation.
Format only unique or duplicate values	That contain data that is either unique in the specified range or that are duplicates of values in other cells in the specified range.
Use a formula to determine which cells to format	That pass a logical test specified by a formula or function.

The **Edit the Rule Description** section displays the commands and options you will use to configure the parameters of whichever rule you select and to customize the display of cell formatting. The commands and options that appear in the **Edit the Rule Description** section vary dramatically depending on the rule type you select in the **Select a Rule Type** list. Typically, you will be presented with options for setting the particular values or content types Excel will use as thresholds/identifiers to apply the selected formatting. The specific formatting options also vary greatly, but selecting several of the rule types will prompt Excel to display the **Format** button in the

Edit the Rule Description section. Selecting the **Format** button opens the **Format Cells** dialog box, providing you with access to a wide array of formatting options. You can access the **New Formatting Rule** dialog box by selecting **Home→Styles→Conditional Formatting→New Rule**.

The Conditional Formatting Rules Manager Dialog Box

You can use the **Conditional Formatting Rules Manager** dialog box to add, delete, edit, and manage conditional formatting rules in your workbooks. The **Conditional Formatting Rules Manager** dialog box contains a number of commands, components, and options that provide you with a high-level of control over your conditional formatting rules. From here, you can simultaneously manage all conditional formatting rules present in an entire workbook. You can access the Conditional Formatting Rules Manager dialog box by selecting **Home→Styles→Conditional Formatting→Manage Rules**.

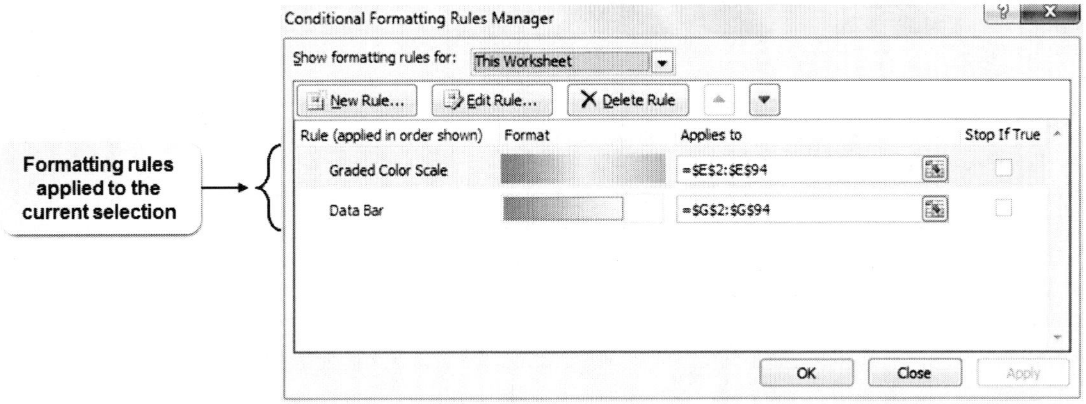

Figure 3-6: Use the Conditional Formatting Rules Manager dialog box to manage all conditional formatting within a particular workbook.

The following table describes the various elements of the **Conditional Formatting Rules Manager** dialog box.

Conditional Formatting Rules Manager Dialog Box Element	Description
Show formatting rules for drop-down menu	Allows you to select which workbook element to display applied formatting rules for. This can be for the currently selected range of cells, any of the worksheets in the workbook, and for particular objects like tables.
New Rule button	Opens the **New Formatting Rule** dialog box, which you can use to create a new conditional formatting rule.
Edit Rule button	Opens the **Edit Formatting Rule** dialog box, which enables you to edit the currently selected rule. This is the same as the **New Formatting Rule** dialog box, only you use it to edit existing conditional formatting rules.
Delete Rule button	Deletes the currently selected rule.
Move Up and **Move Down** buttons	Use these to change the order of rule precedence.
Rule (applied in order) column	Displays all of the specific rules applied to the selection in the **Show formatting rules for** drop-down menu.

Conditional Formatting Rules Manager Dialog Box Element	Description
Format column	Displays a preview of the specific formatting associated with each rule.
Applies to column	Displays the cell or range to which each rule applies.
Stop If True check boxes	Allow you to select how far down the list of displayed rules to stop applying formatting. You use this feature if you need to open a workbook in an earlier version of Excel that does not support the same type or the same number of conditional formatting rules. For example, if you have five conditional formatting rules applied to a particular worksheet, but you have the workbook containing that worksheet open in an older version of Excel that supports only three rules, you could check the **Stop If True** check box for the third rule to tell Excel to apply only the top three rules.

Rule Precedence

The **Conditional Formatting Rules Manager** dialog box displays all rules applied to the selection in the **Show formatting rules for** drop-down menu in order of *rule precedence*. This is the order in which Excel evaluates and applies conditional formatting to the cells. Rules that appear above other rules have a higher precedence.

Where there are no conflicts, all conditional formatting applied to the same range of cells will appear simultaneously. Where there are conflicts, Excel will default to displaying the formatting with a higher precedence. For example, let's say you apply two conditional formatting rules to the same cell, and both of the formats indicate to apply a background fill, one yellow and one red, to the cells. In cells containing data that matches the criteria of both rules, Excel will display the formatting that has a higher precedence in the **Conditional Formatting Rules Manager** dialog box. This is because a cell cannot have two different background fills applied to it at the same time. However, you can, for example, display a data bar on top of a cell background. If those are the two formats applied to a cell, both will appear in the cell and the precedence is moot.

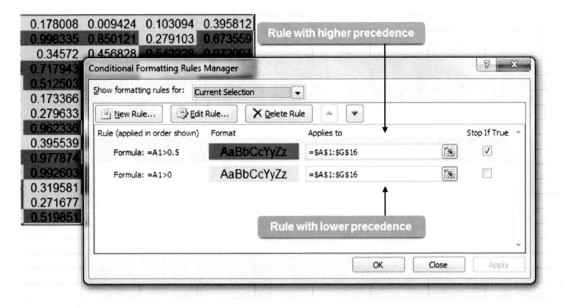

Figure 3-7: Here, all cells meet the criteria for the rule applying yellow fill formatting, but only some cells meet the criteria for the red-fill formatting. As the red fill formatting rule has precedence, the red fill appears in cells that meet its rule's condition.

> Access the Checklist tile on your LogicalCHOICE course screen for reference information and job aids on **How to Apply Advanced Conditional Formatting.**

ACTIVITY 3-3
Applying Advanced Conditional Formatting

Before You Begin
The my_author_data_03.xlsx file is open.

Scenario
You've received another request from your supervisor regarding the author data workbook. Some of F&A's senior leaders would like to review the performance of existing authors before fully integrating the newly acquired authors into the tracking data. Specifically, they have asked to be able to tell, at a glance, where authors lie in terms of overall sales. And, in order to more easily be able to determine who of the existing authors is most worth future investment, they would like to see which authors have had the greatest impact on income per published title. However, they are interested in this only for authors who generate $1,000,000 or more per published title. You decide to apply some of Excel's advanced conditional formatting options to the **Income Earned** and the **Income Per Title** columns to accommodate this request.

1. Use color scales to display the relative performance of each author in terms of overall income earned.
   a) Select the range **G2:G94**.
   b) Select **Home→Styles→Conditional Formatting→Color Scales** and then select the first option in the **Color Scales** gallery.

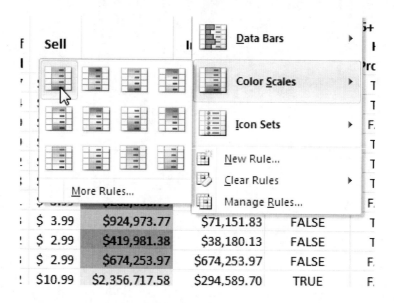

2. Apply custom conditional formatting to include data bars for all authors who generate more than $1,000,000 in income per title.
   a) Select the range **H2:H94**.
   b) Select **Home→Styles→Conditional Formatting→New Rule**.
   c) In the **New Formatting Rule** dialog box, in the **Select a Rule Type** list, ensure that **Format all cells based on their values** is selected.
   d) In the **Format Style** drop-down menu, select **Data Bar**.
   e) In the **Minimum** section, in the **Type** drop-down menu, select **Number**.

f) In the **Value** field, type *1000000*
g) In the **Maximum** section, ensure that **Automatic** is selected in the **Type** drop-down menu.
h) In the **Bar Appearance** section, select the **Color** down arrow and, from the **Standard Colors** section of the **Color** gallery, select **Red**.

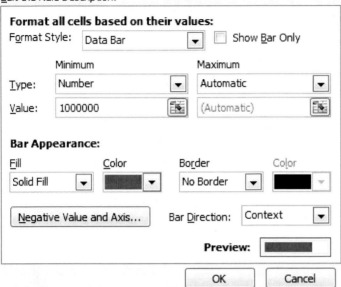

i) Select **OK**.

3. Select any cell to deselect the range **H2:H94** and scroll through the worksheet to review the authors' performance.

4. Save and close the workbook.

Summary

In this lesson, you analyzed data by using text and logical functions, and you applied advanced conditional formatting to a worksheet. Making the transition from using Excel as a data storage tool that performs basic calculations to using it as a tool to extract critical organizational intelligence from your raw data is a major milestone in your development as an Excel user. The ability to ask questions of your data by using the appropriate functions and to display the results in an easily digestible manner are the cornerstones of providing your organizational leaders with the intelligence they need to give you a competitive edge in today's market.

How will the ability to use logical functions change the way you use Excel?

What tasks will Excel's advanced conditional formatting options make easier for you in your current role?

 Note: Check your LogicalCHOICE Course screen for opportunities to interact with your classmates, peers, and the larger LogicalCHOICE online community about the topics covered in this course or other topics you are interested in. From the Course screen you can also access available resources for a more continuous learning experience.

4 Organizing and Analyzing Datasets and Tables

Lesson Time: 2 hours

Lesson Objectives

In this lesson, you will organize and analyze datasets and tables. You will:

- Create and modify tables.
- Sort data.
- Filter data.
- Use the SUBTOTAL and database functions.

Lesson Introduction

Using formulas and functions to analyze data is a powerful way to get a handle on what's really going on in your organization. But you may not always need to analyze all of the data present in your workbooks. Perhaps you're looking for answers to questions regarding only a specific set of data. In extremely large workbooks, applying functions to or reviewing the results of calculations for thousands of rows and columns of data can be a tedious and error-prone process. Your data is most useful when it's presented in a concise, easy-to-digest fashion. Organizational leaders will want to review and consider only the most relevant data. You'll need a way to pare down massive volumes of data to present only the information that is truly important.

This is why Excel 2010 provides you with a number of options for ordering and condensing your data according to a variety of criteria. Taking advantage of this type of functionality will save you time and effort, make your analyzed or raw data easier to review, and allow organizational leaders to focus their efforts on the most important issues.

TOPIC A

Create and Modify Tables

When you need to analyze or review a massive amount of worksheet data, you want to be able to isolate pertinent data as quickly and as easily as possible. One huge advantage would be the ability to treat all of your data as a single chunk of entries paired with the ability to hone in on only the data you need to analyze. Of course, you don't want any of this to disrupt your raw data, as you'll likely need to come back later and focus on something else. Excel 2010 contains a very powerful element of functionality that lets you do all of this in its tables feature.

By converting your raw or analyzed data into tables, you'll be able to leverage Excel's incredibly powerful organizational capabilities without affecting any of the data you've entered into your worksheets. You'll be able to hone in on specific bits of information, regardless of how many entries your worksheets contain. Understanding how all of this works and being able to focus in on just the critical bits of information in your worksheets will give you a huge advantage when it comes to mining your data to get the right people the precise information they need to act in a competitive, fast-changing world.

Tables

In Excel, a *table* is simply a dataset composed of contiguous rows and columns that Excel treats as a single, independent object. Excel tables contain a robust set of functionality that allows you to organize, change the display of, and perform calculations on worksheet data with just a few mouse clicks. Regardless of how many ways you manipulate your table data, the raw data you initially entered remains intact. You can create tables from existing ranges, or create empty tables, and then populate them. You can also revert tables back to simple ranges.

As with cells and ranges, you can apply defined names to tables for ease of reference. When you create a table, Excel automatically assigns it a generic name, such as Table1 or Table2, but you can change these to suit your needs. You can also expand existing tables to accommodate additional data and you can insert or delete columns and rows within tables just as you can in a range.

 Note: Named tables must adhere to the same naming conventions as other named elements.

	A	B	C	D	E	F	G
1	AuthorID	Initial Contract Date	Years Under Contract	Number of Titles in Print	Number of Books Sold	Sell Price	Total Sales
2	1006	6/24/2002	11.56	15	316,237	$ 3.99	$ 1,261,785.63
3	1021	4/19/2007	6.73	14	344,944	$ 5.99	$ 2,066,214.56
4	1024	11/18/2013	0.15	2	255,650	$ 7.99	$ 2,042,643.50
5	1035	11/12/2008	5.16	11	83,399	$ 10.99	$ 916,555.01
6	1042	5/23/2005	8.64	15	16,892	$ 2.99	$ 50,507.08
7	1045	2/4/2006	7.94	7	283,588	$ 10.99	$ 3,116,632.12
8	1048	6/1/2009	4.61	4	43,921	$ 5.99	$ 263,086.79
9	1066	4/29/2011	2.70	13	231,823	$ 3.99	$ 924,973.77
10	1111	9/26/2004	9.30	11	140,462	$ 2.99	$ 419,981.38

Figure 4–1: Data in an Excel table.

Table Components

There is a basic set of table components that Excel tables can contain, but don't necessarily have to. By default, Excel tables contain a header row and appear with banded rows. You can toggle the display of these and other components on or off to suit your needs and to provide access to or suppress various functionality.

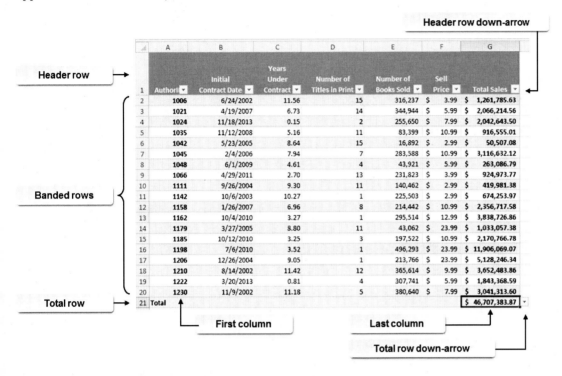

Figure 4–2: An Excel table with all of the components displayed.

The following table describes the various components of Excel tables and their functions.

Excel Table Component	Description
Header row	Displays column headers for the table and provides you with access to some of Excel's table-organization functionality.
Header row down arrow	Displays a drop-down menu that provides you with access to commands you can use to organize and change the display of your table data.
Total row	Displays the results of column-specific calculations and provides you with access to some of Excel's built-in table-function capabilities.
Total row down arrow	Displays a drop-down menu that provides you with quick and easy access to functions for performing calculations on table-column data.
Banded rows	These make it easier to view individual rows of data by applying different formating to alternating table rows.
Banded columns	These make it easier to view individual columns of data by applying different formatting to alternating table columns.
First column	Sets off the display of the first column of data by applying specific formatting, typically bolding, to it.
Last column	Sets off the display of the last column of data by applying specific formatting, typically bolding, to it.

The Create Table Dialog Box

You can use the **Create Table** dialog box to convert simple ranges of data into tables. From here, you can confirm the range selection you wish to convert into a table or modify that range to ensure that the correct data becomes part of the table. The **Create Table** dialog box also enables you to decide whether or not you wish to include the top row of the selected range in the new table as a header row. Typically, you would do this if the selected range contains column labels in the top row. You can access the **Create Table** dialog box by selecting **Insert→Tables→Table**.

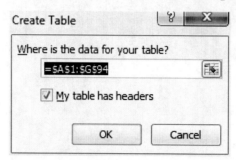

Figure 4–3: Use the Create Table dialog box to convert raw data into a table.

The Table Tools Contextual Tab

The **Table Tools** contextual tab contains various commands and options that are specific to working with tables. It appears when you select a worksheet table, or any part of a table, and disappears when you select an object outside the table. The **Table Tools** contextual tab contains only one tab, the **Design** tab, which is divided into five command groups.

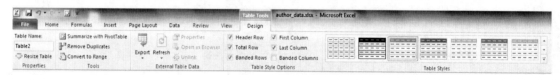

Figure 4–4: The Table Tools contextual tab.

The following table identifies the types of commands and options contained in the various groups on the **Table Tools** contextual tab.

Table Tools Contextual Tab Group	Contains Commands or Options For
Properties	Resizing worksheet tables. This group also displays the name of the currently selected table.
Tools	Removing duplicate values from tables, converting tables back into ranges, and creating PivotTables out of tables.
External Table Data	Exporting table data to external applications and managing data links with external sources.
Table Style Options	Toggling the display of table components on or off.
Table Styles	Applying styles to Excel tables.

Table Styles and Quick Styles

Like cell styles, *table styles* are particular configurations of formatting options you can apply to your worksheet tables. Table styles help make your tables more visually appealing and easier to read. Table styles can consist of font, border, and fill formatting, and you can create your own customized table styles or select from among a variety of pre-configured table styles, which are known as *quick styles*.

	A	B	C	D	E	F	G
1	AuthorID	Initial Contract Date	Years Under Contract	Number of Titles in Print	Number of Books Sold	Sell Price	Total Sales
2	1006	6/24/2002	11.56	15	316,237	$ 3.99	$ 1,261,785.63
3	1021	4/19/2007	6.73	14	344,944	$ 5.99	$ 2,066,214.56
4	1024	11/18/2013	0.15	2	255,650	$ 7.99	$ 2,042,643.50
5	1035	11/12/2008	5.16	11	83,399	$ 10.99	$ 916,555.01
6	1042	5/23/2005	8.64	15	16,892	$ 2.99	$ 50,507.08
7	1045	2/4/2006	7.94	7	283,588	$ 10.99	$ 3,116,632.12
8	1048	6/1/2009	4.61	4	43,921	$ 5.99	$ 263,086.79
9	1066	4/29/2011	2.70	13	231,823	$ 3.99	$ 924,973.77
10	1111	9/26/2004	9.30	11	140,462	$ 2.99	$ 419,981.38
11	1142	10/6/2003	10.27	1	225,503	$ 2.99	$ 674,253.97
12	1158	1/26/2007	6.96	8	214,442	$ 10.99	$ 2,356,717.58
13	1162	10/4/2010	3.27	1	295,514	$ 12.99	$ 3,838,726.86
14	1179	3/27/2005	8.80	11	43,062	$ 23.99	$ 1,033,057.38
15	1185	10/12/2010	3.25	3	197,522	$ 10.99	$ 2,170,766.78
16	1198	7/6/2010	3.52	1	496,293	$ 23.99	$ 11,906,069.07
17	1206	12/26/2004	9.05	1	213,766	$ 23.99	$ 5,128,246.34
18	1210	8/14/2002	11.42	12	365,614	$ 9.99	$ 3,652,483.86
19	1222	3/20/2013	0.81	4	307,741	$ 5.99	$ 1,843,368.59
20	1230	11/9/2002	11.18	5	380,640	$ 7.99	$ 3,041,313.60
21	Total						$ 46,707,383.87

Figure 4-5: A highly stylized Excel table.

The New Table Quick Style Dialog Box

You will use the **New Table Quick Style** dialog box to create and save custom table styles. From here, you can select which table component you wish to apply formatting to; access the **Format Cells** dialog box to configure the desired font, border, and fill formatting; and name and save your custom quick styles. To access the **New Table Quick Style** dialog box, on the **Design** tab of the **Table Tools** contextual tab, in the **Table Styles** group, select the **Table Styles** gallery's **More** button, and then select **New Table Style**.

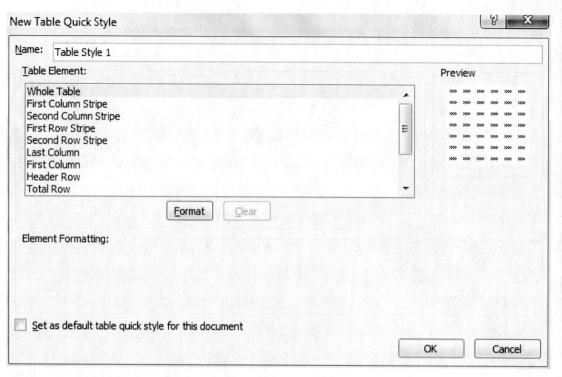

Figure 4-6: The New Table Quick Style dialog box.

Access the Checklist tile on your LogicalCHOICE course screen for reference information and job aids on **How to Create and Modify Tables.**

ACTIVITY 4-1
Creating and Modifying a Table

Data File

C:\091019Data\Organizing and Analyzing Datasets and Tables\author_data_04.xlsx

Before You Begin

Excel 2010 is open.

Scenario

Because Fuller and Ackerman (F&A) acquired two new publishing houses, the author data worksheet has grown considerably in size. You have finished merging all new authors and their data into the workbook, and you have added royalty rate information. As you now have to perform data analysis on a much larger dataset, you decide it would be in your best interest to convert the range on the **Authors** worksheet into a table. You also decide to define a name for the table to make it easier to reference for future data analysis and to apply a table style to the table to better adhere to F&A branding guidelines.

1. Open the **author_data_04.xlsx** workbook file and ensure that the **Authors** worksheet is selected.

2. Convert the dataset into a table.
   a) Select any cell within the dataset.
   b) Select **Insert→Tables→Table**.
   c) In the **Create Table** dialog box, in the **Where is the data for your table?** field, verify that =$A$1:$K$1074 is the displayed range.
   d) Ensure that the **My table has headers** check box is checked and select **OK**.
   e) Adjust the column widths as needed so the header row down arrows do not block any of the column header text.

3. Apply a quick style to the table.
   a) If necessary, select any cell within the table to display the **Table Tools** contextual tab.
   b) Select **Design→Table Styles** and select the **Table Styles** gallery **More** button.

c) In the **Table Styles** gallery, in the **Medium** section, select the **Table Style Medium 11** quick style.

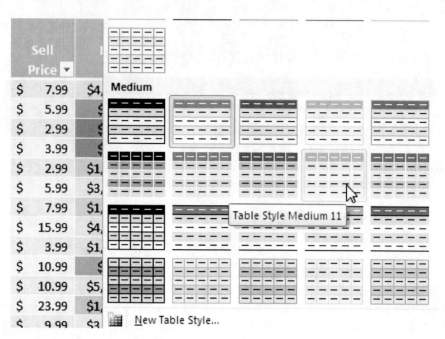

4. Create a defined name for the table.
   a) From the **Table Tools** contextual tab, in the **Properties** group, in the **Table Name** field, type *Table_Author_Totals*
   b) Press **Enter**.

5. Verify Excel created the table name.
   a) Select **Formulas→Defined Names→Name Manager**.
   b) In the **Name Manager** dialog box, ensure that **Table_Author_Totals** appears in the list of defined names, and that it refers to the range **$A$2:$K$1074.**
   c) Close the **Name Manager** dialog box.

6. Save the workbook to the **C:\091019Data\Organizing and Analyzing Datasets and Tables** folder as *my_author_data_04.xlsx*

TOPIC B

Sort Data

Raw data is often entered into Excel worksheets in random order, or at least not in the order you need for a particular data analysis task. For example, sales data may be entered chronologically, but you may need to examine information related to particular products or store locations. Or, you need to review employee data based on hire date, but the entries are listed alphabetically by employee last name. Scouring large worksheets to pick out the necessary entries is tedious, time consuming, and prone to errors. Wouldn't it be easier if you could rearrange your data to help you review only those entries that apply to the task at hand? In Excel, rearranging your data based on particular criteria is straightforward.

By reordering your data, you can more easily locate and interact with specific entries, even in massive worksheets with tens of thousands of entries. In essence, you can provide yourself with a roadmap to get to your destination without having to take a bunch of wrong turns. Placing your data in the proper order will save you time and a few headaches, and will ensure the information you're reporting to organizational leaders contains minimal amounts of errors.

Sorting

Sorting is, quite simply, reordering the data in your worksheets based on some defined criteria, such as alphabetically or from highest value to lowest value. Sorting allows you to put data entries in a sequence that makes sense for a particular task. In Excel, you can sort by row or column, but an overwhelming majoring of sorting is done by column because of the way most people enter worksheet data. You can sort on a single row or column or apply multiple sorts to the same set of data. You can sort either range or table data. Excel can sort data based on a number of different values, such as numeric, alphabetical, date and time, and even by cell color or conditional formatting criteria. If you add data to a sorted range or table, you can re-sort to accommodate the new entries.

It is important to keep in mind that when you sort data, you are not changing the data in your worksheets. You are merely changing the display of the data. So, while you may sort on one particular column in a worksheet, say by numeric value, after the sort, each entry (individual row) will have the same data across the entire row. The rows will just appear in a different order based on the sort criteria. This preserving of data integrity is what makes sorting a powerful, useful feature.

 Note: It's a best practice to select only a single cell within a column or row when sorting. When you do this, Excel will automatically preserve the integrity of your data as described previously. However, if you select an entire column or row and then sort, Excel prompts you to include the surrounding data in the sort. If you do not expand the selection to include the surrounding data, your data integrity will not be maintained.

There are a couple of things about sorting that you should keep in mind. First, you cannot clear sorting, but you can use the **Undo** command to revert sorted data back to its previous state. Second, when you save and close workbook files, you save sorts along with it. So if you want to undo a sort, you must do it before saving and closing the file or before performing more actions than your undo settings allow you to undo. You can access the sort commands in the **Sort & Filter** group on the **Data** tab.

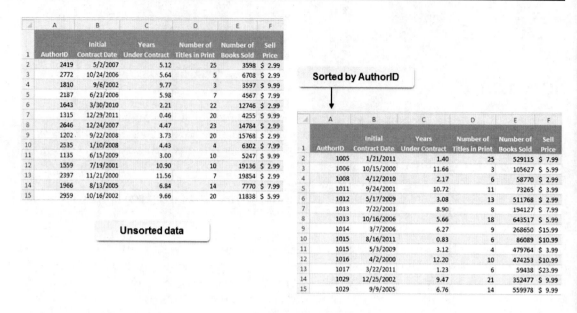

Figure 4-7: The same Excel worksheet both unsorted and sorted.

Multiple Column/Row Sorting

When you sort on multiple columns or rows, it's important to consider that all of the columns or rows on which you're sorting, except for the last one you sort on, should contain some duplicate entries. Otherwise, the sort is of no value. Consider the simple example in the following figure.

	A	B	C	D	E	F	G
1	AuthorID	Initial Contract Date	Years Under Contract	Number of Titles in Print	Sell Price	Number of Books Sold	Total Sales
2	1390	5/30/2001	12.62	1	$ 2.99	202,863	$ 606,560.37
3	1142	10/6/2003	10.27	1	$ 2.99	225,503	$ 674,253.97
4	1928	12/31/2012	1.03	1	$ 2.99	230,678	$ 689,727.22
5	1246	8/20/2013	0.39	1	$ 2.99	269,278	$ 805,141.22
6	1327	3/14/2012	1.83	1	$ 7.99	237,358	$ 1,896,490.42
7	1329	8/8/2007	6.43	1	$ 7.99	325,510	$ 2,600,824.90
8	1699	9/10/2002	11.34	1	$ 7.99	329,506	$ 2,632,752.94
9	1162	10/4/2010	3.27	1	$ 12.99	295,514	$ 3,838,726.86
10	1206	12/26/2004	9.05	1	$ 15.99	213,766	$ 3,418,118.34
11	1755	5/22/2006	7.64	1	$ 15.99	433,029	$ 6,924,133.71
12	1198	7/6/2010	3.52	1	$ 15.99	496,293	$ 7,935,725.07
13	1915	12/5/2010	3.10	2	$ 2.99	53,061	$ 158,652.39
14	1693	9/3/2000	13.36	2	$ 5.99	79,116	$ 473,904.84
15	1024	11/18/2013	0.15	2	$ 7.99	255,650	$ 2,042,643.50
16	1259	5/31/2003	10.62	2	$ 7.99	491,853	$ 3,929,905.47
17	1362	12/6/2003	10.10	2	$ 10.99	189,282	$ 2,080,209.18
18	1262	12/5/2003	10.11	3	$ 2.99	188,565	$ 563,809.35
19	1755	10/12/2010	3.25	3	$ 2.99	478,985	$ 1,432,165.15
20	1747	8/22/2006	7.39	3	$ 3.99	70,283	$ 280,429.17
21	1048	6/1/2009	4.61	3	$ 5.99	43,921	$ 263,086.79

Figure 4-8: Sorting on multiple columns or rows enables you to organize your data in increasingly meaningful ways.

In this example, the dataset is sorted in ascending order on three different columns. First, it is sorted by the number of titles in print, then by sell price, and finally by the number of books sold. This sort can provide some analytical value because there are multiple entries with duplicate values in the first two columns the data is sorted on. For example, of all of the authors with only one title in print, four of them also have books that sell for $2.99. Because of this, there is a meaningful sort on the values in the **Number of Books Sold** column.

Quick Sorts

There are two general categories of sorting in Excel: quick sorts and custom sorts. *Quick sorts* enable you to easily sort the data in a range or table according a set of predefined criteria. Although tables have quick sorting functionality built into them, for ranges, by default, you need to use commands on the ribbon. By using quick sorts, you can sort data one column at a time, in ascending or descending order, according to the type of content stored in the column. So, for example, if the column contains text, you can sort by alphabetical order. If the cells contain numeric values, you can sort lowest to highest or highest to lowest. If the cells contain dates, you can sort based on chronological order. With quick sorts, you can sort only by column, not by row.

 Note: Although tables have built-in sorting capabilities, you can sort them by using ribbon commands as well.

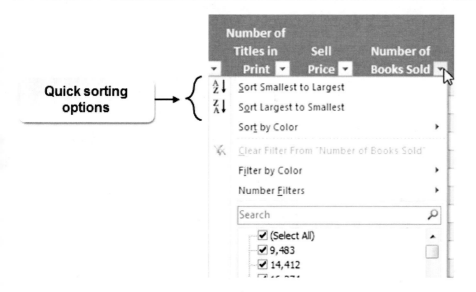

Figure 4-9: Use quick sorts to easily reorder your range or table data.

Custom Sorts

To sort your range or table data by using more highly defined criteria than is possible by using quick sorts, you can define a *custom sort*. Custom sorting enables you to sort by row or column, sort on multiple rows or columns simultaneously, and to define specific sort criteria. In addition to the sort criteria that is available by using quick sorts, custom sorts allow you to sort based on cell and font color, and based on conditional formatting icons.

Each specific criterion you assign to a custom sort is called a *level*. Excel evaluates and sorts your data based on the order in which you assign sort levels to the data. You can add, delete, edit, and reorder sort levels. Custom sorting is only possible by using ribbon commands.

 Note: You cannot apply both column and row sorting to the same data range. Also, you cannot sort tables by row.

The Sort Dialog box

You use the **Sort** dialog box to define and manage your custom sorts. You can access the **Sort** dialog box by selecting **Data→Sort & Filer→Sort**.

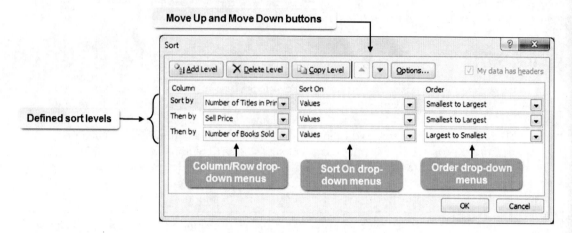

Figure 4-10: The Sort dialog box displaying multiple sort levels for a data range.

The following table describes the functions of the various **Sort** dialog box elements.

Sort Dialog Box Element	Description
Add Level button	Adds new blank sort levels to a custom sort.
Delete Level button	Removes the currently selected sort level from a custom sort.
Copy Level button	Creates a copy of the currently selected sort level and places it immediately after the selected level.
Move Up/Move Down buttons	Allow you to reorder the sort levels in a custom sort.
Options button	Opens the **Sort Options** dialog box.
Column/Row Sort by drop-down menu	Use this to select the column or the row upon which to sort your data. Setting your sort options determines whether you sort by row or column.
Sort On drop-down menu	Use this to select the criteria by which you want to sort your data.
Order drop-down menu	Use this to determine the order in which Excel will display sorted data, for example, alphabetical or oldest to newest. The options that the **Order** drop-down menu displays depend on the selections you make in the **Column/Row Sort by** drop-down menu and the **Sort On** drop-down menu.
Custom sort levels	The sort levels appear in the order in which Excel will evaluate and apply data sorting.

The Sort Options Dialog Box

You use the **Sort Options** dialog box to determine whether Excel will sort by column or row and to define the precedence Excel applies to capitalization while sorting. When the **Case sensitive** check box is unchecked, Excel gives precedence to capital letters. When the **Case sensitive** check box is checked, it gives precedence to lowercase letters. You can access the **Sort Options** dialog box by selecting the **Options** button in the **Sort** dialog box.

Figure 4-11: Use the Sort Options dialog box to assign sorts to rows or columns and to define the precedence Excel applies to capitalization.

 Access the Checklist tile on your LogicalCHOICE course screen for reference information and job aids on How to Sort Data.

ACTIVITY 4–2
Sorting Data

Before You Begin
The my_author_data_04.xlsx file is open.

Scenario
You have been asked to create several reports for company senior leaders for an upcoming meeting. While preparing to create these reports, you notice a few issues in the author data. Specifically, there are several authors who have a negative value in the **Years Under Contract** column, and there are a number of author IDs that appear more than once. You realize that this could be a serious issue, so you consult with a colleague in the HR department and discover that some of the data was corrupted during the author-integration process.

In consultation with HR, you have decided to remove all author entries for authors with a negative value for years under contract and to remove duplicate author ID records. Your colleague in HR has indicated that, for any duplicate author IDs, the oldest record is the valid record.

1. Sort the dataset from highest to lowest on the **Income Earned** column.
   a) In cell **G1**, select the column header down arrow and then select **Sort Largest to Smallest**.
   b) Scroll down slightly and verify that there are several negative values in cells in the **Years Under Contract** column.

    Note: The purpose of this first sort is to simply bring some of the negative values into view. The next sort will arrange the table so you can delete the undesired entries.

2. Delete all entries for authors with a negative value in the **Years Under Contract** column.
   a) In cell **C1**, select the column header down arrow and then select **Sort Smallest to Largest**.
   b) Select the range **C2:C40**.

38	2804	7/1/2012	-0.05	11
39	2984	6/18/2012	-0.01	20
40	2831	6/17/2012	-0.01	22
41	1989	6/12/2012	0.01	22
42	1284	6/9/2012	0.01	18

c) Right-click the selected range and then select **Delete→Table Rows**.

d) Verify that author **1989** is now the first author listed in the table.

3. Sort the table by two columns simultaneously.
   a) Select any cell within the table and then select **Data→Sort & Filter→Sort**.
   b) In the **Sort** dialog box, in the **Sort by** section, from the **Column** drop-down menu, select **AuthorID**.
   c) Ensure that **Values** is selected in the **Sort On** drop-down menu.
   d) Ensure that **Smallest to Largest** is selected in the **Order** drop-down menu.
   e) Select **Add Level** to add another sort level.
   f) In the **Then by** section, from the **Column** drop-down menu, select **Initial Contract Date**.
   g) In the **Sort On** drop-down menu, ensure that **Values** is selected.
   h) In the **Order** drop-down menu, ensure that **Oldest to Newest** is selected.

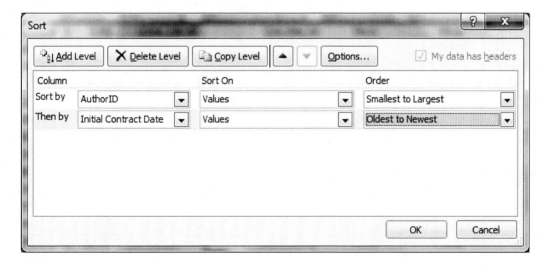

   i) Select **OK**.

4. Highlight the duplicate author ID records to verify the sort worked as expected.
   a) Select the range **A2:A1035**.
   b) Select **Home→Styles→Conditional Formatting→Highlight Cells Rules→Duplicate Values**.
   c) In the **Duplicate Values** dialog box, in the **values with** drop-down menu, select **Yellow Fill with Dark Yellow Text**.
   d) Select **OK**.
   e) Scroll to the top of the worksheet until the range **A18:A21** is visible.

    f) Verify that the entries for rows **18-21** all contain duplicate values and that they appear in chronological order.

17	1033	11/29/2000
18	1034	1/17/2002
19	1034	12/30/2005
20	1034	11/22/2007
21	1034	2/6/2012
22	1037	7/1/2000

5. Remove the duplicate records.

    a) Select **Data→Data Tools→Remove Duplicates**.

 Note: The **Remove Duplicates** command works by deleting all but the first listed duplicate record. This is why you first sorted by author ID, and then sorted by initial contract date. The records Excel will retain will be the earliest of each of the duplicates.

    b) In the **Remove Duplicates** dialog box, select **Unselect All**.

    c) Check the **Author ID** check box.

    d) Select **OK**.

    e) In the **Microsoft Excel** dialog box, verify that Excel deleted 222 duplicate records and then select **OK**.

6. Save the workbook.

TOPIC C

Filter Data

Imagine if you will, you're standing in a field in front of a haystack and a bucket. Somewhere in the haystack is the proverbial needle; in the bucket, there is a baseball and a bunch of marbles. Your job is to locate either the needle or the baseball. Given the choice, which would you rather look for? Now, apply this metaphor to analyzing data in large worksheets. Though sorting can help you locate and review data in large worksheets, it does nothing to cut down on the number of displayed entries. Even with ordered data, you may often still need to sift through large volumes of data, which can be challenging and time consuming. Clearly, it would be far more efficient to review only the data that is absolutely essential to the task at hand. The Excel 2010 filtering feature helps you do exactly that.

By reducing the volume of data entries you need to review and analyze, you cut out extraneous and wasted effort. Paring down massive volumes of data into a small handful of pertinent, useful entries will make your data analysis and reporting tasks faster, easier, and more accurate than they would be if you had to deal with irrelevant entries.

Filtering

As with the sorting feature, you can use the *filtering* feature to make data far easier to work with. Whereas sorting merely rearranges your data based on particular defined criteria, filtering removes from view any data entries that do not match the specified criteria. When you filter data in Excel, you do not affect the actual data entries. You alter only how Excel displays your data. It is important to note that filtering affects entire worksheet rows. If you have data in a range or a table next to data that you filter, rows that are suppressed from view in the data you're filtering are also suppressed from view in the adjacent tables or ranges.

You can filter both tables and data ranges in Excel, and you can filter on more than one column. However, you can filter only by column and not by row. You can combine sorting and filtering to fine tune the display of your data. Typically, when you combine sorting and filtering, it's a best practice to filter first and then sort just the data you wish to work with. Filtering functionality is active in tables by default, but you must turn it on for data ranges. You can toggle filtering on and off for both ranges and tables. To toggle filtering on and off for tables or ranges, select any cell within the desired table or range and select **Data→Sort & Filter→Filter**.

Note: When you turn on filtering for a data range, you also activate quick sorting functionality for the range. In essence, you give it much of the same functionality that tables have, but without the total row and formatting functionality. Be sure that you select either only a single cell within the range or the entire data range when turning on filtering for a range. If you select only certain columns within a range when turning on filtering, when you use quick sorts to sort the range, columns not included in the selection when you turned on filtering will not sort with the rest of the data.

Unlike sorting, filtering can be cleared at any time to re-display all rows that the filtering temporarily suppressed. When you apply functions to or search filtered data, Excel applies the function to or searches through only the data that is displayed. When you clear filters, Excel applies the function to or searches through the entire dataset.

Caution: Filtering data and hiding rows or columns can have a wide range of effects on the **Cut** and **Copy** commands. When cutting or copying and then pasting data from filtered datasets or datasets with hidden columns or rows, always ensure that your pasted values appear as expected.

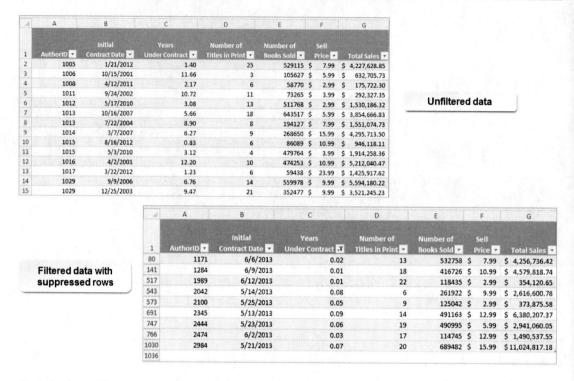

Figure 4-12: Filtering data removes all non-pertinent entries from view, making it easier to review and work with your data.

AutoFilters

AutoFilters enable you to quickly filter datasets and tables based on unique cell entries or applied cell formatting in a column. AutoFilter options appear in two ways: as check boxes or as pop-up menu options in the header row drop-down menu of tables or ranges that have filtering turned on. You use the list of check boxes to filter based on cell values. Checked items will appear in the filtered dataset, unchecked items will not. You can check or uncheck any number of entries for each column, and you can search for specific entry values to pare down the list of AutoFilter options. The search functionality for AutoFilter values is dynamic, so Excel filters the AutoFilter options as you type each character of your search term.

You use the pop-up menu options to filter cells based on font or fill color, or based on icon sets. Again, for whichever formatting criteria you select in the pop-up menu, Excel will display rows containing that particular formatting; all other rows are hidden. You can use AutoFilters to filter blended criteria. In other words, you can filter by cell value and by formatting in the same column but you can filter based on only one formatting criteria at a time.

The AutoFilter feature is most useful in columns that contain multiple duplicate entries or formatting options. Excel will display only one check box for each unique data entry (up to 10,000 unique values) in the column and one formatting option for each unique formatting element. Columns that you have applied filtering to will display a slightly different header row down arrow.

For unfiltered columns, the header row down arrow appears like this ▾; in filtered columns, it looks like this. ▾

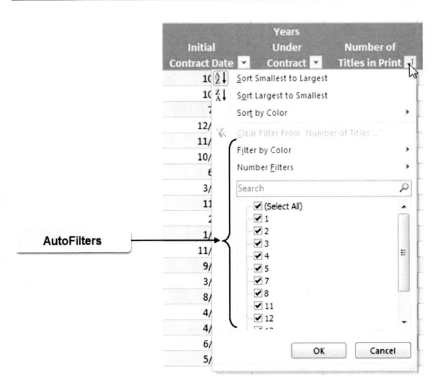

Figure 4-13: AutoFilters enable you to quickly filter datasets based on unique column entries.

Custom AutoFilters

In addition to using the default AutoFilters available in Excel, you can customize AutoFilters to filter datasets by specific criteria. You can use *custom AutoFilters* to filter by such criteria as a particular range of numeric values, text entries that begin with a particular character, or all entries made before or after a particular date. The custom AutoFilter options available to you depend on the type of data stored in the column. You can access these options by selecting either **Text Filters**, **Number Filters**, or **Date Filters** from the header row drop-down menu of ranges or tables that have filtering turned on. Selecting any of these options from the drop-down menu opens a secondary menu. In the secondary menu, some of the filter options have no configurable parameters, such as filtering for the top or bottom 10 percent of numerical values, so selecting them will simply apply the filter. Others do need to be configured, so, when you select them, Excel opens the **Custom AutoFilters** dialog box.

The Custom AutoFilter Dialog Box

You use the **Custom AutoFilter** dialog box to configure the parameters for some of Excel's custom AutoFilters. The options available in the **Custom AutoFilter** dialog box vary depending on the type of data in the column. You can set one or two parameters in the **Custom AutoFilter** dialog box. For example, if you'd like to filter for a certain range of numeric values, you would enter the top and bottom values of the desired range. You can also select whether Excel should filter data based on entries that meet both defined criteria or based on meeting only one of the two criteria. If you don't enter a value in the lower fields, Excel ignores them.

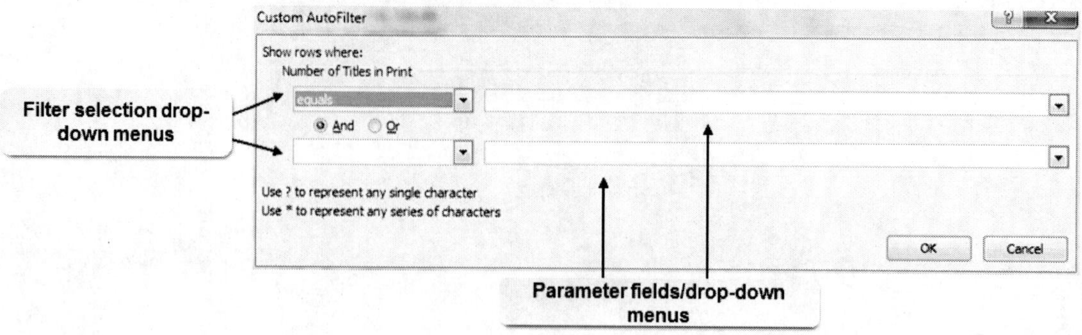

Figure 4-14: Use the Custom AutoFilter dialog box to set the parameters for custom AutoFilters.

The following table describes the function of the various elements of the **Custom AutoFilter** dialog box.

Custom AutoFilter Dialog Box Element	Allow You To
Filter selection drop-down menus	Select the specific custom AutoFilters you wish to apply to your dataset. Typically, Excel automatically populates the top menu with the filter you selected to open the **Custom AutoFilter** dialog box.
And/Or radio buttons	Choose between requiring both filter parameters or applying the filter to entries matching either one or the other.
Parameter entry text fields/drop-down menus	Define the specific criteria for the search. You can manually type the entries or select them from the drop-down menu, which is populated with the column's data entries.

Advanced Filtering

Excel's built-in AutoFilter functionality is a fast and easy way to pare down large volumes of data into manageable, easy-to-view chunks. However, there will likely be times when you will need to filter your data based on much more complex criteria than the AutoFilter options can support. In these cases, you can create advanced filters. When you filter data by using Excel's **Advanced** filtering command, you enter filter criteria directly on the worksheet containing the dataset you want to filter. Advanced filtering uses a set of filter operators that are similar to Excel's logical operators. Although you can filter the original dataset in its original location, you can also ask Excel to return the filtered dataset in a different location within the workbook. This provides you with both an unfiltered and a filtered view of your data simultaneously. You can access the **Advanced** filter command by selecting **Data→Sort & Filter→Advanced**.

> **Note:** Applying advanced filtering to a range or a table with filtering (AutoFilter) turned on automatically turns off filtering.

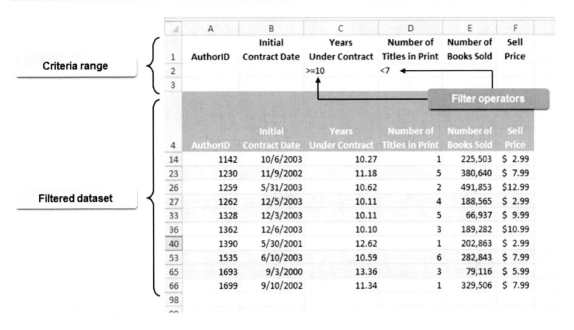

Figure 4–15: The Advanced filtering command enables you to filter your data by using highly complex, user–defined criteria.

The Criteria Range

As previously mentioned, to use advanced filtering, you enter the desired filter criteria directly on the worksheet containing the dataset you wish to filter. The area on the worksheet in which you do this is called the *criteria range*. To properly enter filter criteria in the criteria range, you must follow the correct protocol. Here are the requirements for creating a valid criteria range:

- It is a best practice to have the criteria range be located directly above the dataset you wish to filter.
- The criteria range must contain the same column headings as the columns in the dataset.
- Criteria entered into cells on the same row in the criteria range use the AND operator. In other words, rows displayed in the filtered dataset must meet all of the specified criteria in the criteria range row.
- Criteria entered in different rows use the OR operator.
- Each criterion that you wish to include by using the OR operator must be in its own row in the criteria range.
- You can enter more than one filter operator in the same column. Not all columns have to include a filter operator.
- There must be at least one blank row between the criteria range and the dataset you wish to filter.

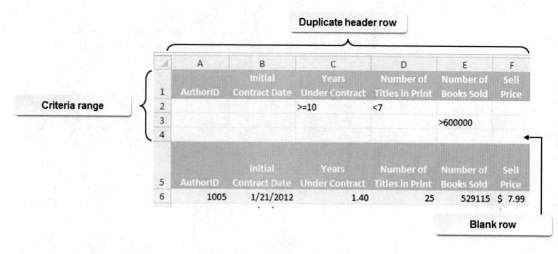

Figure 4-16: Use the criteria range to specify advanced filtering criteria.

Filter Operators

To define the criteria for advanced filtering, you use filter operators. These function very much like the logical operators you use to create logical functions. Filter operators help you narrow your search for specific data, and you can use these in nearly any combination.

 Note: You cannot use cell or range references to define advanced filter criteria. You must manually enter them in the criteria range.

Filter Operator	What It Does
=	Filters data based on an exact content match. As Excel interprets the equal sign as the beginning of a formula or function, you must enclose the = operator in a set of double quotation marks (" "). So, if you want to filter for all entries that include the text *NY*, you must enter the filter criteria as *"=NY"*. To filter for an exact numerical match, you can simply enter the numerical value.
<	Filters for numerical or date and time values that are less than the defined criteria.
>	Filters for numerical or date and time values that are greater than the defined criteria.
<=	Filters for numerical or date and time values that are less than or equal to the defined criteria.
>=	Filters for numerical or date and time values that are greater than or equal to the defined criteria.
<>	Filters for numerical, textual, or date and time values that are not equal to the defined criteria.
?	Serves as a wildcard character for a single character in the same position as the question mark. So, if you want to filter a list of employee numbers that begin with *100*, but can have any number as the last digit, you could type *100?* as the filter criterion.

Filter Operator	What It Does
*	Serves as a wildcard character for multiple characters in the same position as the asterisk. So, if you want to filter a list of product names for entries that begin with the letter *S* and end with the letter *L*, you could enter **"=S*L"** as the criterion. In this case, both *sail* and *stool* would appear in the filtered dataset.

 Access the Checklist tile on your LogicalCHOICE course screen for reference information and job aids on How to Filter Data.

ACTIVITY 4-3
Filtering Data

Before You Begin
The my_author_data_04.xlsx workbook file is open.

Scenario
Now that you have resolved the data errors, you're ready to apply filters to the dataset to answer questions from company senior leaders to include in your report. These are the questions they have asked:

- How many titles that sell at the highest price are currently in publication?
- Who are the top five authors by income earned?
- How many authors have been with the company for one year or less?
- Which authors have been with the company for fewer than five years and have sold 500,000 or more books?

---

1. Use an AutoFilter to answer the question "How many titles that sell at the highest price are currently in publication?"
   a) In cell **F1**, select the column header down arrow.
   b) Uncheck the **Select All** check box.
   c) Check the **$23.99** check box and select **OK**.
   d) Scroll to the bottom of the table.
   e) Ensure that any cell in the table is selected, and then display the tables total row by checking the **Total Row** check box in the **Table Style Options** group on the **Table Tools** contextual tab.
   f) Select cell **F814** and then select the total row down arrow.

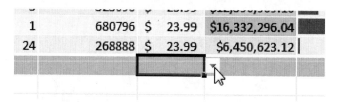

1	680796	$ 23.99	$16,332,296.04	
24	268888	$ 23.99	$6,450,623.12	

   g) From the drop-down menu, select **Count**.

2. **How many titles sell at the highest price?**

3. Scroll to the top of the table, select the column header down arrow in cell **F1**, and then select **Clear Filter From "Sell Price."**

4. Use an AutoFilter to answer the question "Who are the top five authors by income earned?"
   a) In cell **G1**, select the column header down arrow.
   b) Select **Number Filters→Top 10**.
   c) In the **Top 10 AutoFilter** dialog box, in the **Show** section, set the value in the spin box to **5**.
   d) Select **OK**.
   e) Review the author IDs to determine the top five authors.
   f) Clear the filter from the **Income Earned** column.

5. Use advanced filtering to answer the question "How many authors have been with the company for one year or less?"

   a) Insert three empty rows above the table's header row.

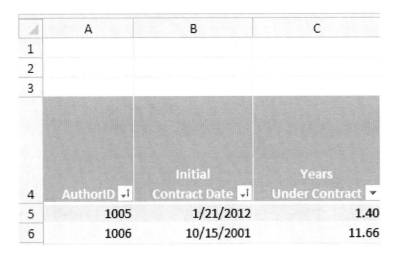

   b) Copy and paste all of the table's column headers into the top row directly above the existing headers.

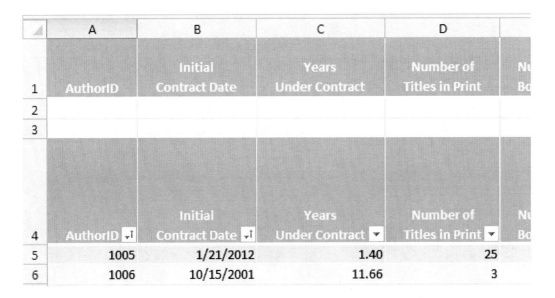

   c) In cell **C2**, type *<=1* and then press **Enter**.
   d) Select any cell within the table and then select **Data→Sort & Filter→Advanced**.
   e) In the **Advanced Filter** dialog box, in the **List range** field, verify that **$A$4:$K$816** appears.
   f) In the **Criteria range** field, select the **Collapse Dialog** button, select the range **A1:K2** on the worksheet, and then press **Enter**.
   g) Select **OK**.

   > **Note:** Remember that using advanced filtering automatically turns off the table's built-in filtering functionality. You can turn this back on by selecting **Data→Sort & Filter→Filter**.

h) Scroll to the bottom of the table.

796	2948	7/5/2012	0.94	9	215893	$	5.99
812	2984	5/21/2013	0.07	20	689482	$	15.99
817	Total						48

6. Does the COUNT function result in the Sell Price column answer the question "How many authors have been with the company for one year or less?"

7. Select **Data→Sort & Filter→Clear** to clear the filter.

8. Scroll to the top of the table and delete the filter operator in cell **C2**.

9. Use advanced filtering to answer the question "Which authors have been with the company for fewer than five years and have sold 500,000 or more books?"
   a) If necessary, re-select cell **C2**, type *<5* and then press **Tab** twice.
   b) Ensure that cell **E2** is selected, type *>=500000* and then press **Enter**.
   c) Select any cell within the table and then select **Data→Sort & Filer→Advanced**.
   d) In the **Advanced Filter** dialog box, in the **List range** field, change the entry to *$A$4:$K$816*
   e) Ensure that **$A$1:$K$2** appears in the **Criteria range** field.
   f) Select **OK**.
   g) Scroll through the filtered table to confirm the filter worked as planned and to review the author IDs for the authors who meet these criteria.

10. Select cell **F817** and press **Delete**.

11. Clear the filter and save the workbook.

TOPIC D

Use SUBTOTAL and Database Functions

The ability to sort and filter your data makes sifting through large volumes of entries and applying calculations to only particular sets of data fast and easy. But what if you need to perform calculations on a variety of subsets of data at once? For example, let's say your organization has branch offices all over the country. What if you want to find the total or the average sales for the sales reps in each of these regions? Filtering your data for each region, and then applying functions to the data subsets becomes a repetitive, tedious process. This is especially true if your organization is divided into 20 or 30 regions. Or, perhaps, you want to analyze the total or average sales for a variety of products or services at once. If your organization offers thousands of products, this could become a nightmare. And, if you want to perform some type of analysis on a very particular subset of data, one that meets incredibly precise criteria, drilling down into your data to perform the calculations could involve a lot of work or be nearly impossible.

What all of this means is you're going to need a more efficient, accurate way to drill down into your data to analyze it on a granular level. Excel provides you with a number of ways to do this. The more comfortable you become with Excel's ability to focus on specific, fine detail in massive datasets, the better able you'll be to ask specific questions and get the answers you need to make sound organizational decisions.

SUBTOTAL Functions

Before you look at two key elements of Excel functionality that will help you analyze your data on a more granular level, it will be helpful to look at a different type of Excel function, one that lies at the core of this functionality: SUBTOTAL functions. *SUBTOTAL functions* are a specific set of Excel functions that perform calculations on a subset of data.

 Note: Although it is important to have an understanding of how SUBTOTAL functions work in terms of syntax, most users take advantage of them through ribbon commands and other UI-based functionality as opposed to entering them manually by typing.

The most common calculation you will likely make by using SUBTOTAL functions is, not surprisingly, finding subtotals. Take a look at this example to get a sense of how useful these functions can be.

	A	B	C	D	E
4	Sales Rep	Region	Commission Scale	Years w/ Company	Total Sales
5	Allen, S	AP	1	2	$45,123.00
6	Garcia, B	AP	1	3	$99,852.30
7	Smith, J	AP	1	4	$235,441.00
8	Cobbs, D	AP	2	11	$91,778.75
9					**$472,195.05**
10	Smith, T	AR	3	12	$100,021.30
11	Sharpe, L	AR	3	1	$63,258.30
12	Jones, A	AR	1	1	$47,986.25
13	Chen, L	AR	2	3	$55,154.32
14	Rivas, I	AR	3	5	$78,456.60
15	Ailes, E	AR	3	18	$125,101.10
16	Toner, R	AR	1	2	$45,612.30
17					**$515,590.17**
18	Jacobs, J	FM	2	8	$78,698.45
19	Odin, L	FM	2	11	$189,654.75

In this example, a range of sales data has been sorted by region. To find the sales totals by region, we've added extra rows in the worksheet, and used the SUM function to calculate each region's total sales, which are subtotals of the company's overall sales. This is simple enough to do if you're dealing with a relatively small worksheet, but this could quickly become quite a chore in larger ones. So, having a function that can perform the subtotal calculation on a very large dataset can be quite advantageous.

Technically speaking, SUBTOTAL functions are not really a group of functions; rather, this is a single function that calls one other function out of a set of available functions, such as SUM, AVERAGE, MAX, and MIN, depending on the specific calculation you want Excel to perform. It then performs the selected function on the range or ranges you stipulate in the arguments. Here is the function's syntax:

=SUBTOTAL(function_num, ref1, [ref2], ..., [ref254])

In the function's syntax, the reference arguments, **ref1**, **ref2**, and so on, simply tell the function which ranges to perform the calculations on. The **function_num** argument calls the specific function you want to use to calculate your subtotals. You express this argument as a single numeric value of 1 to 11 or 101 to 111. Of the available functions the SUBTOTAL function can call, there are two different groups, hence the two sets of possible values for the **function_num** argument. These are two identical sets of functions: If you enter a value from 1 to 11 as the argument, the selected function will include hidden values (because of hidden rows or columns in your worksheet); if you enter a value from 101 to 111 as the argument, the selected function will ignore hidden values.

The following table outlines the functions each value in the **function_num** argument calls.

Function_num Argument (Includes Hidden Values)	Function_num Argument (Ignores Hidden Values)	Called Function
1	101	AVERAGE
2	102	COUNT
3	103	COUNTA
4	104	MAX
5	105	MIN
6	106	PRODUCT

Function_num Argument (Includes Hidden Values)	Function_num Argument (Ignores Hidden Values)	Called Function
7	107	STDEV
8	108	STDEVP
9	109	SUM
10	110	VAR
11	111	VARP

So, if you have a large set of data in column A of a worksheet, and you want the subtotal for the first 20 values, you would enter the following function: *=SUBTOTAL(9, A1:A20)*. If you wanted to find the average value of that same range, you would enter *=SUBTOTAL(1,A1:A20)*. If that range contained hidden rows that you wanted to ignore while performing the same calculations, you would use *109* and *101* for the **function_num** arguments, respectively.

 Note: Both sets of SUBTOTAL functions ignore values removed from view because of filtering.

The Subtotals Feature

As previously mentioned, although it's good to have a grasp of the SUBTOTAL function's syntax, it isn't necessary to manually enter these functions. This is because Excel 2010 includes several features that enter the appropriate function for you automatically. One of these is the *Subtotals feature*. Selecting the **Subtotals** command enables you to automatically perform SUBTOTAL function calculations on subsets of data within a particular dataset. The Subtotals feature does not work on tables.

 Note: Although it is possible to enter SUBTOTAL functions in a table manually, they are rather difficult to work with in that environment. It is generally recommended that you convert the table to a dataset or copy it as a dataset and then use the Subtotals feature.

One of the most important things to remember about the Subtotals feature is that it is most effective when you have included column headers in the dataset and you have already sorted your data by some specific criteria, for example, region or financial period, for which you wish to calculate subtotals. This is because the Subtotals feature looks for changes in the column entries of one column, and then performs the desired calculation on the corresponding values in another column.

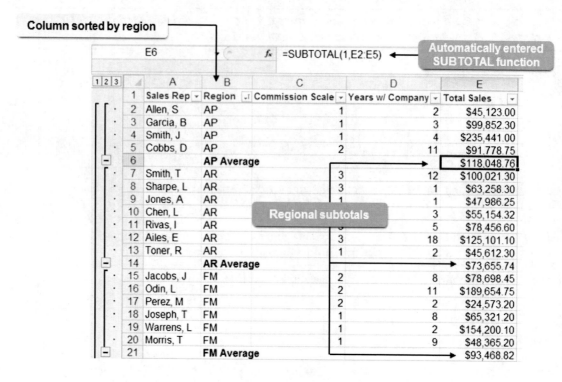

Figure 4-17: The Subtotal feature applied to a dataset. Here, the data is sorted by region and the Subtotal feature has applied the AVERAGE function to the values in the Total Sales column.

The Subtotal Dialog Box

You can use the **Subtotal** dialog box to perform SUBTOTAL function calculations on data ranges without having to manually enter the desired SUBTOTAL function. From here, you specify the criteria by which Excel will organize subsets of data, select the desired function, and select the column on which the calculation will be performed. The **Subtotal** dialog box also includes several options for configuring the display of subtotals. You can access the **Subtotal** dialog box by selecting **Data→Outline→Subtotal**.

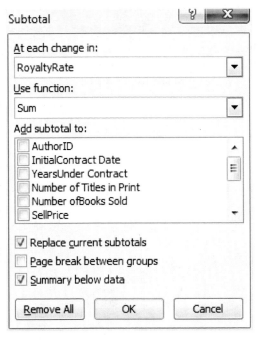

Figure 4-18: Use the Subtotal dialog box to configure your subtotal calculations.

The following table describes the function of the various elements of the **Subtotal** dialog box.

Subtotal Dialog Box Element	Allows You To
At each change in drop-down menu	Select the criteria by which to organize subsets of data. You do this by selecting the column that contains the desired entries. For example, you can tell Excel to perform subtotal calculations on data entries based on a particular region, department, or product. Remember to first sort your data on the column you will select in the **At each change in** drop-down menu and then apply the subtotal calculation.
Use function drop-down menu	Select the desired SUBTOTAL function.
Add subtotal to menu	Select the column on which you wish to perform the calculation. Like the **At each change in** drop-down menu, this drop-down menu is populated with the column headers in the selected dataset.
Replace current subtotals check box	Decide between replacing existing subtotals with new subtotal calculations or including multiple subtotals in your dataset.
Page break between groups check box	Place a page break after each subtotal so you can print each subset of data separately.
Summary below data check box	Include a summary row at the bottom of the table. This will include the grand total from all of the individual subtotals.
Remove All button	Clear all subtotals and subsets from the original dataset.

Outlines

You may have already noticed that when Excel applies subtotal functions to a range of data, it automatically creates a layered hierarchy of the various data subsets along the left side of the worksheet. This hierarchy is called an *outline*. In an outline, subtotaled datasets are arranged into groups of varying levels of detail that you can expand or collapse depending on how much detail you want to see. For example, if you want to carefully analyze individual data entries for the worksheet, you would want to expand all levels in the hierarchy so that all populated cells appear in the worksheet. But if you want to present summary data to your supervisor on a per-region basis, you may want to display only the subtotal rows that contain the summary information.

Outlines can contain up to eight levels of detail. Each level is nested within the previous level. The level buttons along the top of the **Outline** panel allow you to instantly change the view of your worksheet to display only the summary information of that level. The higher the number of the level button, the more detailed a view of your data you will see. Data subsets are represented in the outline by square brackets. These brackets display plus and minus buttons that enable you collapse and expand individual data subsets as desired.

Although Excel automatically creates outlines in datasets containing subtotals, you can also manually organize your datasets according to your needs. You will find the commands to do this in the **Outline** group on the **Data** tab.

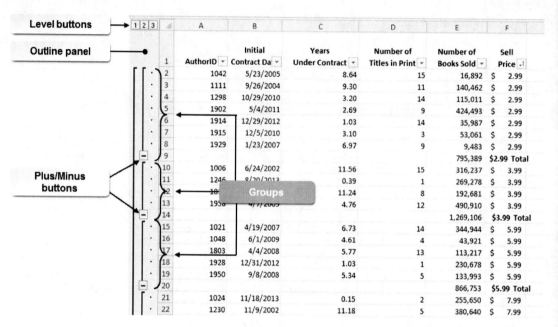

Figure 4-19: Outlines enable you to control how much detail is displayed in worksheets containing subtotals.

Summary Functions

Summary functions automatically perform SUBTOTAL function calculations in tables, much as the Subtotals feature does in datasets. But summary functions do not automatically create data subsets in tables. You can, however, calculate subtotals in tables by applying a summary function and then filtering the table to display only the data subset you wish to perform the calculation on.

You perform summary function calculations in tables in much the same way as you filter and sort data in tables. The best way to do this is to include a total row in the desired table and then select the desired function from the total row down arrow in the desired column. This returns the result of the selected function in the total row of the that column, which includes all displayed values in the calculation. Once you have applied the function, you can filter the table data to reapply the calculation to only the desired values. You can also manually type SUBTOTAL functions into any worksheet cell, referencing the desired table range, if you wish.

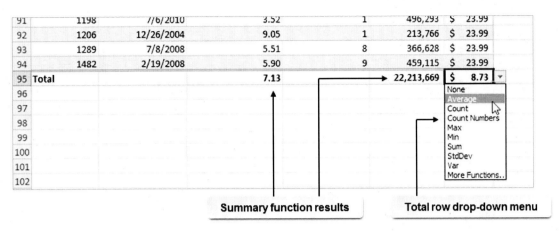

Figure 4-20: You can automatically apply summary functions to table columns in tables that contain total rows.

 Access the Checklist tile on your LogicalCHOICE course screen for reference information and job aids on How to Summarize Data with **SUBTOTAL** and Summary Functions.

ACTIVITY 4–4
Using Subtotals to Summarize Data

Before You Begin

The my_author_data_04.xlsx workbook file is open.

Scenario

You're on your way to a meeting. You have been asked to report on the total income generated by Fuller and Ackerman's authors. But you have also been asked to give detailed information on income generated by authors at each of the royalty rate levels. Rather than take the time to filter the table numerous times and recalculate the income totals for each group, you decide to use the Subtotals feature to provide all of the summary information at once. You realize you will have to convert your table back to a range to do this, but you also suspect you will need the table for future calculation. So, you decide to make a copy of the **Authors** worksheet and convert the table to a range on the worksheet copy. This way, you'll have easy access to your data as both a range and as a table.

---

1. Make a copy of the **Authors** worksheet on which to convert the table to a range.
   a) Right-click the **Authors** worksheet tab and select **Move or Copy**.
   b) In the **Move or Copy** dialog box, in the **Before sheet** list, select **Statistics**.
   c) Check the **Create a copy** check box and select **OK**.
   d) Rename the **Authors(2)** worksheet tab to *Authors_Range*

2. Convert the table on the **Authors_Range** worksheet to a range.
   a) Ensure that the **Authors_Range** worksheet is selected.
   b) Select any cell within the table.
   c) From the **Table Tools** contextual tab, select **Design→Tools→Convert to Range**.
   d) In the **Microsoft Excel** dialog box, select **Yes**.

3. Delete the first three worksheet rows to remove the criteria range.

4. Sort the dataset by royalty rate.
   a) Select any cell within the dataset and then select **Data→Sort & Filter→Filter**.

    Note: This enables quick sorting and AutoFilters for the dataset without converting it to a table.

   b) In cell **K1**, select the column header down arrow and then select **Sort Smallest to Largest**.

5. Add subtotals to the dataset.
   a) Ensure a cell within the dataset is selected and then select **Data→Outline→Subtotal**.
   b) In the **Subtotal** dialog box, from the **At each change in** drop-down menu, select **RoyaltyRate**.
   c) Ensure that **Sum** is selected in the **Use function** drop-down menu.
   d) In the **Add subtotal to** list, check the **IncomeEarned** check box and ensure that all other check boxes are unchecked.

e) Ensure the **Replace current subtotals** check box and the **Summary below data** check boxes are both checked, and that the **Page break between groups** check box is unchecked.

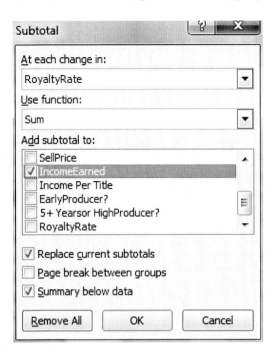

f) Select **OK**.

6. Collapse the detailed view of the dataset to view only the subtotals.

   a) At the top of the **Outline panel**, select the **2** button.

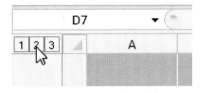

   b) If necessary, adjust the width of column **G** to view the summarized data.

7. Save the workbook.

ACTIVITY 4–5
Using Summary Functions in Tables

Before You Begin

The my_author_data_04.xlsx workbook file is open and the Authors_Range worksheet is selected.

Scenario

You've just returned to your office from the meeting at which you presented the subtotals for income earned by royalty rate. During the meeting, someone asked how much income F&A has generated from authors who signed their initial contracts during the 2012 calendar year and how many authors fit that criteria. You suspect company leaders will be looking for further information as they decide how to handle relationships with both legacy and newly acquired authors. You decide to take advantage of the dynamic nature of Excel tables to answer these, and potentially future, questions.

---

1. Select the **Authors** worksheet tab and ensure that the **Total** row is still visible.

2. Make sure all previous filters have been cleared from the table.

3. Turn AutoFiltering back on for the table by selecting **Data→Sort & Filter→Filter**.

4. Filter the table and use summary functions to answer the questions "How many authors signed their initial contracts in 2012?" and "What is the total income generated by these authors?"

    a) Select the **Column** header down arrow in cell **B4**.
    b) In the drop-down menu, select **Date Filters→Between**.
    c) In the **Custom AutoFilter** dialog box, in the **is after or equal to** field, type *1/1/2012*
    d) Ensure that the **And** radio button is selected and then, in the **is before or equal to** field, type *12/31/2012*

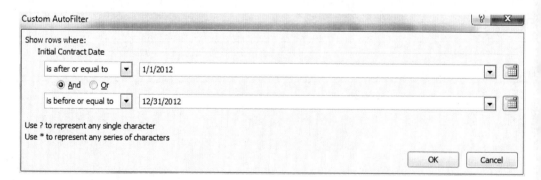

    e) Select **OK**.
    f) Scroll to the bottom of the table.

g) Select the cell that is in the **Total** row of the **Initial Contract Date** column (cell **B817**).

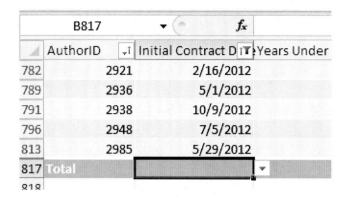

h) Select the **Total** row down arrow and then select **Count**.
i) Select the **Total** row down arrow in cell **G817** and then select **Sum**.
j) If necessary, adjust the width of column **G** to accommodate the new figure.

5. How many authors signed their initial contracts in 2012?

6. How much income did those authors produce?

7. Clear all filters and save the workbook.

Database Functions

Excel 2010 provides you with a powerful set of functions that can help you drill down into your data to ask highly focused questions: *database functions*. Database functions enable you to perform calculations on ranges of data based on specific criteria. Essentially, these allow you to perform calculations on particular data by incorporating a database query-like level of functionality. Basically, you query the dataset to find a particular value or set of values, and then perform some calculation on only the specific data.

Mathematically speaking, the calculations that database functions perform are similar to their standard counterparts. Database functions, essentially, combine the functionality of Excel functions with the functionality of advanced filters. Database functions use the same operators that advanced filters use to identify the specific data you wish to perform a calculation on. To enter criteria for database functions, you must follow the same rules as you do for creating advanced filters.

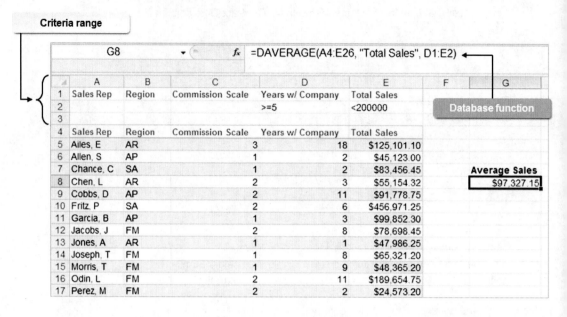

Figure 4-21: The database function in cell G8 returns the average sales for sales reps who have been with the company for five or more years and who have total sales of less than $200,000.

The following is a list of all of the database functions in Excel 2010.

- DAVERAGE
- DCOUNT
- DCOUNTA
- DGET
- DMAX
- DMIN
- DPRODUCT
- DSTDEV
- DSTDEVP
- DSUM
- DVAR
- DVARP

Database Function Syntax

You can distinguish database functions from their counterparts because the function names all begin with the letter "D." The database function equivalent of the SUM function is the DSUM function, and the database function equivalent of the AVERAGE function is the DAVERAGE function. All database functions have the same three arguments, which are all required. Let's look at the DSUM function as an example.

Syntax: =DSUM(database, field, criteria)

Description: The DSUM function calculates the sum of values within a range that all meet the specified criteria. In the function's arguments, **database** is the reference to the range of cells that make up the entire dataset. This range should include column labels (headers).

The **field** argument specifies the column the function will perform a calculation on. You can include this argument in one of three ways. The first is by enclosing the column label in double quotation marks (example: "Total Sales"). The second is by entering the cell reference of the cell containing the column label. Or, you can simply refer to the column by its numerical place in the dataset. So, if you want the function to perform the calculation on the third column in a table or dataset, you would enter *3* as the **field** argument.

The **criteria** argument specifies the criteria range. You enter this argument as a range of cells; the range must include the duplicate header row and all criteria you wish to include. It does not have to include the empty row between the criteria range and the dataset.

Let's take another look at the previous example, which uses the DAVERAGE function.

As you can enter the field argument in three different ways, this function could be entered in any of the following ways.

=DAVERAGE(A4:A26, "Total Sales", D1:E2)

=DAVERAGE(A4:A26, E4, D1:E2)

=DAVERAGE(A4:A26, 5, D1:E2)

In the first example, the **field** argument is specified by the column's label. The second example uses the label's cell reference. The third example specifies the argument by the column's position in the dataset. As the **Total Sales** column is the fifth column in the dataset, you can simply enter *5* to define the **field** argument.

 Note: For more information on data calculation in tables, watch the LearnTO **Use Structured References to Calculate Data in an Excel Table** presentation from the **LearnTO** tile on the LogicalCHOICE Course screen.

 Access the Checklist tile on your LogicalCHOICE course screen for reference information and job aids on How to Use Database Functions.

ACTIVITY 4-6
Using Database Functions

Before You Begin

The my_author_data_04.xlsx workbook file is open, and the **Authors** worksheet is selected.

Scenario

As suspected, you are being asked more and more often for summary data about Fuller and Ackerman (F&A) authors based on a wide variety of criteria. Although you've been able to use sorting, filtering, and summary functions to find the answers company leaders are seeking, you feel it would be much faster to simply type the criteria in a criteria range and use database functions to return the desired answers.

You decide to create an answer cell to the right of the table on the **Authors** worksheet and use that to query your data whenever senior leaders ask for specific information. Currently, they are looking for answers to the following questions:

- What is the average number of books sold for authors who signed their initial contract before 2010 and who have generated more than $1 million in income?
- What is the total income earned by books that were written by authors who have been with F&A for fewer than three years or who have authored five or fewer books?

1. Create an answer cell to the right of the table to return results of database functions.
   a) Change the magnification level of the worksheet to **90%**.
   b) Select cell **M5** and type *Answer*
   c) Press **Ctrl+Enter**.
   d) Select **Home→Styles→Cell Styles→Accent3** to apply the Accent 3 cell style to the **Answer** label.

2. Write a database function to answer the question "What is the average number of books sold for authors who signed their initial contract before 2010 and who have generated more than $1 million in income?"
   a) Delete the filter criteria from cells **C2** and **E2**.
   b) Select cell **B2**, type *<1/1/2010* and press **Tab**.
   c) Select cell **G2**, type *>1000000* and press **Enter**.
   d) Select cell **N5**, type *=DAVERAGE(A4:K816, E4, B1:G2)* and press **Enter**.

3. **What is the average number of books sold for these authors?**

4. Write a database function to answer the question "What is the total income earned by books that were written by authors who have been with F&A for fewer than three years or who have authored five or fewer books?"
   a) Delete the contents of cells **B2**, **G2**, and **N5**.
   b) Select cell **C2**, type *<3* and press **Enter**.
   c) Select cell **E3**, type *<=5* and press **Enter**.

d) Add a new row between rows **3** and **4**.

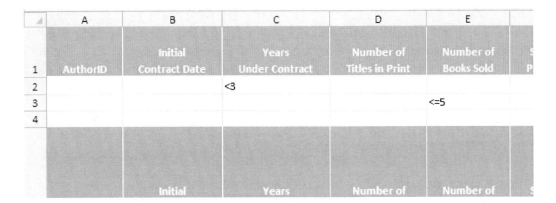

e) Select cell **N6**.
f) Type *=DSUM(A5:K817, G5, C1:E3)* and press **Enter**.

5. What is the total income earned by these authors?

6. Save and close the workbook.

Summary

In this lesson, you organized and analyzed datasets and tables. With the massive volume of data many organizations are storing these days, the ability to organize and filter that data is a critical element of making sense of it all. The ability to pare down your data into manageable chunks and to ask very specific questions about subsets of massive worksheets allows you to home in on what's really important to organizational leaders. Taking advantage of these data analysis features means you can get the answers you need quickly, avoid errors, and move on to other important tasks.

What advantages do you see tables providing over data ranges?

Which of the data-analysis tools covered in this lesson do you think will have the greatest impact on your daily tasks?

Note: Check your LogicalCHOICE Course screen for opportunities to interact with your classmates, peers, and the larger LogicalCHOICE online community about the topics covered in this course or other topics you are interested in. From the Course screen you can also access available resources for a more continuous learning experience.

5 | Visualizing Data with Basic Charts

Lesson Time: 30 minutes

Lesson Objectives

In this lesson, you will visualize data with basic charts. You will:

- Create charts.

- Modify and format charts.

Lesson Introduction

Excel 2010 provides you with a powerful array of functionality for organizing and analyzing your data. As you become more familiar with these features, you'll find you can ask Excel an astonishingly vast array of questions and get the answers you need. But not everyone who you report to or present data to will have the same comfort level or expertise when it comes to viewing worksheets. Viewing information in the form of ranges of data entries is simply not natural for many people. You may find yourself presenting information to large audiences on a regular basis. In these cases, you don't want people scanning lines of data on a worksheet when you're trying to present. You want to give them a simple, easy-to-digest view of important data so they can quickly understand what's really important.

In short, you need a way to generate visual representations of your data. Excel 2010 includes some handy functionality that can convert your raw or analyzed data into visually clear, easy-to-interpret diagrams with just a few steps. Taking the time to understand how this functionality works will give you the ability to generate high-impact visuals to present to nearly any audience, nearly any time, almost instantly.

TOPIC A

Create Charts

Let's face it, long strings of data are simply difficult for people to read and interpret. And, in today's data-driven, high-pace world, most people don't have the time to sit down and pore over worksheets to get the information they need. Often, decision makers are looking for only a snapshot of just the most relevant information. And, as an Excel user, it's likely your job to provide that snapshot for them.

Now that you've amassed, organized, and analyzed your data, you need to convert all of the figures and labels into a picture that makes a clear, simple statement. The good news is that, in Excel, this is quite simple to do. And, what's even better, is once you convert your data in to easy-to-view visuals, you can keep those visuals up to date just as easily as you can your data.

Charts

Charts are graphical representations of the numeric values and relationships in a dataset. Charts help worksheet viewers to quickly and easily interpret the data in a worksheet.

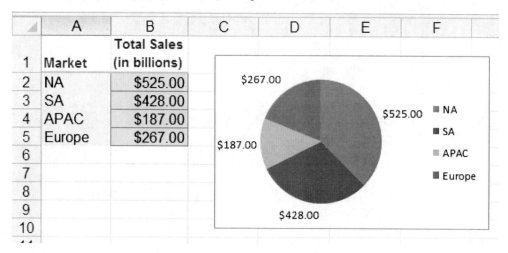

Figure 5–1: A pie chart on an Excel worksheet.

In this figure, while you can tell from the values in the **Total Sales (in billions)** column what the sales are for each market, the pie chart to the right of the data is much easier to interpret. With just a glance, you can tell that North American sales account for more sales than the other three regions, and that they account for more than a third of all sales. Getting this information from the raw data would require a bit of analysis and some calculating.

Chart Basics

Although there is a wide variety of charts available in Excel 2010 to chart a number of different types of data, most of the chart types follow the same basic conventions. Most of the commonly used chart types in Excel plot data along two axes, the X axis and the Y axis. The X axis is the one that runs horizontally along the chart. It is typically used to represent a category of information, such as fiscal quarter or department. The Y, or vertical, axis is typically used to represent values within your dataset, such as sales totals or number of products shipped. The objects displayed in the chart, such as bars, columns, or lines, typically represent the individual items, or series, for which you wish to represent the data, such as particular regions or individual sales reps.

Because Excel pulls data from your worksheets to create charts, it's important to understand how Excel reads your data in order to create them. Excel pulls the elements plotted along the X axis, or the categories, from your column labels. It identifies a data series based on the row labels from the selected dataset. Excel reads the values in the remaining cells as the values to plot against the Y axis.

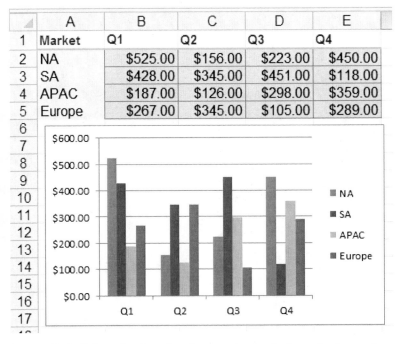

Figure 5-2: Using simple sales data to chart relative sales by region.

Note that, in the figure, the categories along the X axis correspond to the worksheet column labels, which in this case are fiscal quarters. The data series, represented by the columns on the chart, represent different global regions, which Excel pulled from the row labels. The data entered into the remaining cells are the values against which the series are plotted.

Of course, not all charts work exactly like this, but most of the commonly used charts do. The most notable exceptions are the pie chart, which you will typically use only to chart a single column of data, and the bar chart, which essentially turns a column chart on its side.

Chart Types

Excel 2010 includes 11 different chart types, each of which is ideal for displaying a particular type of data or set of relationships. Each type of chart contains a variety of specific sub-types that you can use to tailor the presentation of your data. You can access the chart types and sub-types in the **Insert Chart** dialog box, which you can use to insert charts in your worksheets. You can access the **Insert Chart** dialog box by selecting the **Insert→Charts** dialog box launcher, or by selecting **All Chart Types** from any of the chart type drop-down menus in the **Charts** group on the **Insert** tab.

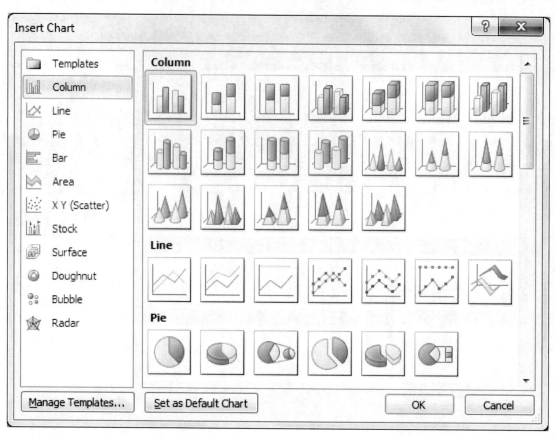

Figure 5-3: Use the Insert Chart dialog box to select the desired chart type and sub-type to suit your needs.

The following table describes the ideal uses for the various Excel chart types.

Chart Type	Is Best Used to Display
Column	Relationships among values in a number of categories or changes in values over time.
Line	Trends in data over a period of time at consistent intervals, for example quarterly or annually.
Pie	The relative size of values compared to the whole and to other parts of the whole. This is the best chart to use when you are charting only a single column or row of data.
Bar	Relationships among values in a number of categories.
Area	Relationships among values in a number of categories over time with visual emphasis on the magnitude of each data category.
X Y (Scatter)	The relationship between two categories of measured data, as opposed to one category of measured data across evenly spaced periods of time. Use this chart type to determine if there is a trend in the relationship between two sets of variables.
Stock	The change in stock prices over time or other similar fluctuating sets of values, such as daily or annual temperatures.

Chart Type	Is Best Used to Display
Surface	Three-dimensional representations of data. Typically, you would use a surface chart when working with three sets of data. An example of this would be charting the relative change in density of several materials, at a variety of temperatures, over a period of time.
Doughnut	The relative size of values compared to the whole and to other parts of the whole. The doughnut chart type is similar to the pie chart type except you can use this to compare relative values for more than one data series.
Bubble	The relationships among three categories of measured data. The bubble chart type is similar to the X Y (Scatter) chart type. The difference is that in a bubble chart, each data point on the chart also has a relative size compared to the other data points. Bubble charts are often used to display demographic data.
Radar	The aggregate relational sizes of multiple data categories in terms of multiple criteria. For example, you could use a radar chart to track the popularity of a particular item in multiple countries for each year in a decade.

Chart Insertion Methods

Before inserting a chart into a worksheet, you should select the dataset the chart will be based on. If you select a single cell within the desired dataset, Excel will try to guess at the proper range. This does not always generate the desired outcome, so it's a best practice to manually select the desired dataset.

It's important to remember to include row and column labels in your selection and to have your data entered correctly. For example, the categories you want plotted along the X axis should be your column labels, and the desired data series should be the row labels. Once you have ensured that your data is properly entered on the worksheet, and you have selected the desired range, you have three general options for inserting a chart: ribbon commands, the **Insert Chart** dialog box, or inserting the default chart type. For either of the first two methods, simply select the desired chart type from the **Insert Chart** dialog box or from the chart type drop-down menus in the **Charts** group on the **Insert** tab.

If you know you will be inserting a number of the same type of chart in your workbook, you can set that chart type as the default chart type. Then you can use one of two keyboard shortcuts to instantly create the default chart type out of any selected dataset.

Note: Use the **Set as Default Chart** command on the **Insert Chart** dialog box to set the default chart type. This is an application-level setting, so what you set here will be the default chart type for any workbook file until you change the default chart type.

Keyboard Shortcut	Inserts
Alt+F1	The default chart type on the same worksheet the dataset is on.
F11	The default chart type on a new worksheet.

Access the Checklist tile on your LogicalCHOICE course screen for reference information and job aids on How to Create Charts.

ACTIVITY 5-1
Creating a Chart

Data File

C:\091019Data\Visualizing Data with Basic Charts\sales_dashboard.xlsx

Before You Begin

Excel 2010 is open.

Scenario

In addition to tracking total income by author, you also track the sales for each title by calendar year. In preparation for a big meeting with Fuller and Ackerman (F&A) leadership, you are developing a sales dashboard workbook. Your goal is to create a workbook you can use to answer nearly any question company leaders may have about F&A book sales. You have already organized some of the raw sales data into tables, and you have created a few charts to display overall sales information by market, format, and genre. Now you want to create a chart that illustrates total sales by format per fiscal year. You plan to add the chart and then position it next to the others.

1. Open the **sales_dashboard.xlsx** workbook file and ensure that the **Sales Dashboard** worksheet is selected.

    Note: You may find it helpful to zoom out a bit on screen while performing this activity.

2. Create a line chart to display per-year sales information for the electronic and print formats.
   a) Scroll to the right and then select the range **Y2:Z15**.
   b) Select **Insert→Charts→Line** and, in the **2-D Line** section, select the **Line** chart type.

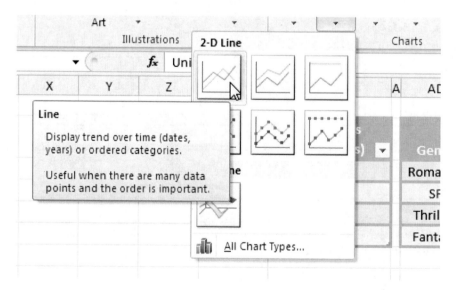

3. Position the mouse pointer at the chart's border until it appears as the **Move** cursor ✛ and then drag the chart so it appears below the **Total Sales by Format (in millions)** chart.

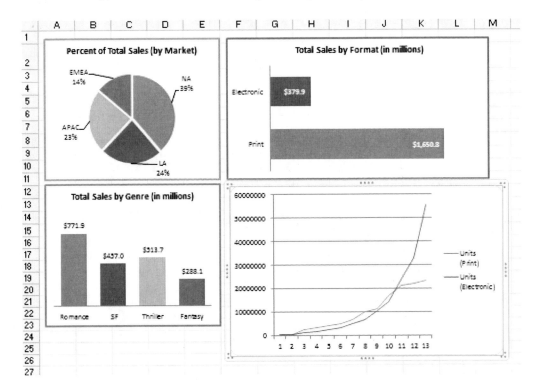

4. Save the workbook to the **C:\091019Data|Visualizing Data with Basic Charts** folder as *my_sales_dashboard.xlsx*

TOPIC B

Modify and Format Charts

Although you can create charts with just a few mouse clicks, the default chart configurations aren't always exactly what you need to present your data. Depending on your audience and the venue, you may want to include more or less information than the default configurations include, present your data with organizational branding, or simply make your charts larger or easier to read.

Excel 2010 provides you with a vast array of options when it comes to modifying and formatting your charts. By configuring the display of your charts, you take full control over the message your charts convey and their overall visual impact. A well-formatted chart can mean the difference between simply delivering information and making an impact on your audience.

Modification vs. Formatting

Modifying and formatting charts go hand-in-hand. Although many people use these terms synonymously, they are actually two different things. Modifying a chart includes making changes such as moving chart elements, adding or removing chart elements, turning the display of particular data on or off, and changing the chart type. Think of modifying a chart as working with the display of data. You modify a chart to change the audience's understanding of the information you're presenting.

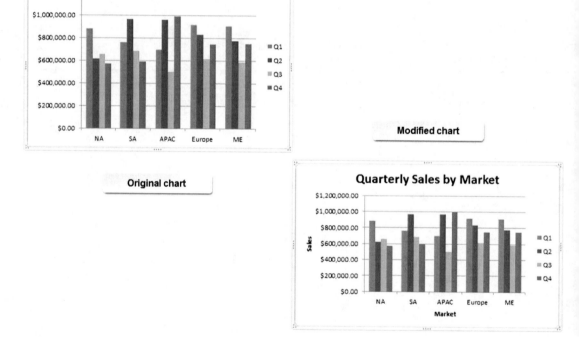

Figure 5–4: This chart has been modified to make the data easier to interpret.

Formatting refers to altering the overall look and feel of a chart. Formatting a chart typically includes tasks such as changing the color scheme or the font and altering the size of the chart. You format a chart to comply with branding standards or to convey a particular mood or feel.

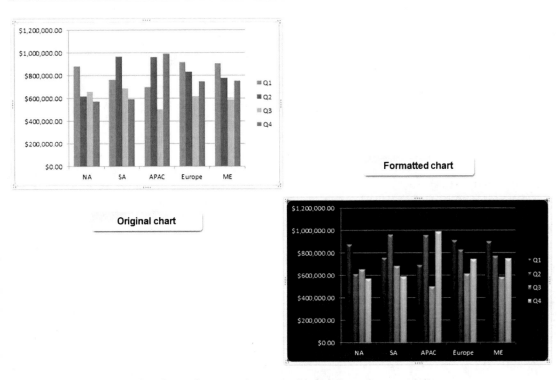

Figure 5-5: This chart has been formatted to comply with branding guidelines.

Chart Elements

Chart elements are the individual objects that can appear on charts and that convey some level of information to a viewer about the chart's data. While all Excel charts contain at least one chart element, by default, the various chart types display different chart elements. For example, while bar and column charts typically display an X and a Y axis, surface charts display three axes. Pie and doughnut charts don't contain axes as they deal with only a single column of data. Each chart element serves a different role in visually communicating information about data and trends.

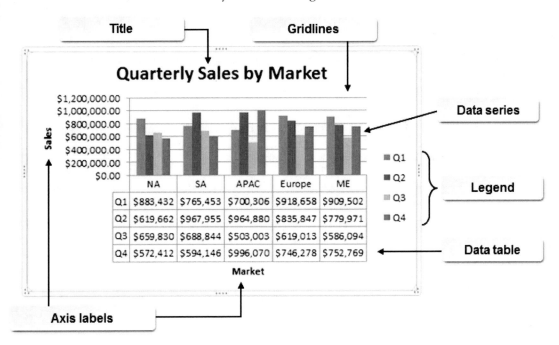

Figure 5-6: Chart elements help the audience interpret chart data.

Guidelines for Including Chart Elements

 Note: All of the Guidelines for this lesson are available as checklists from the **Checklist** tile on the LogicalCHOICE Course screen.

Formatting charts has relatively little impact on an audience's ability to interpret your data. Modifying chart elements, on the other hand, can have a significant impact. As a general rule, it's best to include only those chart elements that are absolutely necessary for conveying meaning. Cluttered charts can muddy your main point and make the chart confusing to view, which is exactly what you create charts to avoid. However, some chart elements do actually help add meaning. Until you gain an intuitive sense of what chart elements to include for various purposes, you may want to consider adding chart elements that you feel will help your target audience interpret your data, analyze your chart, and then remove anything that doesn't directly contribute to the message you intend to deliver. When analyzing your charts, ask yourself questions, such as:

- If I remove the gridlines, will the chart still convey meaning?
- Do I need a legend? Can I remove the legend and use data labels instead?
- How much precision do I need for axis labels?
- Do the axes really need titles?
- Will using a three-dimensional layout enhance visual appeal or distort proportions?
- Does including the data table aid understanding?
- Do I really need major and minor tick marks on the axes?
- Before finalizing your charts, keep the old adage "less is more" in mind. If the audience needs an element to acquire meaning, keep it. Otherwise, remove it.

The Chart Tools Contextual Tab

You can access all of the commands you will use to modify and format your charts on the **Chart Tools** contextual tab. Similar to other contextual tabs, the **Chart Tools** contextual tab appears whenever you select a chart or a chart element, and it disappears when you select a worksheet element outside the chart. The **Chart Tools** contextual tab contains three tabs that each contain task-related groups and commands for working with your charts. Let's take a look at the various command groups on each of these tabs.

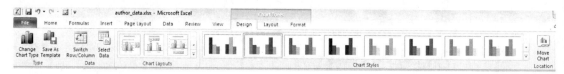

Figure 5-7: The Design tab.

Use the commands on the **Design** tab to quickly change the overall look and feel of your charts.

Design Tab Command Group	Contains Commands For
Type	Changing the chart type and saving a particular chart as a template.
Data	Changing the chart's dataset range and switching the row and column data. Keep in mind that this does not switch the data that is displayed on the X axis with the data that is displayed on the Y axis. This switches the categories with the data series.
Chart Layouts	Quickly configuring the display of chart elements according to predefined configurations.
Chart Styles	Quickly formatting a chart by using predefined sets of formatting options.

Design Tab Command Group	Contains Commands For
Location	Moving charts to different worksheets within a workbook.

Figure 5-8: The Layout tab.

Use the commands on the **Layout** tab to work with individual chart elements and to name charts.

Layout Tab Command Group	Contains Commands For
Current Selection	Selecting particular chart elements and accessing the **Format Selection** dialog box.
Insert	Adding images, shapes, and text boxes to your charts.
Labels	Toggling on or off and configuring the display of chart elements.
Axes	Toggling on or off and configuring the display of axes and gridlines.
Background	Configuring the display of chart background elements.
Analysis	Adding and configuring data analysis chart elements.
Properties	Naming charts.

Figure 5-9: The Format tab.

Use the commands on the **Format** tab to configure chart formatting.

Format Tab Command Group	Contains Commands For
Current Selection	Selecting particular chart elements and accessing the **Format Selection** dialog box.
Shape Styles	Configuring formatting options for chart elements.
WordArt Styles	Configuring formatting options for chart text.
Arrange	Changing the front-to-back placement of chart elements and configuring the orientation of chart elements.
Size	Changing the size of chart elements.

The Select Data Source Dialog Box

You will use the **Select Data Source** dialog box to manage Excel chart data. From here, you can edit the entire dataset feeding the chart, or you can edit the data feeding any of the individual data series. You can also remove from or add back to the chart any of the individual data series, reorder how the data series appear on the chart, or switch the chart's X and Y axes. You can access the **Select Data Source** dialog box from the **Chart Tools** contextual tab by selecting **Design→Data→Select Data**.

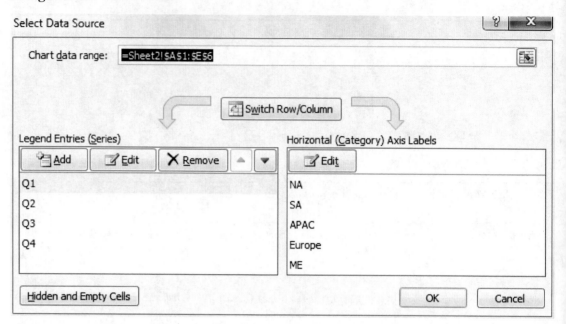

Figure 5-10: Use the Select Data Source dialog box to manage the data displayed by Excel charts.

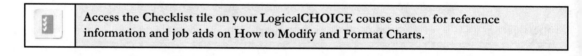

Access the Checklist tile on your LogicalCHOICE course screen for reference information and job aids on **How to Modify and Format Charts.**

ACTIVITY 5-2
Modifying and Formatting a Chart

Before You Begin
The my_sales_dashboard.xlsx workbook file is open and the **Sales_Dashboard** worksheet is selected.

Scenario
Your new line chart is in place alongside the other charts in your sales dashboard workbook. It doesn't blend visually with the other charts on the worksheet, so you decide to format it to match the others. You also feel the **Total Sales by Format (in millions)** chart doesn't quite visually convey the message you want to send, which is how much of overall sales are made up of each format. You decide to convert that bar chart into a pie chart.

---

1. Add a title to the line chart.
   a) Ensure the line chart is selected and, on the **Chart Tools** contextual tab, select the **Layout** tab.
   b) In the **Labels** group, select **Chart Title→Centered Overlay Title**.
   c) In the **Formula Bar**, type *Unit Sales by FY (in millions)* and press **Enter**.
   d) With the chart title still selected, right-click the title and, by using the **mini toolbar**, change the font size to *12*

2. Edit the chart legend to make it easier to read.
   a) From the **Chart Tools** contextual tab, select **Design→Data→Select Data**.
   b) In the **Select Data Source** dialog box, in the **Legend Entries (Series)** section, select **Units(Print)** and then select **Edit**.
   c) In the **Edit Series** dialog box, delete the contents of the **Series name** field, type *Print* and select **OK**.

    Note: When you edit legend entries in this way, as opposed to changing the labels in the source dataset, Excel breaks the link between the label in the dataset and the legend entry. If you modify the label in the original dataset, the new text will not update in the legend.

   d) Use the same method to change **Units(Electronic)** to *Electronic*
   e) In the **Select Data Source** dialog box, select **OK**.
   f) Verify that the changes reflect in the chart legend.

3. Remove the chart's gridlines.
   a) Ensure that the chart is still selected and, on the **Chart Tools** contextual tab, select the **Layout** tab.

b) In the **Current Selection** group, select the **Chart Elements** down arrow above the **Format Selection** command.

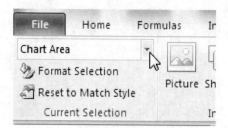

> **Note:** The selection in the **Chart Elements** drop-down menu may be different in this image if you inadvertently selected a chart element manually.

c) From the **Chart Elements** drop-down menu, select **Vertical (Value) Axis Major Gridlines** and press **Delete**.

4. Edit the horizontal axis.
   a) Select the down arrow in the **Current Selection** group and select **Horizontal (Category) Axis**.
   b) From the **Chart Tools** contextual tab, select **Design→Data→Select Data**.
   c) In the **Select Data Source** dialog box, in the **Horizontal (Category) Axis Labels** section, select **Edit**.
   d) In the **Axis Labels** dialog box, in the **Axis label range** field, select the **Collapse Dialog** button.
   e) Select the range **X3:X15** and press **Enter**.
   f) In the **Axis Labels** dialog box, select **OK** and, in the **Select Data Source** dialog box, select **OK**.
   g) Verify that the horizontal axis is now labeled with the calendar years.

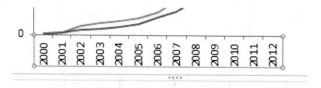

> **Note:** The original chart didn't contain the year labels because the original data selection did not contain the year labels. This is due to the table layout and the chart type used here.

5. Edit the vertical axis.
   a) Ensure that the chart is still selected.
   b) From the **Chart Tools** contextual tab, select the **Layout→Current Selection** down arrow and then select **Vertical (Value) Axis**.
   c) Select **Layout→Current Selection→Format Selection**.
   d) In the **Format Axis** dialog box, select the **Number** tab.
   e) In the **Category** section, select **Custom**.
   f) Clear the contents of the **Format Code** field and type *##0,,*

   g) Select **Add**.

h) In the **Format Axis** dialog box, select **Close**.

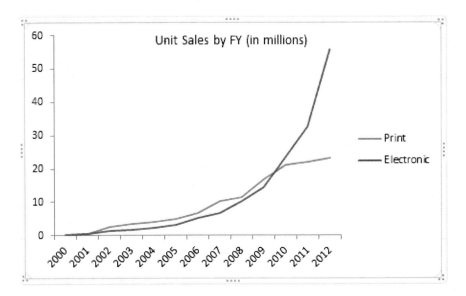

6. Resize the chart.
   a) Select the chart border to ensure that the entire chart, and not the vertical axis, is selected; then select the **Format** tab on the **Chart Tools** contextual tab.
   b) In the **Size** group, set the value in the **Height** spin box to **2.5**.
   c) Set the value in the **Width** spin box to **4.8**.

7. Edit the chart to make it more easily read.
   a) Right-click the legend and select **Format Legend**.
   b) In the **Format Legend** dialog box, make sure the **Legend Options** tab is selected.
   c) In the **Legend Position** section, select the **Top** radio button and then select **Close**.
   d) Drag the legend so it is centered directly below the chart title.

   Unit Sales by FY (in millions)
   ——— Print   ——— Electronic

   e) Right-click the horizontal axis and select **Format Axis**.
   f) In the **Format Axis** dialog box, make sure the **Axis Options** tab is selected.
   g) At the bottom of the **Axis Options** pane, in the **Position Axis** section, select the **On tick marks** radio button and select **Close**.

8. Add a border to the chart.
   a) With the chart still selected, if necessary, select **Chart Area** from the **Chart Elements** drop-down menu.
   b) In the **Current Selection** group, select **Format Selection**.
   c) In the **Format Chart Area** dialog box, select the **Border Color** tab.
   d) Ensure that the **Solid line** radio button is selected and select the **Color** down arrow.
   e) From the **Color** gallery, in the **Standard Colors** section, select **Light Green**.
   f) Select the **Border Styles** tab.
   g) Set the value in the **Width** spin box to **2** and select **Close**.

9. Deselect the chart to view the border.

10. Save and close the workbook.

Summary

In this lesson, you gave your worksheet data visual interest by using basic charts. You did this by creating charts to display your data and formatting and modifying them to make them easier to read and interpret. Providing your audience members with a visual snapshot of your data enables them to quickly see the overall impact raw data, recognize trends, make easy comparisons, and focus on your message instead of your worksheets.

What are a couple of reasons you anticipate for including charts in your workbooks?

Which chart type do you expect to use most often?

Note: Check your LogicalCHOICE Course screen for opportunities to interact with your classmates, peers, and the larger LogicalCHOICE online community about the topics covered in this course or other topics you are interested in. From the Course screen you can also access available resources for a more continuous learning experience.

6 | Analyzing Data with PivotTables, Slicers, and PivotCharts

Lesson Time: 1 hour

Lesson Objectives

In this lesson, you will analyze data with PivotTables, Slicers, and PivotCharts. You will:

- Create a PivotTable.

- Analyze PivotTable data.

- Present data with PivotCharts.

- Filter data by using slicers.

Lesson Introduction

You've already seen the way Excel functions and features, such as sorting, filtering, and summary functions, can help you drill down into your data to get answers to very specific questions. Although using these features is often a good option for attaining specific answers, these aren't necessarily the best options if you need to frequently change the questions you're asking of your data. To change the question you're asking when using functions, sorting, and filtering, you often need to rewrite functions, adjust criteria, or re-filter you data; sometimes, you need to use several of these methods at the same time. You certainly could take this route, but it isn't the most efficient way to re-query your data to get the variety of answers you need. If you work in a high-paced, data-intensive environment, you simply may not have the time needed to recalculate every time a supervisor asks you a different question. You need something a little more dynamic.

Excel 2010 includes a powerful feature that enables you to ask any number of questions of your data; get detailed, specific answers; and do it all over again in just a matter of moments. By using PivotTables to analyze your data, you will take the next major step toward Excel mastery. This functionality gives you a staggering level of control over data analysis. You can get critical, time-sensitive organizational intelligence to the people who need it quickly, easily, and with a high-level of flexibility.

TOPIC A

Create a PivotTable

To take advantage of the functionality and flexibility of PivotTables, you must first understand how to create them. Although this is a relatively simple process, you must also know a bit about the type of data that works best for PivotTables. By taking a few moments to gain this foundational level of understanding, you'll be preparing yourself to create useful, effective PivotTables that you can use to analyze your raw data in incredibly fine detail.

Pivoting

Pivoting allows you to view your data from a variety of new perspectives. In Excel, pivoting is a form of data manipulation that can take a column of data and pivot it into a row and vice versa. While this may not seem highly useful at first, think about it in terms of reorganizing and summarizing data based on a number of criteria. For example, let's say you have a dataset that contains rows of data, each representing a single event, such as a sale, a shipment, or a financial transaction. Each row would be composed of cells in a series of columns that each represent a single aspect of the individual events, say a particular date, dollar amount, or location. If you want to compile particular data about these events as a whole, say to find total sales that occurred at each of the various locations, you could take the location column and pivot it so that it appears as a series of rows with each unique location being represented by an individual row. Location is your first criterion.

Your second criterion is sales figures. In the original dataset, each row represents a single sale. The sales figures for all of the sales were in the same column, and each was associated with one of the locations. Now that the locations are represented by individual rows in the pivoted dataset, you want to know the total value of all sales from the dataset for each location. Manually calculating this would take some time; however, asking Excel to look at every sales entry for each location, sum the values together, and then return the total value for each location in the new rows would save all that manual effort. Once done, you would have just successfully pivoted a single column into multiple rows and summarized a particular data entry for each to answer a very specific question: How much in total sales was generated for each location? This simple example shows the power of pivoting.

 Note: As with filtering and sorting, pivoting does not affect your raw data; it only modifies your view of the data.

Here's a look at how the previous example would work in a worksheet.

⁄	A	B	C	D	E
1	Transaction Date	Location Code	Units Sold	Sell Price	Total Sale
2	1/4/2013	115	27	$9.99	$269.73
3	1/4/2013	117	17	$9.99	$169.83
4	1/4/2013	122	53	$9.99	$529.47
5	1/14/2013	117	44	$23.95	$1,053.80
6	1/14/2013	115	34	$23.95	$814.30
7	1/14/2013	117	46	$23.95	$1,101.70
8	1/15/2013	122	73	$7.99	$583.27
9	1/15/2013	115	61	$9.99	$609.39
10	1/15/2013	122	60	$7.99	$479.40
11	1/15/2013	117	39	$9.99	$389.61
12	1/15/2013	131	57	$9.99	$569.43
13	1/15/2013	122	16	$7.99	$127.84
14	1/16/2013	131	24	$7.99	$191.76
15	1/16/2013	117	22	$7.99	$175.78
16	1/16/2013	117	34	$7.99	$271.66
17	1/17/2013	122	31	$11.99	$371.69
18	1/17/2013	115	38	$11.99	$455.62
19	1/17/2013	122	54	$11.99	$647.46
20	1/22/2013	115	6	$6.99	$41.94
21	1/22/2013	122	22	$23.95	$526.90
22	1/22/2013	131	30	$8.99	$269.70
23	1/22/2013	115	6	$6.99	$41.94
24	1/22/2013	122	19	$23.95	$455.05

Original dataset

Location Code ▾	Sum of Total Sale
115	$3,077.98
117	$3,825.63
122	$5,044.79
131	$2,036.79
Grand Total	**$13,985.19**

Pivoted data

Here, you can see that, in the original dataset, each sale is listed as a separate entry. Store locations, in the form of location codes, appear within a single column. In the pivoted dataset, that column has been pivoted into rows, with each location being represented by a single row. For each location, Excel has summed each sale and calculated the total sales per store. Excel also calculated the total of all sales for all locations.

PivotTables

A *PivotTable* is a dynamic Excel data object that enables you to analyze data by pivoting columns and rows of raw data without altering the raw data. PivotTables are effective for summarizing large volumes of data according to two or more criteria to return specific answers to your questions. PivotTables combine some of the most powerful and useful types of Excel functionality, such as sorting, filtering, summary functions, and subtotals, to give you an incredible level of control over how you view your data.

When you create a PivotTable, Excel enables you place it on the same worksheet as the original data, or you can insert it on a new worksheet. Once the PivotTable is created, you can re-pivot, re-sort, re-summarize, and re-filter you data any number of times without affecting the original dataset. In addition to pivoting columns and rows, you can nest columns and rows within one another to create a hierarchy, much as you do when using subtotals. You can expand or collapse levels of hierarchy to view more or less detail in your PivotTables. And you can use any of the available summary functions to summarize your pivoted data for a variety of purposes. You can also create PivotTables out of either data in the same workbook or data from other workbooks and external data sources.

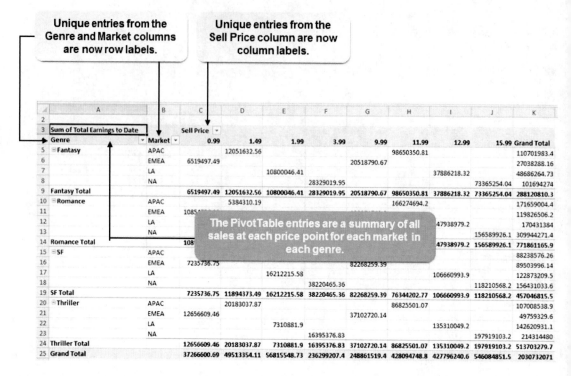

Figure 6-1: A PivotTable containing a hierarchy of raw data. In this example, genre, market, sell price, and total earnings to date are all column labels in the original dataset.

Transactional Data

There is an extremely important consideration for you to keep in mind when creating and working with PivotTables: your data format. PivotTables are designed to work with, and work best with, raw *transactional data*. Transactional data is not summarized in any way, so it does not contain row labels, only column labels. Columns in a transactional dataset are also known as *fields*. The best way to visualize transactional data is to examine the root word "transaction." In a transactional dataset, each transaction, or *entry*, is located in its own separate row. To carry on the example from earlier, of sales transactions at a variety of locations, each sale, regardless of when or where it took place, would be entered as an individual row of data. The dataset columns represent the specific elements of each transaction: date, time, location, amount, and so on.

In a summarized dataset, even a raw one, the data has already been compiled in some way and will have row labels as well as column labels. For example, you may have raw sales data for each sales rep in your organization. Because each rep has his or her own row of data, the dataset would likely contain the total of each person's sales, as opposed to each sale regardless of the rep. Although you can create PivotTables from summary data, they will never give you as much granular insight into your data as PivotTables created from transactional data.

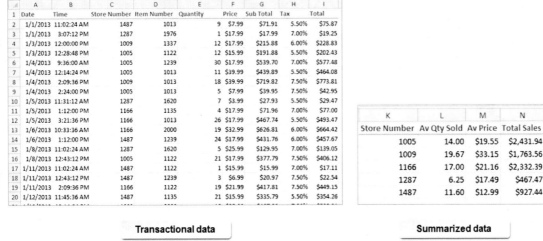

Transactional data   Summarized data

Figure 6-2: Transactional data shows each event, whereas summary data compiles it in some way.

The Create PivotTable Dialog Box

You use the **Create PivotTable** dialog box to insert PivotTables into your worksheets. From here, you can select the desired dataset or include a reference to a named range or table. You can also select a location for the PivotTable, which can be on the same worksheet as the dataset or on another worksheet in the same workbook. You can access the **Create PivotTable** dialog box by selecting **Insert→Tables→PivotTable**.

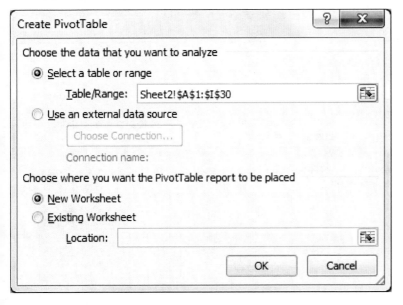

Figure 6-3: The Create PivotTable dialog box.

> Access the Checklist tile on your LogicalCHOICE course screen for reference information and job aids on How to Create a PivotTable.

ACTIVITY 6-1
Creating a PivotTable

Data File

C:\091019Data\Analyzing Data with PivotTables, Slicers, and PivotCharts \sales_dashboard_06.xlsx

Before You Begin

Excel 2010 is open.

Scenario

Your supervisor and other senior managers at Fuller and Ackerman continue to come to you for answers to questions they have about authors and book sales. Given the frequency with which you find yourself analyzing data, you decide it would be most efficient to add a PivotTable to your sales dashboard workbook. With such a PivotTable, you'll be able to answer any number of questions without having to significantly revise your worksheets. You have already defined a name for the raw sales data on the Sales worksheet in the sales dashboard workbook, so you will create the PivotTable by using that defined name.

---

1. Open the **sales_dashboard_06.xlsx** workbook file.

    Note: You may find it helpful to zoom out slightly during this activity.

2. Insert a PivotTable by using a defined name.

   a) Scroll to the right and select cell **AD2**.

   b) Select **Insert→Tables→PivotTable**.

   c) In the **Create PivotTable** dialog box, in the **Choose the data that you want to analyze** section, ensure that the **Select a table or range** radio button is selected.

   d) In the **Table/Range** field, type *RawSalesData*

   e) In the **Choose where you want the PivotTable report to be placed** section, make sure the **Existing Worksheet** radio button is selected.

f) In the **Location** field, verify that **'Sales Dashboard'!$AD$2** is displayed.

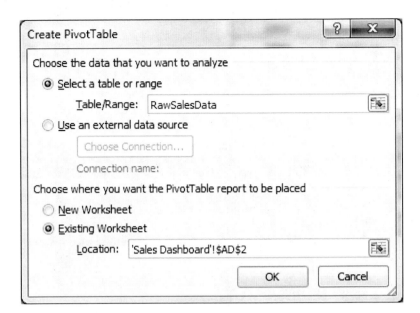

g) Select **OK**.

3. If necessary, scroll to the right so the PivotTable is fully visible and not obstructed by the **PivotTable Field List** pane.

4. In the **PivotTable Field List** pane, verify that the **Choose fields to add to report** list displays a list of all of the fields in the dataset on the **Sales** worksheet.

5. Save the workbook to the **C:\091019Data\Analyzing Data with PivotTables, Slicers, and PivotCharts** folder as *my_sales_dashboard_06.xlsx*

TOPIC B

Analyze PivotTable Data

Now that you have created your PivotTable, you're ready to dive right in and crunch the numbers to gain the organizational insight that can help you succeed. As with all Excel data analysis tasks, creating and configuring effective PivotTables is a matter of asking the right questions to glean the necessary information. When working with PivotTables, this all boils down to structure. You already know PivotTables allow you to reorganize and re-analyze your data as many times as necessary to get all of the answers you're looking for. How do you translate your questions into a PivotTable structure? Actually, it's relatively simple.

Excel 2010 provides you with a number of different tools and commands you can use to organize the structure of your PivotTables. Knowing how these tools work, and understanding how PivotTable structure translates into actionable intelligence, are the keys to getting the answers you seek.

Start with Questions, End with Structure

To create PivotTables that will be useful to you, begin by thinking about the types of questions you would like your raw data to answer. This is precisely that same type of initial analysis you perform when determining which functions or formulas to include in worksheets. The only difference here is that you will use your questions as a basis for organizing your PivotTables, not to enter a function or a formula. Once you've determined what question you want Excel to answer, you can begin to design the structure of your PivotTable.

There are a couple of items to keep in mind before beginning this process. First, it's typically best to create rows and columns out of fields that have a fairly finite set of entries, such as sales reps, regions, or products. You may not, for example, find it very useful to create rows out of dates that occurred over a 10-year span of time as you could end up with thousands of rows of data. Second, you should create rows out of the field for which you are primarily interested in determining some fact, and create columns out of your secondary criterion. For example, if you want to know the total sales per product for each sales rep in your department, you would typically create rows out of sales reps (your primary concern) and columns out of the products (the items for which you are measuring performance). Then you would ask Excel to use the SUM function to total the sales for each rep per product.

Let's take a look at a simple example. This is the beginning of a table with about 100 entries of sales data.

	A	B	C	D	E
1	Date	Rep	Region	Product	Sale
2	2/2/2008	Toner, R	NE	Camera	$336.00
3	3/8/2008	Toner, R	East	Fax	$509.00
4	4/7/2008	Smith, F	NE	Phone	$287.00
5	4/17/2008	Rios, J	SW	Camera	$457.00
6	5/25/2008	Toner, R	Central	Scanner	$673.00
7	7/3/2008	Allen, P	East	Scanner	$350.00
8	7/19/2008	Rios, J	West	Printer	$286.00
9	7/24/2008	Toner, R	Central	Camera	$376.00
10	8/22/2008	Toner, R	SW	Phone	$510.00
11	10/5/2008	Toner, R	West	Camera	$467.00
12	10/14/2008	Smith, F	East	Printer	$262.00
13	11/27/2008	Chan, G	Central	Phone	$537.00
14	12/1/2008	Rios, J	West	Camera	$702.00
15	12/19/2008	Smith, F	East	Scanner	$565.00
16	12/23/2008	Rios, J	SW	Camera	$681.00
17	1/12/2009	Rios, J	West	Scanner	$261.00
18	3/15/2009	Smith, F	West	Camera	$334.00
19	3/31/2009	Smith, F	East	Phone	$694.00
20	4/11/2009	Rios, J	NE	Camera	$758.00

Now, here's a PivotTable created from the entire dataset that answers this question: What are the total sales for each sales rep by product?

Sum of Sale	Column Labels						
Row Labels	Camera	Copier	Fax	Phone	Printer	Scanner	Grand Total
Allen, P	$2,152.00	$1,406.00	$2,222.00	$485.00	$1,831.00	$1,506.00	$9,602.00
Chan, G	$2,315.00	$1,454.00	$588.00	$1,500.00			$5,857.00
Rios, J	$5,107.00	$578.00	$1,061.00	$1,110.00	$2,195.00	$713.00	$10,764.00
Smith, F	$3,942.00	$1,777.00	$2,199.00	$1,593.00	$1,685.00	$565.00	$11,761.00
Toner, R	$3,800.00	$1,240.00	$2,844.00	$1,093.00	$3,664.00	$1,718.00	$14,359.00
Grand Total	$17,316.00	$6,455.00	$8,914.00	$5,781.00	$9,375.00	$4,502.00	$52,343.00

Notice that the sales reps are listed by row and the products are listed by column. The PivotTable returns the total sales, indicating the use of the SUM function, for each sales rep for each product.

Now, let's say you'd like Excel to answer the following question: How many of each product was sold in each region? As you are primarily concerned with what is happening on a per-region basis, you would make regions the rows and keep the products in columns. Then you would ask Excel to count the number of each product sold in each region, indicating the use of the COUNT function.

Count of Product	Column Labels						
Row Labels	Camera	Copier	Fax	Phone	Printer	Scanner	Grand Total
Central	5	1	1	2	9	1	19
East	4		3	4	7	3	21
NE	8	5	3	1	1		18
SW	4	2	5	2	1	2	16
West	11	5	3	2	1	4	26
Grand Total	32	13	15	11	19	10	100

Notice that the rows and columns in each of these examples represent two of the criteria on which you are analyzing the data. The values throughout the rest of the table represent the third criterion, the values you are asking Excel to calculate based on the other two criteria. This is the basic structure you will use to create most PivotTables. The keys to structuring your PivotTables are to determine the question you want Excel to answer, to visualize the table you wish to create, and to determine what calculation you want Excel to perform.

The PivotTable Field List Pane

Once you create a PivotTable, you will use the **PivotTable Field List** pane to configure the PivotTable and perform data analysis tasks. Excel automatically opens **PivotTable Field List** pane when you insert a PivotTable in a worksheet. The top half of the pane, the **Choose fields to add to report** section, displays a list of all of the fields (columns) from the original dataset; Excel pulls the names for these from the column labels. The bottom half of the pane, the **Drag fields between areas below** section, displays a series of four areas that you use to configure the PivotTable. By dragging the various fields to the various areas, you configure the structure of the PivotTable and select the values upon which Excel performs calculations.

As PivotTables are dynamic, by default, you can drag fields to the various areas of the **PivotTable Field List** pane as necessary and your PivotTable will update automatically. You can move the fields around as often as you like, and you can include more than one field in each area. When you drag more than one field into the same area, Excel creates a hierarchy in the PivotTable with items on top of the area representing higher levels in the hierarchy. This works much like using subtotals and outlines in ranges.

Each field that you have dragged into an area displays a field down arrow. This provides you with access to context menus and dialog boxes that enable you to configure your PivotTables further.

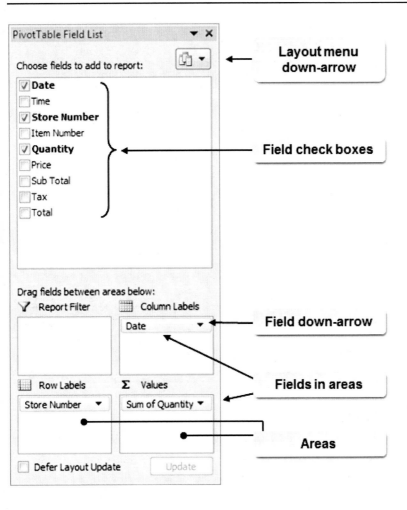

Figure 6-4: Use the elements of the PivotTable Field List pane to configure the structure of PivotTables.

The following table provides a brief description of the various elements of the **PivotTable Field List** pane.

PivotTable Field List Pane Element	Description
Layout menu down arrow	Provides you with access to a menu that contains various pre-configured **PivotTable Field List** pane layouts. Select from among these options to customize the **PivotTable Field List** pane to suit your needs.
Field check boxes	These allow you to add or remove fields from the various areas. Checking a field's check box adds it to an area, whereas unchecking it removes the field from all areas. You have no control over where Excel places a field when you check its check box, so many users prefer to simply drag the fields to the desired areas.

PivotTable Field List Pane Element	Description
Field down arrow	Selecting a field's down arrow displays a context menu that provides you with various options for configuring your PivotTables. For example, you can move fields to another area (again, this can also be done simply by dragging the field to another area), move fields within a hierarchy, or access the **Field Settings** or **Value Field Settings** dialog boxes.
Report Filter area	Drag fields here to include field values as filter criteria for the PivotTable.
Column Labels area	Drag fields here to create columns out of the unique entries in a field.
Row Labels area	Drag fields here to create rows out of the unique entries in a field.
Values area	Drag fields here to have Excel perform calculations on, or summarize, their values.

 Note: To learn more about tailoring PivotTables to suit your specific needs, watch the LearnTO **Customize the View of a PivotTable** presentation from the **LearnTO** tile on the LogicalCHOICE Course screen.

The PivotTable Tools Contextual Tab

The **PivotTable Tools** contextual tab displays commands and options that are specific to working with PivotTables. In a similar way as other contextual tabs, the **PivotTable Tools** contextual tab appears when you select a PivotTable and disappears when you select outside the PivotTable. The **PivotTable Tools** contextual tab contains two tabs: the **Options** tab and the **Design** tab.

Figure 6-5: The Options tab.

The following table identifies the types of commands you will find in the various groups on the **Options** tab.

Options Tab Group	Contains Commands For
PivotTable	Accessing the PivotTable **Options** dialog box, which allows you to change global PivotTable settings. This also displays the name of the currently selected PivotTable.
Active Field	Changing the currently selected field's settings.
Group	Grouping various elements within a PivotTable and managing those groups.
Sort & Filter	Accessing and managing sorting and filtering commands and options.
Data	Refreshing PivotTable data when the source dataset has been updated, and for modifying the dataset that feeds PivotTables.
Actions	Clearing filtering, selecting elements of a PivotTable, and moving PivotTables in your workbooks.

Options Tab Group	Contains Commands For
Calculations	Configuring PivotTable calculations.
Tools	Creating PivotCharts, performing data analysis tasks, and working with a particular type of external database.
Show	Toggling the display of PivotTable elements on and off.

Figure 6-6: The Design tab.

The following table identifies the types of commands you will find in the various **Design** tab groups.

Design Tab Group	Contains Commands For
Layout	Toggling particular functionality on or off, and for modifying the overall layout of PivotTables.
PivotTable Style Options	Toggling the display of PivotTable elements on or off.
PivotTable Styles	Selecting and configuring PivotTable formatting options.

The Value Field Settings Dialog Box

When you select the field down arrow of a field in the **Value** area of the **PivotTable Field List** pane, Excel opens the **Value Field Settings** dialog box. You will use the commands and options in the **Value Field Settings** dialog box to configure the calculations Excel performs on field data in PivotTables, and to configure how Excel displays the results of those calculations. The **Value Field Settings** dialog box is divided into two tabs: the **Summarize Values By** tab and the **Show Values As** tab.

Figure 6-7: The Value Field Settings dialog box.

The **Summarize Values By** tab enables you to select which function Excel uses to summarize the data in your PivotTables. The available functions here are the same as those available for creating subtotals and for summarizing table data. For example, you could use the SUM function to find the total of all values that meet the criteria outlined in the PivotTable rows and columns. Or, you could use the AVERAGE function to find the average values of the entries that meet the criteria.

 Note: The default summary function to numerical values is the SUM function. The default summary function for all other values is the COUNT function.

The **Show Values As** tab provides you with access to options for how you wish to display your summarized PivotTable data. By default, the value here is **No Calculation**, which means the PivotTable will simple summarize your data according to the function selected on the **Summarize Values By** tab. You can also choose to have Excel display the summary data in a variety of other ways. For example, you may wish to show the summarized data as a percentage of the grand total or as a percentage of column or row totals. This could be helpful if you want to know what percentage of your total sales came from a particular region or which sales rep generated the highest percentage of your total or regional sales. Or, you may wish to show a relative comparison between values. For example, you may wish to see how far behind the sales leader other sales reps are in terms of total sales.

One other handy feature of the **Value Field Settings** dialog box is the **Number Format** button. Selecting this will open a scaled-down version of the **Format Cells** dialog box, which contains only the **Number** tab. Use this to change the cell formatting in your PivotTables to accommodate the various types of values you ask Excel to calculate.

Summarize and Show Combinations

Combining the options from the **Summarize Values By** tab and the **Show Values As** tab enables you to gain a deeper understanding of the information in your raw data. Here is a simple example that shows how the summary functions and the **Show Values As** tab options work together to give you new perspectives on your data. Take a look at this PivotTable that displays sales totals for sales reps per region. Here, the sales figures have been dragged to the **Values** area of the **PivotTable Field List** pane, and the default SUM function and **No Calculation** option are selected.

Sum of Sale	Column Labels ▾					
Row Labels ▾	Central	East	NE	SW	West	Grand Total
Allen, P	$2,292.00	$1,147.00	$1,013.00	$3,831.00	$1,319.00	$9,602.00
Chan, G	$488.00	$671.00	$1,228.00	$537.00	$2,933.00	$5,857.00
Rios, J	$1,248.00	$1,498.00	$2,975.00	$2,593.00	$2,450.00	$10,764.00
Smith, F	$1,700.00	$4,476.00	$1,861.00	$1,462.00	$2,262.00	$11,761.00
Toner, R	$3,606.00	$3,228.00	$2,278.00	$1,770.00	$3,477.00	$14,359.00
Grand Total	$9,334.00	$11,020.00	$9,355.00	$10,193.00	$12,441.00	$52,343.00

Now take a look at how selecting the **% of Grand Total** option from the **Show Values As** tab changes your view of the data; the summary function is still the SUM function.

Sum of Sale	Column Labels ▾					
Row Labels ▾	Central	East	NE	SW	West	Grand Total
Allen, P	4.38%	2.19%	1.94%	7.32%	2.52%	18.34%
Chan, G	0.93%	1.28%	2.35%	1.03%	5.60%	11.19%
Rios, J	2.38%	2.86%	5.68%	4.95%	4.68%	20.56%
Smith, F	3.25%	8.55%	3.56%	2.79%	4.32%	22.47%
Toner, R	6.89%	6.17%	4.35%	3.38%	6.64%	27.43%
Grand Total	17.83%	21.05%	17.87%	19.47%	23.77%	100.00%

You can see what percentage of all sales is comprised of each rep's sales in each region. Notice also that the grand totals for each row and for each column add up to 100 percent of all total sales. You now have a clear picture of which regions and which sales reps are generating your sales.

Now take a look at what happens when you change the summary function to the AVERAGE function and change the **Show Values As** tab option to **Difference From**. Here, all sales rep's sales averages are being compared to Robert Toner's sales, as he has the highest percentage of overall sales. You could compare the values to any individual sales rep.

Average of Sale	Column Labels ▾					
Row Labels ▾	Central	East	NE	SW	West	Grand Total
Allen, P	-$28.00	-$155.67	-$63.00	-$42.71	-$57.05	-$46.90
Chan, G	-$113.00	$133.00	-$160.17	-$53.00	-$7.88	-$64.19
Rios, J	-$185.00	-$38.67	$25.50	$58.25	-$6.71	-$14.07
Smith, F	-$176.00	$21.50	-$104.25	$141.00	-$44.31	-$40.92
Toner, R						
Grand Total						

Notice that there are no values for Robert Toner, as his values are the ones the PivotTable is comparing the other values to. By looking at this PivotTable, you can see how far behind the sales leader all other reps are in terms of average regional and overall sales. You can even tell that J. Rios is actually ahead of Robert Toner in two regions, the Northeast and the Southwest. Combining summary functions with the show values as options is an effective way to gain a deep, granular understanding of the information hidden in your raw data.

 Access the **Checklist** tile on your **LogicalCHOICE** course screen for reference information and job aids on **How to Analyze PivotTable Data.**

ACTIVITY 6-2
Analyzing PivotTable Data

Before You Begin
The my_sales_dashboard_06.xlsx workbook file is open.

Scenario
With your PivotTable in place, you're now ready to answer some of the questions Fuller and Ackerman senior managers have been asking. Here is a list of their current requests:

- What is the total number of units sold per genre in each of the markets served?
- Which genre is the biggest overall seller?
- For the APAC and EMEA markets, what is the combined number of total units sold in the romance and fantasy genres?
- What percentage of total sales is made up of fantasy sales in the LA market?
- Which market has the highest percentage of science fiction sales?
- For each author and book, what are the total sales of electronic books versus the total sales of print books?
- Which author has the lowest total sales?
- For the lowest-selling author, which book has generated the most sales?
- What percentage of author 1048's total sales are electronic book sales?

---

1. Structure the PivotTable to answer the question "What is the total number of units sold per genre in each of the markets served?"

   a) Ensure the **Sales Dashboard** worksheet is selected, and then select any cell within the PivotTable.

   b) In the **PivotTable Field List** pane, drag the **Genre** field from the **Choose fields to add to report** list to the **Row Labels** area.

   c) Drag the **Market** field to the **Column Labels** area.

d) Drag the **Total Units to Date** field to the **Values** area.

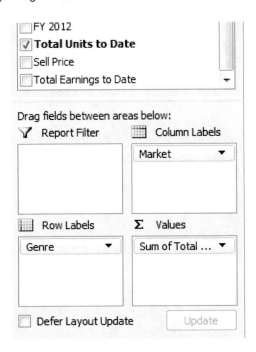

e) If necessary, scroll to the right so the PivotTable is visible.

2. Review the totals in the data cells to determine the total number of units sold per genre in each market.

3. Use the PivotTable to answer the question "Which genre is the biggest overall seller?"
   a) Select any cell in the range **AI4:AI7**.
   b) On the **PivotTable Tools** contextual tab, select **Options→Sort & Filter→Sort Largest to Smallest**. $\begin{smallmatrix} Z \downarrow \\ A \end{smallmatrix}$

4. **Which genre is the biggest overall seller?**

5. Use the PivotTable to answer the question "For the APAC and EMEA markets, what is the combined number of total units sold in the romance and fantasy genres?"

a) From the **Column Labels** drop-down menu on the PivotTable, uncheck the **(Select All)** check box, and then check both the **APAC** check box and the **EMEA** check box.

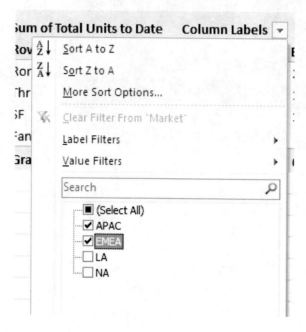

b) Select **OK**.

c) From the **Row Labels** drop-down menu, uncheck the **(Select All)** check box and then check the **Fantasy** and **Romance** check boxes.

d) Select **OK**.

6. What is the total number of units of fantasy and romance books sold in the APAC and EMEA markets?

7. Use the PivotTable to answer the question "What percentage of total sales is made up of fantasy sales in the LA market?"

a) Clear all filters in the **Row Labels** drop-down menu and in the **Column Labels** drop-down menu.

b) In the **PivotTable Field List** pane, in the **Values** area, select the **Sum of Total** down arrow.

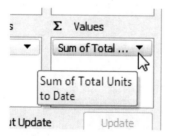

c) In the drop-down menu, select **Value Field Settings**.

d) In the **Value Field Settings** dialog box, select the **Show Values As** tab.

e) In the **Show values as** drop-down menu, select **% of Grand Total** and then select **OK**.

8. What percentage of total sales is made up of fantasy sales in the LA market?

9. Use the PivotTable to answer the question "Which market has the highest percentage of science fiction sales?"

a) In the **PivotTable Field List** pane, in the **Values** area, select the **Sum of Total** down arrow, and then select **Value Field Settings**.

b) Select the **Show Values As** tab and then select **% of Row Total** from the **Show values as** drop-down menu.

c) Select **OK**.

d) Filter the PivotTable to display only the science fiction (SF) genre.

10. **Which market has the highest percentage of science fiction sales?**

11. Clear the filter.

12. Restructure the PivotTable to answer the question "For each author and book, what are the total sales of electronic books versus the total sales of print books?"

a) Drag the **Genre** field, the **Market** field, and the **Total Units to Date** field back to the **Choose fields to add to report** list.

b) Drag the **Author** field to the **Row Labels** area.

c) Drag the **Title** field to the **Row Labels** area, making sure you drop it below the **Author** field.

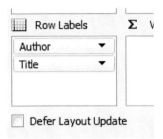

d) Drag the **Format** field to the **Column Labels** area.

e) Drag the **Total Earnings to Date** field to the **Values** area.

f) Right-click any data cell within the PivotTable and select **Value Field Settings**.

g) In the **Value Field Settings** dialog box, select **Number Format**.

h) In the **Format Cells** dialog box, in the **Category** list, select **Currency** and then select **OK**.

i) Select **OK**.

j) Scroll down the PivotTable to review the total sales of electronic and print books for each author and title.

13. Use the PivotTable to answer the question "Which author has the lowest total sales?"

a) Select cell **AG4**.

b) On the **PivotTable Tools** contextual tab, select **Options→Sort & Filter→Sort Smallest to Largest**.

14. **Which author has the lowest total sales?**

15. Sort the results for author 1017 to answer the question "For the lowest-selling author, which book has generated the most sales?"

a) Select any cell within the range AG5:AG10.

b) On the **PivotTable Tools** contextual tab, select **Options→Sort & Filter→Sort Largest to Smallest**.

16. **Which book for author 1017 has generated the most sales?**

17. Use the PivotTable to answer the question "What percentage of author 1048's total sales are electronic book sales?"

a) Select the **Row Labels** down arrow and type *1048* in the **Search** field.

b) Ensure that the **(Select All Search Results)** check box and the **1048** check box are checked, and that the **Add current selection to filter** check box is unchecked.

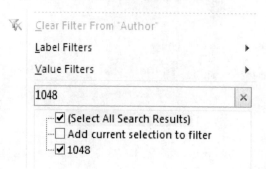

c) Select **OK**.

d) Right-click any data cell within the PivotTable, and then select **Show Values As→% of Row Total**.

18. What percentage of author 1048's total sales are electronic book sales?

19. Save the workbook file.

TOPIC C

Present Data with PivotCharts

Although PivotTables provide you with an amazing array of options for analyzing your data, they have one downfall in common with other worksheet data: They can be difficult to read. You know you can convert the data in your worksheet ranges and tables into visually appealing, easy-to-interpret charts. You also know that doing so makes it easier for your audience to gather meaning from all of that data with just a glance. Wouldn't it be nice if you could do the same with PivotTable data?

The good news is that Excel 2010 provides you with a quick and easy ways to translate your PivotTable data into charts just as you can do with your other data. Taking the time to familiarize yourself with this functionality will provide you with all of the benefits of Excel charts when it comes to presenting the data you analyze by using PivotTables.

PivotCharts

Like standard Excel charts, *PivotCharts* are graphical representations of numeric values and relationships among those values. The main difference is simply that PivotCharts are linked to PivotTable data, whereas standard charts are linked to either a range of data or a table. As with charts, when you alter the data in a PivotTable, PivotCharts update automatically to reflect the changes. As you drag fields from one area to another, update the PivotTable data, and modify the summary function and Show Values As options, your PivotCharts will dynamically change to reflect the changes in the PivotTable.

Excel provides you with many of the same options for formatting your PivotCharts, including the ability to change chart types, as it does with charts. And, the same considerations apply for deciding which chart type to select and which chart elements you should include in your PivotCharts. You use the **Insert Chart** dialog box to create PivotCharts from PivotTables. To create a PivotChart, you can access the **Insert Chart** dialog box from the **Charts** group on the **Insert** tab, or by selecting **Options→Tools→PivotChart** from the **PivotTable Tools** contextual tab.

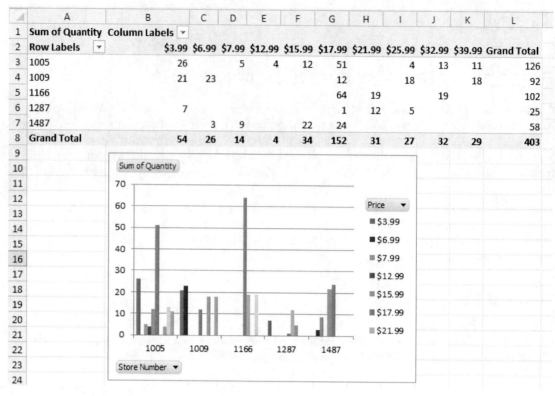

	A	B	C	D	E	F	G	H	I	J	K	L
1	Sum of Quantity	Column Labels ▾										
2	Row Labels ▾		$3.99	$6.99	$7.99	$12.99	$15.99	$17.99	$21.99	$25.99	$32.99	$39.99 Grand Total
3	1005		26		5	4	12	51		4	13	11 126
4	1009		21	23				12		18		18 92
5	1166							64	19		19	102
6	1287		7					1	12	5		25
7	1487			3	9		22	24				58
8	Grand Total		54	26	14	4	34	152	31	27	32	29 403

Figure 6-8: A PivotChart and its associated PivotTable.

PivotChart Filters

One of the added benefits of PivotCharts is that they include their own set of filters, which are linked to the filters on the associated PivotTable. These filters correspond to the fields you drag to the **Column Labels** and **Row Labels** areas in the **PivotTable Field List** pane, and they display the same filter and sorting options available on the PivotTable. Whether you filter or sort your data by using the options on the PivotTable or the options on the PivotChart, Excel updates both objects simultaneously. By right-clicking the PivotChart filters, you have access to the same context menus that open when you select fields in the various areas at the bottom of the **PivotTable Field List** pane.

PivotCharts also display a **Value field label**. This corresponds to the field that you dragged to the **Values** area in the **PivotTable Field List** pane. Right-clicking the **Value field label** provides you with access to the **Value Field Settings** dialog box and the associated context menu options.

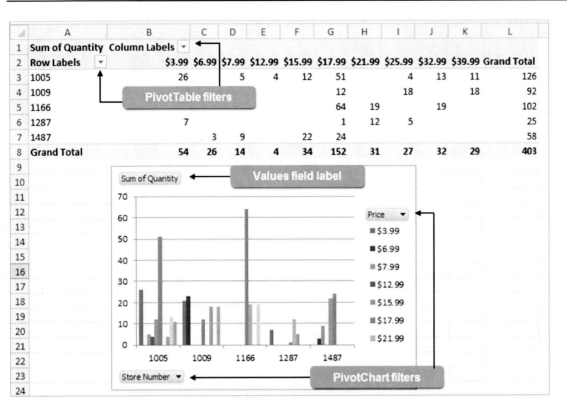

Sum of Quantity	Column Labels										
Row Labels	$3.99	$6.99	$7.99	$12.99	$15.99	$17.99	$21.99	$25.99	$32.99	$39.99	Grand Total
1005	26		5	4	12	51		4	13	11	126
1009						12		18		18	92
1166						64	19		19		102
1287	7					1	12	5			25
1487		3	9		22	24					58
Grand Total	54	26	14	4	34	152	31	27	32	29	403

Figure 6-9: Changes made with either the PivotTable filters or the PivotChart filters reflect in both objects.

 Access the Checklist tile on your LogicalCHOICE course screen for reference information and job aids on **How to Create and Work with a PivotChart.**

ACTIVITY 6-3
Presenting Data with PivotCharts

Before You Begin

The my_sales_dashboard_06.xlsx workbook file is open and the **Sales Dashboard** worksheet is selected.

Scenario

You've had a number of meetings with Fuller and Ackerman (F&A) senior management to report back on your analysis in response to their questions. Several members of the senior management team have asked that you also provide your analysis in the form of charts. As you know Excel's PivotCharts are dynamic and they will continually present updated sales data as you configure it in your PivotTable, you decide that adding a PivotChart would be the best way to accommodate this request. You have been asked to display an overview of how many units of each genre sell in the various markets F&A serves at an upcoming meeting. You decide that this would be the ideal configuration for your PivotChart.

---

1. Insert a column PivotChart.
   a) Select any cell within the PivotTable.
   b) On the **PivotTable Tools** contextual tab, select **Options→Tools→PivotChart**.
   c) In the **Insert Chart** dialog box, from the **Column** section in the right pane, verify that **Clustered Column** is selected and then select **OK**.

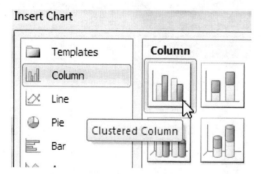

   d) Drag the PivotChart to the left of the PivotTable so you can view both simultaneously.

    Note: It is okay for now if the PivotChart covers up the tables on the worksheet.

2. Structure the PivotTable to display information about the number of units sold for each genre in the various markets.
   a) Select any cell within the PivotTable.
   b) In the **PivotTable Field List** pane, drag all of the fields from the **Column Labels**, **Row Labels**, and **Values** areas back to the **Choose field to add to report** list.
   c) Drag the **Genre** field to the **Row Labels** area, the **Market** field to the **Column Labels** area, and the **Total Units to Date** field to the **Values** area.

3. **Which genre/market pair is the most successful in terms of number of units sold?**

4. Filter out the romance genre to get a better understanding of how the other genres compare to each other.

   a) On the PivotChart, select the **Genre** down arrow.

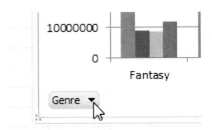

   b) Uncheck the **Romance** check box and select **OK**.

   c) Verify that Excel filtered the **Romance** genre out of both the PivotChart and the PivotTable.

5. Use the PivotChart to compare the average number of units sold for the remaining genres.

   a) On the PivotChart, right-click **Sum of Total Units to Date** and select **Value Field Settings**.

   b) In the **Value Field Settings** dialog box, from the **Summarize Values By** tab, select **Average** and then select **OK**.

   c) Verify that both the PivotChart and the PivotTable display the average number of units sold for the remaining genres.

6. Clear the filter on the **Genre** field and drag the PivotChart to the empty space between the standard charts and the tables on the worksheet.

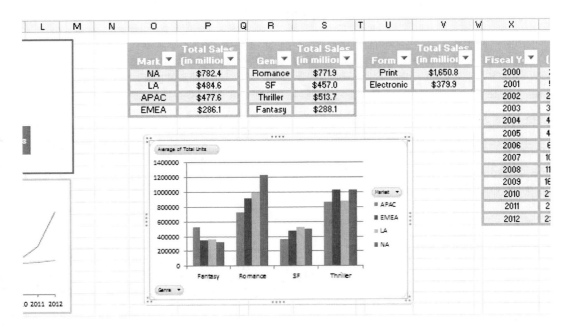

7. Save the workbook.

TOPIC D

Filter Data by Using Slicers

The ability to filter your PivotTables enables you to drill down into your raw data to view the fine detail that lies within. As you likely have many questions to ask of your data, it can quickly become tedious to have to open drop-down menus, determine what items are filtered out, clear the filtering, and then re-filter your data to find the next answer. This is especially true if data analysis is one of your key functions. If you fall into this category of Excel users, you'll likely appreciate the ability to quickly and easily re-filter your PivotTables on any number of fields. In addition, the ability to quickly view the filters applied to the current dataset could come in handy if you're returning to a worksheet after having not worked in it for a while.

In short, you need some type of tool that gives you a high level of control over PivotTable filtering, one that is easy to work with and easy to interpret regardless of how many filters you apply to your PivotTables. Excel 2010 includes such a tool. Gaining an understanding of how this feature works will give you a greater level of control over your PivotTable filtering and the peace of mind of knowing that you have filtered your data in precisely the manner you meant you.

Slicers

Slicers are PivotTable filtering tools that you can link to various PivotTables in your worksheets. You can create a slicer out of any of the fields associated with a PivotTable, and then you can use those slicers to filter each field by any of its unique entries. Although a slicer is typically associated with a single PivotTable, you can link slicers to multiple PivotTables; this is typically done for PivotTables that are associated with the same raw dataset. This can be handy, for example, if you want to create multiple versions of the same PivotTable, create a unique structure for each to answer various questions about your data, and then filter them by the same criteria simultaneously.

Each unique value in a field appears as a separate button on the associated slicer. By default, slicer buttons appear highlighted in blue when the filter is inactive, meaning the associated value will appear in the PivotTable. When the filter is active, meaning the value has been removed from the PivotTable, the button appears white. When you first create a slicer, all filters are inactive, so all of the buttons are highlighted in blue. Selecting a slicer button activates all of the other filters, meaning only the value you selected will appear in the table. This may, at first, seem counterintuitive, but it makes sense when you think about it in this way: Selecting a button displays the associated value in a PivotTable. To select multiple slicer buttons simultaneously, press and hold down the **Ctrl** key while making your selections. Selecting the **Clear Filter** button deactivates all filters on a slicer, meaning all values will appear in the PivotTable.

Slicer buttons may also appear slightly grayed-out. Excel does this when some active filter has removed the associated values from view. Grayed-out slicer buttons are inactive, as you cannot filter on values that do not appear in the PivotTable. Clearing the filter that is suppressing the values from view will reactivate the associated slicer button(s).

The default slicer formatting is blue and white but you can customize the display of slicers to match your worksheet formatting. You can place slicers anywhere on your worksheets or resize them as you like. You can even place copies of slicers in multiple locations. The original slicer and the copies remain linked, so whatever you do to one affects the others. This is true only of filtering tasks, not visual formatting.

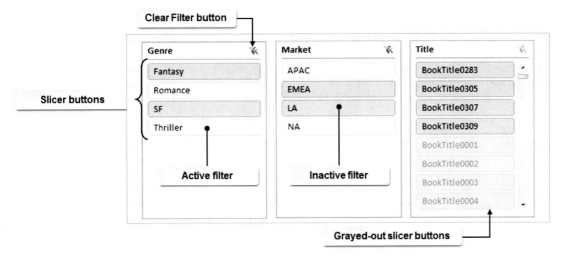

Figure 6-10: Use slicers to quickly and easily apply multiple filters to your PivotTables.

 Note: For information on an alternate way to filter PivotTables, watch the LearnTO **Add a Report Filter to an Excel PivotTable** presentation from the **LearnTO** tile on the LogicalCHOICE Course screen.

The Insert Slicers Dialog Box

You use the **Insert Slicers** dialog box to create slicers out of the various fields in your PivotTables. Each field appears as a check box option in the dialog box. To create a slicer out of a particular field, check the associated check box. You can access the **Insert Slicers** dialog box from the **PivotTable Tools** contextual tab by selecting **Options→Sort & Filter→Insert Slicer**.

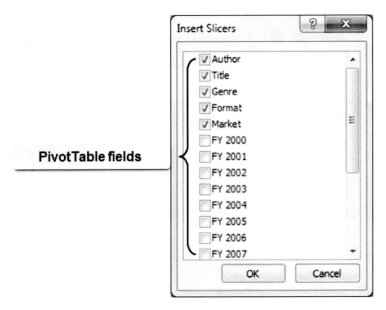

Figure 6-11: The Insert Slicers dialog box enables you to create slicers out of any PivotTable field.

The Slicer Tools Contextual Tab

You can access the commands you will use to work with PivotTable slicers on the **Slicer Tools** contextual tab. The **Slicer Tools** contextual tab appears when you select a slicer and disappears when you select any non-slicer object. If you select multiple slicers simultaneously, some of the commands on the **Slicer Tools** contextual tab remain active and others become deactivated. For example, you can typically resize or apply formatting to multiple slicers at the same time, but you can only manage slicer connections one at a time.

Figure 6-12: The Slicer Tools contextual tab.

The following table describes the types of commands you will find in the command groups on the **Slicer Tools** contextual tab.

Slicer Tools Contextual Tab Group	Contains Commands For
Slicer	Renaming slicers, accessing slicer options, and managing slicer connections to PivotTables.
Slicer Styles	Applying formatting to slicers.
Arrange	Configuring the arrangement of slicers on screen. You can use the commands in this group to order slicers from front to back, align slicers with other objects, and rotate the display of slicers.
Buttons	Modifying the size and alignment of slicer buttons. Changes you make here can also affect the size of the slicers themselves.
Size	Modifying the size of slicers. Changes you make here can also affect the display of slicer buttons.

The PivotTable Connections Dialog Box

You can use the **PivotTable Connections** dialog box to manage slicer connections. All PivotTables that are associated with the same raw dataset can share slicers. These *shared slicers* affect all PivotTables that share them, so what you filter in one PivotTable is filtered in all PivotTables that share the slicer. It is important to note that PivotTables that are associated with the same raw dataset do not have to share slicers. You can create unique slicers for each PivotTable that filter the same fields independently on each PivotTable. It is only the slicers that you connect to multiple PivotTables that will affect those PivotTables simultaneously. You can access the **PivotTable Connections** dialog box from the **Slicer Tools** contextual tab by selecting **Options→Slicer→PivotTable Connections**.

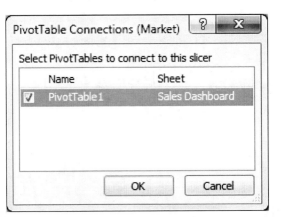

Figure 6-13: Use the PivotTable Connections dialog box to manage slicer connections.

Access the Checklist tile on your LogicalCHOICE course screen for reference information and job aids on How to Insert and Work with Slicers.

ACTIVITY 6-4
Filtering Data by Using Slicers

Before You Begin
The my_sales_dashboard_06.xlsx workbook file is open, and the **Sales Dashboard** worksheet is selected.

Scenario
There has been even more of an increase in demand for analysis on the raw sales data in your sales dashboard workbook. With requests for information coming it at an ever-faster pace, you'd like to find a faster way to filter your PivotTable so you can provide answers to questions more quickly and easily. You feel that adding slicers would be the best approach. You decide to add slicers for each of the fields you commonly filter on and use the slicers to filter the PivotTable to answer the following questions from senior managers:

- How many romance print books has author 1029 sold in the APAC market?
- Of author 1056's NA electronic format sales for fantasy and science fiction, what percentage is from the science fiction genre?

1. Insert slicers for the commonly filtered fields.
   a) Select any cell within the PivotTable.
   b) From the **PivotTable Tools** contextual tab, select **Options→Sort & Filter→Insert Slicer**.
   c) In the **Insert Slicers** dialog box, check the **Author**, **Title**, **Genre**, **Format**, and **Market** check boxes.
   d) Select **OK**.

2. Reposition the slicers to the right of the PivotTable on the **Sales_Dashboard** worksheet.

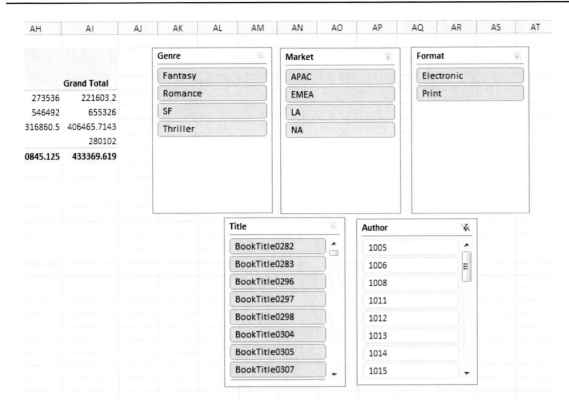

3. Select any cell within the PivotTable and then drag all fields from the various areas back to the **Choose fields to add to report** list.

4. Structure and filter the PivotTable to answer the question "How many romance print books has author 1029 sold in the APAC market?"

    a) Drag the **Author** field to the **Row Labels** area, the **Market** field to the **Column Labels** area, and the **Total Units to Date** field to the **Values** area.

    b) On the **Author** slicer, scroll down and select **1029**.

    c) On the **Format** slicer, select **Print** and, on the **Genre** slicer, select **Romance**.

5. How many romance print books has author 1029 sold in the APAC market?

6. Clear all filters by selecting the **Clear Filter** button  on the **Format, Genre,** and **Author** slicers.

7. Structure and filter the PivotTable to answer the question "Of author 1056's NA electronic format sales for fantasy and science fiction, what percentage is from the science fiction genre?"

    a) Select any cell within the PivotTable, and then drag the **Genre** field to the **Row Labels** area, placing it below the **Authors** field.

    b) On the **Author** slicer, select **1056** and, on the **Format** slicer, select **Electronic**.

    c) On the **Genre** slicer, select **Fantasy**, press and hold **Ctrl**, and then select **SF**.

    d) Right-click any data cell within the PivotTable and select **Show Values As→% of Column Total**.

8. Of author 1056's electronic fantasy and science fiction book sales in the NA market, what percentage is represented by science fiction sales?

9. Save and close the workbook.

Summary

In this lesson, you used PivotTables, PivotCharts, and slicers to analyze and present your data. The ability to crunch and re-crunch your numbers, ask incredibly detailed questions of your data, present your results in an easily digestible manner, and do it all over again without affecting your raw data puts the power of information right in the palm of your hand. As the volume of data, and the speed at which organizations generate it, continues to grow, your ability to mine actionable intelligence from it becomes increasingly critical and can give you the competitive edge to succeed.

How do you see PivotTables and PivotCharts helping you with your regular tasks?

When might you use slicers?

 Note: Check your LogicalCHOICE Course screen for opportunities to interact with your classmates, peers, and the larger LogicalCHOICE online community about the topics covered in this course or other topics you are interested in. From the Course screen you can also access available resources for a more continuous learning experience.

Course Follow-Up

Congratulations! You have completed the *Microsoft® Office Excel® 2010: Part 2 (Second Edition)* course. You have successfully customized the Excel environment to suit your needs, and used advanced formulas and analysis tools to extract actionable organizational intelligence from Excel data.

To gain a competitive edge in today's market, decision makers need to have a keen understanding of what's happening within their organizations. They need to be able to ask specific questions and get specific answers even when sifting through massive amounts of data. Becoming proficient at engaging your data in an ongoing dialog to find these answers means you'll be able to provide the decision makers within your organization with the intelligence they need to keep you ahead of the competition. The more you know about Excel's analysis tools and formula and function syntax, the better you'll be able to analyze and examine your raw data to find the nuanced patterns and opportunities that could mean the difference between running with the pack and staying one step ahead of everyone else.

What's Next?

Microsoft® Office Excel® 2010: Part 3 (Second Edition) is the next course in this series. In that course, you will build upon the skills you have acquired by automating a number of Excel tasks, applying conditional logic to your analysis, auditing and troubleshooting your workbooks to identify and correct errors, and presenting your analysis with advanced chart features. You are also encouraged to explore Excel further by actively participating in any of the social media forums set up by your instructor or training administrator through the **Social Media** tile on the LogicalCHOICE Course screen.

Financial Functions

Finance and accounting professionals are most likely to use Excel's financial functions. These specialized functions are useful for calculating a variety of financial values, such as payments, interest, and investment values over time. The following are overviews of some of the more commonly used Financial functions not directly covered in the course.

 Note: These function overviews assume some prior knowledge of finance.

The IPMT Function

Syntax: =IPMT(rate, per, nper, pv, [fv], [type])

Description: This function returns the interest payment due for a particular period on an investment or a loan with regular payments and a fixed interest rate. Here is a breakdown of the function's syntax.

Required arguments:

- **rate**: The interest rate per period. It's important to be specific about the payment period here. If your interest rate is 10 percent and payments are made monthly, the **rate** value should be 10 percent divided by 12, or 0.10/12. If payments are annual, the **rate** value would simply be 10 percent, or 0.10.
- **per**: The period for which you wish to calculate the interest. Take note that this is not a range of dates or a specific date, but rather the payment number itself. So if payments are monthly on a four-year investment, the **per** value will have to be somewhere between 1 and 48. If you're calculating the interest for the first month of year 2, the **per** value is 13.
- **nper**: The total number of payments for the investment. For example, if payments are monthly on a five-year investment, the **nper** value is 60. Literally, this is the number of payment periods for the duration of the investment.
- **pv**: The principal, or lump-sum, value. This is the present value of all remaining payments.

 Note: For all arguments in the IPMT function, use positive numbers for any money you must pay out, and use positive numbers for any money you take in.

Optional arguments:

- **fv**: The future value of the investment after all payments have been made. If you do not enter a value for the **fv** argument, Excel treats it as zero. This may be easier to think of in terms of a loan. Typically, you are interested in values associated with paying a loan off in full, so the final, or future, value is 0.
- **Type**: Designates when payments are due within a particular period. This argument can have one of two values: 0 or 1. A value of 0 indicates payments are due at the end of the given period, for example, the last day of the month. A value of 1 indicates payments are due at the beginning of the period, for example, the first day of the year. If you do not enter a value, Excel treats it as 0.

Example: In the following example how much interest a borrower would owe in the first month of the second year of a five-year, $10,000 loan is being calculated. Payments are due at the end of each month.

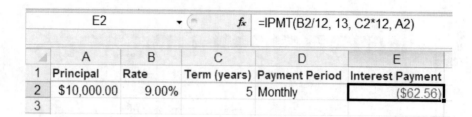

If you were making the same calculation from the bank's perspective, you would have entered -$10,000 for the principal, as you would have paid the money out to the borrower. Excel would return $62.50, not -$62.50, because the interest payment would be owed to you from the borrower. The value *13* is entered for the **per** argument because the first month of the second year represents the 13th payment period.

The PPMT Function

Syntax: =PPMT(rate, per, nper, pv, [fv], [type])

Description: The PPMT function calculates the amount owed against the principal for a particular period on an investment or a loan with regular payments and a fixed interest rate. The arguments for the PPMT function are exactly the same as those for the IPMT function. If you add the values returned for the same period of the same loan by the IPMT function and the PPMT function, you will calculate the total payment, less any fees, for the period.

Example: This is what the PPMT function would return for the aforementioned example for the principal payment due in the same period.

	E2			f_x	=PPMT(B2/12, 13, C2*12, A2)
	A	B	C	D	E
1	Principal	Rate	Term (years)	Payment Period	Principal Payment
2	$10,000.00	9.00%	5	Monthly	($145.02)
3					

The NPV Function

Syntax: =NPV(rate, value1, [value2], ..., [value254])

Description: The NPV function calculates the net present value of an asset or an investment given the estimated or known future cash flows and the discount rate per period. In the function's syntax, **rate** is the discount rate per period, and the **value**X arguments represent the future cash flows. For this function, the cash flow, or **value** argument, period must be fixed and the cash flows must occur at the end of each period.

 Note: The NPV function does not take into account the initial cost of the investment, or the cash flow at Time 0. You must subtract this from the value returned by the NPV function manually to calculate the actual increase or decrease in net value from the investment.

Example: In the following example, assume an annual discount rate of 9 percent and the given estimated cash flows.

	B8	▼	f_x	=NPV(B1,B3:B6)	

▲	A	B	C	D
1	Discount Rate	9.00%		
2	Initial Cost	$(100,000.00)		
3	Cash Flow Yr. 1	$ 60,000.00		
4	Cash Flow Yr. 2	$ 40,000.00		
5	Cash Flow Yr. 3	$ 30,000.00		
6	Cash Flow Yr. 4	$ 25,000.00		
7				
8	NPV	$129,589.21		
9				

Notice that the initial cost is not included in the function, this is not factored in. To calculate the true NPV of the investment, you must subtract the initial cost of the investment from the value returned by the NPV formula. In this case, the NPV for the investment is $29,589.21.

The FV Function

Syntax: =FV(rate, nper, pmt, [pv], [type])

Description: This function calculates the future value of an investment with fixed, periodic payments and a fixed interest rate. Here is a breakdown of the function's syntax.

Required:

- **rate**: The interest rate per period. As with some of the other financial functions, it's important to be specific about the period here. If the interest rate is 10 percent and payments are made monthly, the **rate** value should be 10 percent divided by 12, or 0.10/12. If payments are annual, the **rate** value would simply be 10 percent, or 0.10.
- **nper**: The number of periods from now for which you wish to calculate the future value. Make sure the periods for this argument are the same as those used in the **rate** argument.
- **pmt**: the payment made each period. For example, if you invest $200 a month from your paycheck toward a retirement investment for 20 years, the **pmt** value should be 200 and the **nper** value should be 240 (12 months × 20 years).

> **Note:** Although the **pmt** argument is considered to be required, that's not exactly true. You could also use the FV function to calculate the future value of a lump-sum investment. For example, if you put $10,000 in a fixed-rate investment, without making additional periodic contributions, you could simply enter 10000 in the **pv** argument, and leave the **pmt** argument blank. The FV function would then return the future value of that lump sum if it sat untouched in the same investment.

Optional:

- **pv**: The present value of the investment. Use this argument to determine the future value of a one-time, lump-sum investment into a fixed-rate asset. Or, you can use this in addition to the **pmt** argument to determine the future value of an investment in which you already have money, but plan to add to on a regular basis over time.
- **type**: Designates when payments are made within a particular period. This argument can have one of two values: 0 or 1. A value of 0 indicates payments are made at the end of the given period, for example, the last day of the month. A value of 1 indicates payments are made at the beginning of the period, for example, the first day of the year. If you do not enter a value, Excel treats it as 0.

Example: In the following example, assume the investor put $10,000 into an investment with an annual fixed-rate of return of 8 percent. Also assume the investor plans to contribute another $1,500 each month for 30 years with payments made at the end of each month.

| | B5 | ▾ | *fx* | =FV(B1/12, 30*12, B3, B2, 1) |

◢	A	B	C	D	E
1	**Rate**	8.00%			
2	**Intial Investment**	$ 10,000.00			
3	**Monthly Contribution**	$ 1,500.00			
4					
5	**Future Value**	($2,359,800.06)			
6					

B | Date and Time Functions

Excel's date and time functions are often used by business analysts, human resources professionals, and project managers, who all frequently deal with scheduling and analyzing data for particular periods of time. But there are also a couple of handy functions for simply entering the current date or time. The following are overviews of some of the more commonly used in date and time functions.

The TODAY Function

Syntax: =TODAY()

Description: This function enters the current date in a cell. This function has no arguments. Simply enter it into a cell to return the current date in whatever date format you have applied to the cell. You can use the value returned by this function to perform other calculations related to durations of time.

Example: In the following example, the TODAY function is entered into two cells, one with the default date format and one with a different format applied.

A1	▾	f_x	=TODAY()

	A	B	C	D	
1	10/24/2013	24-Oct			
2					

The NOW Function

Syntax: =NOW()

Description: Like the TODAY function, this function has no arguments; it simply returns the current date and time in the cell you enter in into. You can use the value returned by this function to perform other calculations related to durations of time.

 Note: When you enter the NOW function in a cell, Excel automatically formats the cell with a custom cell format used to accommodate both the date and the time. Here is the format: m/d/yyyy h:mm. Although the format displays only a single *m* for month and a single *d* for day, dates will appear in cells with both numbers for months and dates that contain two digits. If you alter the format to a different date or time format, you will alter the value in the cell.

Example: In the following example, the NOW function is entered in cell **A1**.

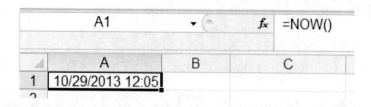

The DATE function

Syntax: =DATE(year, month, day)

Description: The DATE function returns the serial number for the date entered in the arguments. This is because Excel uses a serial number system to represent dates and times. January 1, 1900 is represented by the number 1. Each day after that increases by one whole number. So, January 12, 1900 is represented by the number 12. This is how Excel is able to display dates in a number of different formats as the underlying serial number is always the same. Although the DATE function technically returns the specified date's serial number, it displays the date in whatever date format is applied to your worksheet cells.

 Note: Times are represented by decimal places that follow the date's whole number and represent the number of hours and minutes that have passed in a day up to the desired or calculated time.

In the DATE function's syntax, the **year** argument is the four-digit year you wish to enter, the **month** argument is the calendar month represented in numbers from 1 to 12, and the **day** argument is the desired date. You use the DATE function largely to make calculations using other date and time functions, as using plain text or simply entering the date and time values can return errors.

Example: In the following example, the DATE function has been used to return the date September 27, 2003, and a specific date format has been applied to the cell.

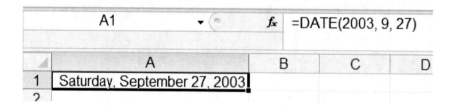

The NETWORKDAYS Function

Syntax: =NETWORKDAYS(start_date, end_date, [holidays])

Description: The NETWORKDAYS function returns a count of the number of work days between two specific dates. You would use this function, for example, to determine how many working days you'll have to complete a project from now until a specific date in the future, or to calculate how much of a particular benefit employees have accrued. In the function's syntax, the **start_date** argument is the first date of the range for which you wish to count the number of work days. The **end_date** argument is the last day of the range. The optional **holidays** argument allows you to exclude known holidays so they are not counted as work days. The NETWORK days function automatically excludes weekends from the calculation.

Example: In the following example, the number of working days are being counted in a project, which starts on June 12, 2008 and ends on December 15, 2008. The project team will all be off on Thanksgiving and the day after. The cells in the range B1:B4 have all been entered using the DATE function.

B5	▾	*fx*	=NETWORKDAYS(B1, B2, B3:B4)

	A	B	C	D	E
1	Project Start Date	6/12/2008			
2	Project End Date	12/15/2008			
3	Thanksgiving	11/27/2008			
4	Day After Thanksgiving	11/28/2008			
5	Total Work Days	131			
6					

C | Working with Graphical Objects

Appendix Introduction

Although data is king in Excel, there are a number of reasons you may need to add graphical objects, outside of charts or PivotCharts, to your worksheets. You may want to simply enhance the visual appeal of your worksheets, or you may wish to include some type of "info-graphic" that simply can't be created with a chart. Perhaps you want to include your company logo in a visible location when sharing your screen with potential clients. Or, you may wish to include screenshots of relevant computer applications or websites when presenting related information.

Whatever the case, at some point you'll likely need to insert graphical support for the data in your workbooks. Excel 2010 provides you with a number of tools for inserting, modifying, and even editing a variety of graphical objects that can not only enhance the visual appeal of a document, but can also serve as interactive data objects. Understanding what these objects are, how they work, and how you can integrate them with your data can help you elevate your workbooks to a new level of sophistication.

TOPIC A

Insert Graphical Objects

Before you can use graphical objects to enhance the visual appeal of your workbooks or present your data with greater impact, you must first be able to insert them into your worksheets. Excel 2010 provides you with a variety of tools and commands that enable you to add a variety of graphical objects to your worksheets. Understanding the differences among the various types of graphical objects and the various methods for inserting them is a key first step in using graphical objects to enhance your workbooks.

Graphical Objects

There are five basic types of graphical objects that you can insert into your workbooks: pictures, clip art, shapes, SmartArt, and screenshots. Each of these is suited to particular purposes. It's important to understand that these objects, much like charts, are separate data objects that lie on top of worksheets; you do not insert them in cells. All of these graphical objects can be resized, modified, and moved. Some of them can also contain text or display the content of worksheet cells. You can access the commands for inserting graphical objects in the **Illustrations** group on the **Insert** tab.

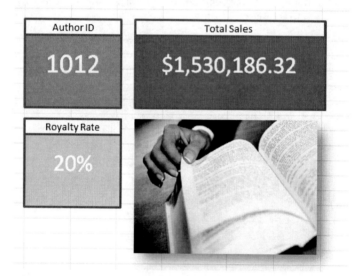

Figure C-1: Graphical objects enable you to add appeal to your worksheets and present data visually.

The following table describes each of the types of graphical objects in some detail.

Graphical Object Type	Description
Pictures	These are image files created outside of Excel, such as images from digital cameras, pictures downloaded from the web, or graphics and art saved as image files. Excel 2010 supports a variety of common image file formats.
Clip art	Simple artwork graphics or images that are pre-loaded into Excel or that are downloaded from Office.com. Clip art objects behave differently depending on the type of graphical object you select, but they are all still generically referred to as clip art.

Graphical Object Type	Description
Shapes	Simple graphical objects, such as circles, squares, rectangles, text callouts, and arrows, that are generated within Excel and that you manually draw on your worksheets. Excel 2010 comes loaded with a wide variety of shapes. Shapes can also display text or the contents of worksheet cells.
SmartArt	Pre-configured graphics that you can use as graphical representations of textual content. You will typically use SmartArt to represent processes, procedures, cycles, or hierarchies. Common uses of SmartArt include creating organizational charts and representing sales or business cycles. As with shapes, you can use SmartArt to display text, but you cannot link cell content to SmartArt graphics.
Screenshots	Images taken from the current display of your computer monitor. You capture these images directly within Excel, which can be of either entire windows or particular regions of your screen. Excel enables you to screen capture any currently open windows that are not minimized.

The Clip Art Pane

You will use the **Clip Art** pane to insert clip art objects, or clips, into your workbooks. From here, you can enter search criteria for the clips you wish to use, select from among a variety of media types, and insert the desired clips. Typically, clips will be in the form of simple illustrations or photographs. You can also search for and insert audio and simple video clips, although you will likely need to play these back in a separate application. You can access the **Clip Art** pane by selecting **Insert→Illustrations→Clip Art**.

Figure C–2: The Clip Art pane.

The following table describes the functions of the various **Clip Art** pane elements.

Clip Art Pane Element	Use This To
Search for field	Enter search criteria for the desired clip art.
Go button	Execute a search for clip art.
Results should be drop-down menu	Select the desired media type for your clip art.
Include Office.com content check box	Decide whether Excel will search for clip art only on your computer or on your computer and from Office.com. When you install Excel, a library of clip art is installed along with it.
Search results	Review search results and select the desired clip art.
Find more at Office.com link	Navigate to Office.com to search for a wide variety of available clip art.
Hints for finding images link	Open Excel Help to an article specific to searching for and adding clip art.

The Shapes Gallery

You will select the particular shapes you wish to add to your worksheets by using the **Shapes** gallery. The **Shapes** gallery is divided into a series of nine categories of related shape types. These include simple lines and arrows, basic geometric shapes, flowchart elements, and text callout boxes. Shapes you have recently used in your workbooks appear in the **Recently Used Shapes** section at the top of the **Shapes** gallery. You can access the **Shapes** gallery by selecting **Insert→Illustrations→Shapes**.

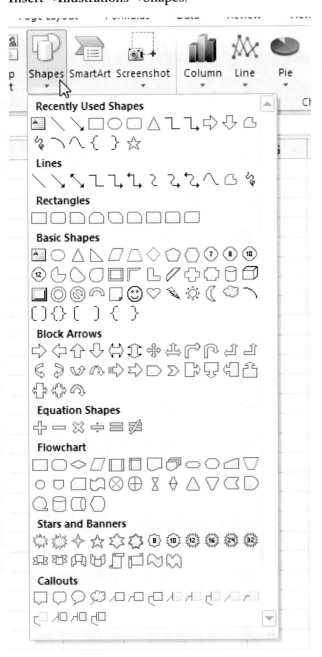

Figure C–3: The Shapes gallery.

The Screenshot Command

The **Screenshot** command enables you to capture an image from an open application on your computer. You can capture either an entire application window or a particular region of the screen.

The **Screenshot** tool enables you to screen capture open applications that are not minimized to the task bar. When you select the **Screenshot** command, Excel opens the **Available Windows** gallery, from which you can select an open application to capture. This method captures an image of the entire window of the selected application. To capture only a portion of the application window, select the **Screen Clipping** command from the bottom of the **Available Windows** gallery. Excel then activates the **Screen Clipping** tool, enabling you to select the particular region of your screen that you wish to capture. This allows you to select the particular region of your screen that you wish to capture. The **Screen Clipping** tool also allows you to capture screenshots of your desktop, which is not possible from the **Available Windows** gallery. You cannot capture an image of Excel from within Excel. You can access the **Screenshot** tool by selecting **Insert→Illustrations→Screenshot**.

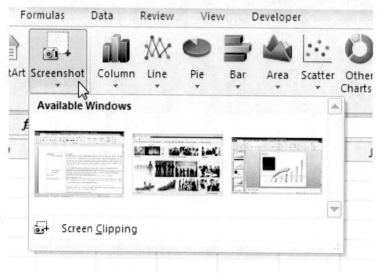

Figure C-4: The Screenshot command.

 Access the Checklist tile on your LogicalCHOICE course screen for reference information and job aids on How to Insert Graphical Objects.

TOPIC B

Modify Graphical Objects

Inserting graphical objects is a great way to enhance the visual appeal and impact of your workbooks. However, many of the raw images or basic shapes you insert may not suit your particular needs. For instance, you may need to ensure that all shapes adhere to your organization's branding guidelines. Or you may want to remove distracting background elements from images to focus your audience's attention on only the most important aspects of pictures. Whatever the reason, taking the time to gain the foundational knowledge needed to modify and edit your graphical objects will give you the flexibility you need to ensure your images deliver the proper message and have the desired impact.

 Note: While there are no formal activities for this lesson, a sample data file has been provided that you can use to practice adding shapes and connecting them to cell data in the **C: \091019Data\Appendix E** folder. Use the **graphic_objects.xlsx** file to practice adding, modifying, and connecting data to shapes; one has been included in the workbook as an example. You can also practice adding images or SmartArt as well. A sample solution file has been provided in the **C:\091019Data\Appendix E\solutions** folder.

Pictures and Drawings

There is an important distinction to understand before you modify the graphical objects in your workbooks. With the exception of SmartArt, although there are four types of graphical objects in Excel, pictures, clip art, shapes, and screenshots, Excel recognizes only two types of images in terms of editing and modifying graphical objects: pictures and drawings.

 Note: Although, technically, the individual elements of a SmartArt graphic are the same as shapes, SmartArt has a separate set of tools that you will use to modify your SmartArt graphics.

In terms of modifying graphical objects, Excel considers pictures, screenshots, and some clip art to be pictures, whereas it considers shapes and some other clips to be drawings. Each has its own unique set of tools for working with and modifying the various types of graphical objects. In general terms, the clip art images you can search for by checking **Illustrations** in the **Results should be** drop-down menu of the **Clip Art** pane are considered drawings. On the other hand, clip art images you search for by checking **Photographs** are considered pictures.

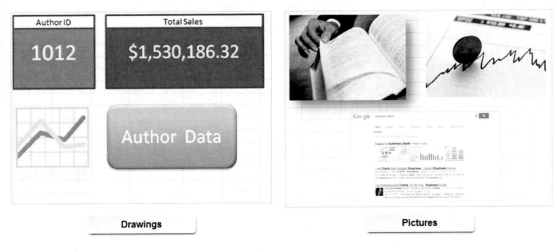

Figure C–5: Excel draws a distinction between drawings and pictures.

The Picture Tools Contextual Tab

Excel displays the **Picture Tools** contextual tab when you select a graphical object it considers to be a picture. The **Picture Tools** contextual tab contains only one tab, the **Format** tab, which displays the tools and commands you will use to edit, modify, and add effects to the pictures in your workbooks.

Figure C-6: The Picture Tools contextual tab.

The Image Editor

The **Adjust** group on the **Format** tab of the **Picture Tools** contextual tab contains a set of commands and tools sometimes referred to collectively as the image editor. These commands and tools enable you to perform image editing tasks, such as adjusting the brightness, contrast, or sharpness of a picture, that you might otherwise need a separate application to perform.

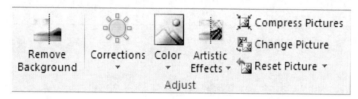

Figure C-7: The Adjust group's imaging editing tools.

The following table describes the type of image-correction and -modification tasks you can perform by using the tools and commands available in the image editor.

Image Editor Command/Tool	Use This To
Remove Background tool	Remove unwanted background elements from a picture. The **Remove Background** tool will attempt to guess at the main subject of an image and remove all other background elements. You can also manually select which regions of an image Excel will keep and which elements it will remove.
Corrections command	Adjust the sharpness, brightness, or contrast of an image.
Color command	Adjust the color tone or saturation of an image, recolor an image, or select a particular color to make transparent in an image.
Artistic Effects command	Apply a particular artistic effect to an image, such as making an image look like a pencil sketch, adding a blur effect, adding a pixelated effect, or turning a color image into a black-and-white image.
Compress Picture command	Reduce the overall file size of your Excel workbook by compressing the images it contains.
Change Picture command	Replace a picture with another image file.
Reset Picture command	Remove any formatting changes you've made to a picture.

The Drawing Tools Contextual Tab

Excel displays the **Drawing Tools** contextual tab when you select a graphical object it considers to be a drawing. The **Drawing Tools** contextual tab contains only one tab, the **Format** tab, which displays the tools and commands you will use to edit, modify, and add effects to the drawings in your workbooks.

Figure C-8: The Drawing Tools contextual tab.

The **Format** tab on the **Drawing Tools** contextual tab is divided into five command groups. Each of these groups displays functionally related commands for working with drawings in Excel.

Format Tab Group	Contains Commands For
Insert Shapes	Inserting additional shapes, changing the outline (shape) of a shape, and inserting text boxes.
Shape Styles	Applying a variety of pre-configured or custom styles to drawings.
WordArt Styles	Applying a variety of pre-configured or custom styles to text you add to drawings.
Arrange	Changing the placement of drawings on worksheets, arranging multiple drawings front-to-back, grouping drawings together, and rotating drawings.
Size	Modifying the size of drawings.

The Selection and Visibility Pane

Although you can use the commands on the **Picture Tools** or the **Drawing Tools** contextual tabs to arrange images front to back on your worksheets, Excel 2010 includes a tool that makes doing so easier: the **Selection and Visibility** pane. The **Selection and Visibility** pane enables you to easily view the front-to-back order of graphical objects on your worksheets, view which objects are grouped together, change the order of objects and groups (and individual objects within groups), and hide from view or display any of the graphical objects on your worksheets.

It may not appear as such when objects are separated from each other, but all objects on a worksheet are arranged in a front-to-back order as if each exists on its own plane. This fact becomes evident, however, when you overlap objects on screen. Objects that are in front of other objects will obscure the view of the objects behind them. Objects appear in the **Selection and Visibility** pane from top to bottom as they appear on the worksheet from front to back. In other words, the object at the top of the **Selection and Visibility** pane is in front of all other objects on the worksheet.

When you group objects together, they behave as one independent object that you can move, arrange, resize, or modify collectively. You are, however, able to select individual objects within a group to perform modifications on it separate from the group. Grouped objects appear in the **Selection and Visibility** pane in a hierarchical fashion with the group existing at the same level as other independent objects, and the objects in the group appearing one level down in the hierarchy within the group.

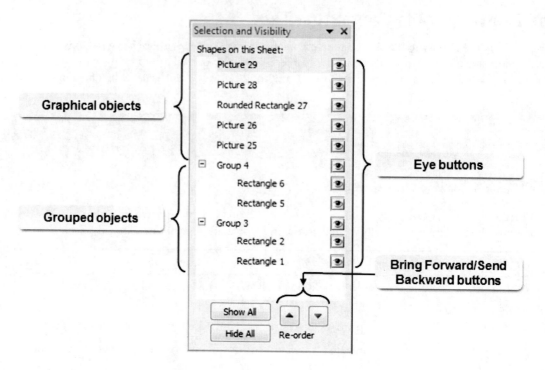

Figure C-9: The Section and Visibility pane.

The following table describes the functions of the various elements of the **Selection and Visibility** pane.

Selection and Visibility Pane Element	Description
Shapes on this Sheet section	Displays the order of all objects and groups on a worksheet as well as the order in which individual objects appear within a group.
Eye buttons	Enable you to hide or show any object or group.
Show All button	Turns on the display of all objects and groups on a worksheet.
Hide All button	Turns off the display of all objects and groups on a worksheet.
Bring Forward and **Send Backward** buttons	Enable you to move objects or groups up or down in the **Selection and Visibility** pane, which changes their order on the worksheet.

 Access the Checklist tile on your LogicalCHOICE course screen for reference information and job aids on **How to Modify Graphical Objects**.

TOPIC C

Work with SmartArt

Creating complex graphical representations of textual information can be a daunting task. You must decide what shapes to include, how to size and format them, and how to arrange them on the slide so they make sense. You may know what you would like to communicate, but be unsure of how to say it visually. So, how do you go about designing and building your graphic? You don't have to do all of the work yourself.

The SmartArt tools within Excel 2010 give you a vast array of options for creating graphics that are well suited to a variety of needs. Understanding how to insert SmartArt into your workbooks and how to decide which layout to use will save you the effort of tirelessly adding and formatting individual shapes to create a complex graphic.

SmartArt Graphics

SmartArt graphics are visual representations of textual content that typically represent a process, a cycle, a hierarchy, or relationships. Excel 2010 contains eight different categories of SmartArt graphics that you can use to display a variety of textual information. In addition, you can download a number of other SmartArt templates from Office.com. Like other objects, SmartArt graphics are individual objects that can be moved, resized, arranged, and formatted in a variety of ways.

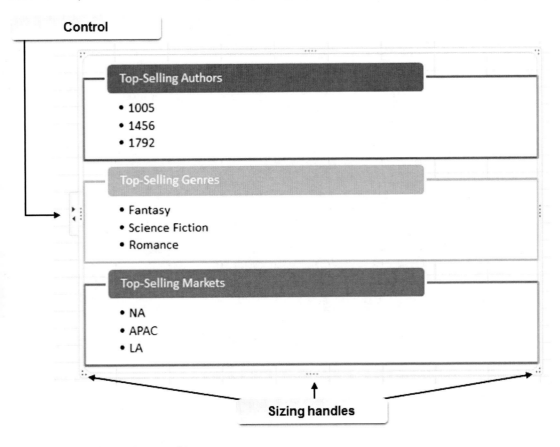

Figure C-10: A SmartArt graphic.

The following table describes some of the common uses for SmartArt graphics in the various SmartArt graphic categories.

SmartArt Category	Is Used to Create Diagrams for Displaying
List	Information that does not need to be shown in sequential order. Lists are ideal for content such as bulleted lists.
Process	Information that needs to be shown in sequential order, such as a manufacturing process or a task procedure.
Cycle	A continuous process, such as an annual performance-review system or annual sales cycles.
Hierarchy	Steps in a decision process or an organizational chart.
Relationship	How various elements of a system interconnect with each other.
Matrix	How various elements of a system relate to the system as a whole.
Pyramid	How elements of varying degrees of importance or size relate, proportionally, to each other as part of the whole.
Picture	Content as a combination of text and graphics.

SmartArt Shapes

The individual elements of a SmartArt graphic are known as shapes. This can be a bit confusing as they share a name with the shapes you manually draw onto your Excel worksheets. Essentially, the individual elements of SmartArt are the same objects as shapes. But, to differentiate the two, from this point forward, the term *shapes* will be used to refer to the objects you manually draw and the elements of SmartArt graphics will be referred to as **SmartArt shapes**.

It is the SmartArt shapes that display the text in SmartArt graphics. And, although they are typically formatted in much the same way as other SmartArt shapes in a SmartArt graphic, you can individually format, move, and resize them to suit your needs. Much as with grouped objects, to select a SmartArt shape, you first select the SmartArt graphic it is a part of, and then select the individual SmartArt shape you wish to interact with.

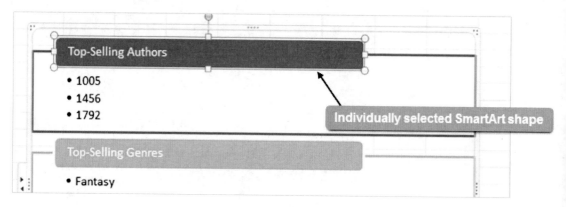

Figure C–11: A SmartArt shape.

The Choose a SmartArt Graphic Dialog Box

You will use the **Choose a SmartArt Graphic** dialog box to insert SmartArt graphics into you workbooks. The **Choose a SmartArt Graphic** dialog box is divided into a series of tabs that organize the available SmartArt graphics by category. As you select the various categories of SmartArt in the left pane, the dialog box displays the available SmartArt graphic layouts in the middle pane as thumbnail images. Selecting one of the thumbnail images displays a preview of the selected SmartArt layout along with a brief description of its common uses. To display the **Choose a SmartArt Graphic** dialog box, select **Insert→Illustrations→SmartArt**.

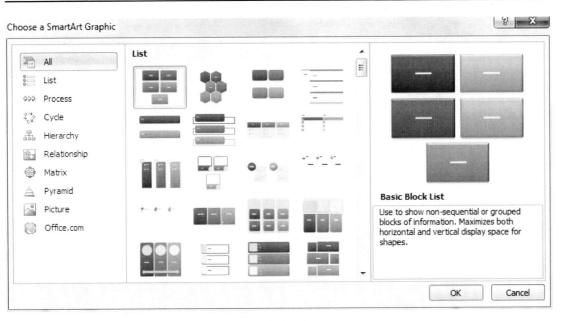

Figure C-12: The Choose a SmartArt Graphic dialog box.

The Text Pane

There are two methods you can use to add text to your SmartArt graphics. The first is to simply select the default text on the SmartArt shapes and then enter the text. The second method is to use the *Text pane*. With the **Text** pane open, you can still select the text placeholders directly in the SmartArt shapes to enter or edit text, but you can also place the insertion point in the various text placeholders within the **Text** pane to do the same.

Many SmartArt graphics are hierarchical in nature. This is especially beneficial when creating graphics for, say, bullet list content and organizational charts. As such, Excel provides you with functionality to control and arrange the hierarchical relationships among the various bits of text in your SmartArt graphics. Once you enter text in the **Text** pane, pressing the **Enter** key will add a new text placeholder at the same hierarchical level, both in the **Text** pane and in the SmartArt graphic. You can also promote or demote text in the graphic's overall hierarchy. Depending on the particular SmartArt graphic you're working with, adding more lines of text may simply add bullet items within a SmartArt shape, or it may add new SmartArt shapes to contain the text. To open the **Text** pane, select the SmartArt graphic and then select the **control**.

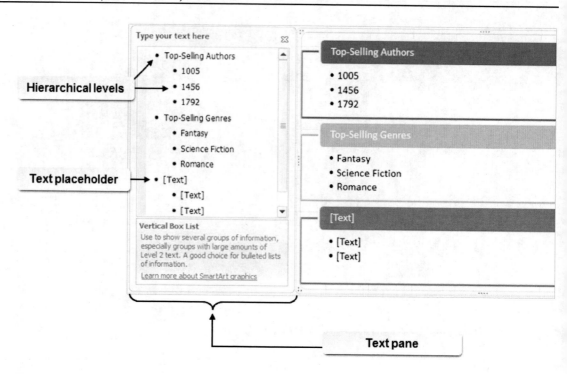

Figure C–13: The Text pane.

The SmartArt Tools Contextual Tab

You will find the commands and tools specific to working with and modifying SmartArt graphics on the **SmartArt Tools** contextual tab. The **SmartArt Tools** contextual tab is divided into two tabs: the **Design** tab and the **Format** tab. The **Design** tab contains the commands you will use to configure the overall structure of your SmartArt graphics, and to apply particular style elements to entire SmartArt graphics.

Figure C–14: The Design tab.

The **Design** tab is divided into four command groups.

Design Tab Group	Contains Commands For
Create Graphic	Adding SmartArt shapes to SmartArt graphics, adding additional text panes to SmartArt shapes, and managing the hierarchical structure of SmartArt graphics.
Layouts	Modifying the overall layout of SmartArt graphics.
SmartArt Styles	Changing the overall color scheme of SmartArt graphics and applying stylistic elements, such as 3-D effects, beveling, and drop shadows, to SmartArt graphics.
Reset	Removing customization from SmartArt graphics and converting SmartArt graphics to standard Excel shapes.

The **Format** tab contains the commands you will use to apply formatting to the individual SmartArt shapes and their text within your SmartArt graphics.

Figure C-15: The Format tab.

The **Format** tab is divided into five functional groups.

Format Tab Group	Contains Commands For
Shapes	Changing the shape of and modifying the size of individual SmartArt shapes.
Shape Styles	Applying pre-configured or customized formatting to individual SmartArt shapes.
WordArt Styles	Applying pre-configured or customized formatting to the text within SmartArt shapes.
Arrange	Configuring the placement of, arranging, and rotating SmartArt shapes.
Size	Modifying the size of overall SmartArt graphics or individual SmartArt shapes.

 Access the Checklist tile on your LogicalCHOICE course screen for reference information and job aids on How to Insert and Modify SmartArt.

D | Microsoft Office Excel 2010 Exam 77-882

Selected Logical Operations courseware addresses Microsoft Office Specialist certification skills for Microsoft Office 2010. The following table indicates where Excel 2010 skills that are tested in Exam 77-882 are covered in the Logical Operations Microsoft Office Excel 2010 series of courses.

Objective Domain	Covered In
1. Managing the Worksheet Environment	
1.1 Navigate through a worksheet	
1.1.1 Use hot keys	Part 1
1.1.2 Use the name box	Part 1; Part 2, Topic -A
1.2 Print a worksheet or workbook	
1.2.1 Print only selected worksheets	Part 1
1.2.2 Print an entire workbook	Part 1
1.2.3 Construct headers and footers	Part 1
1.2.4 Apply printing options	
1.2.4.1 Scale	Part 1
1.2.4.2 Print titles	Part 1
1.2.4.3 Page setup	Part 1
1.2.4.4 Print area	Part 1
1.2.4.5 Gridlines	Part 1
1.3 Personalize the environment by using Backstage	
1.3.1 Manipulate the Quick Access Toolbar	Part 2, Topic 1-B
1.3.2 Customize the ribbon	
1.3.2.1 Tabs	Part 2, Topic 1-B
1.3.2.2 Groups	Part 2, Topic 1-B
1.3.3 Manipulate Excel default settings (Excel Options)	Part 2, Topic 1-A
1.3.4 Import data to Excel	Part 3
1.3.5 Import data from Excel	Part 3
1.3.6 Manipulate workbook properties	Part 1

Objective Domain	Covered In
1.3.7 Manipulate workbook files and folders	Part 1
1.3.8 Apply different name and file formats for different uses	Part 1
1.3.9 Using save and save as features	Part 1
2. Creating Cell Data	
2.1 Construct cell data	
2.1.1 Use paste special	
2.1.1.1 Formats	Part 1
2.1.1.2 Formulas	Part 1
2.1.1.3 Values	Part 1
2.1.1.4 Preview icons	Part 1
2.1.1.5 Transpose rows and columns	Part 1
2.1.1.6 Operations	Part 1
2.1.1.7 Comments	Part 1
2.1.1.8 Validation	Part 1
2.1.1.9 Paste as a link	Part 1
2.1.2 Cut, move, and select cell data	Part 1
2.2 Apply AutoFill	
2.2.1 Copy data using AutoFill	Part 1
2.2.2 Fill series using AutoFill	Part 1
2.2.3 Copy or preserve cell format with AutoFill	Part 1
2.2.4 Select from drop-down list	Part 1
2.3 Apply and manipulate hyperlinks	
2.3.1 Create a hyperlink in a cell	Part 1
2.3.2 Modify hyperlinks	Part 1
2.3.3 Modify hyperlinked cell attributes	Part 1
2.3.4 Remove a hyperlink	Part 1
3. Formatting Cells and Worksheets	
3.1 Apply and modify cell formats	
3.1.1 Align cell content	Part 1
3.1.2 Apply a number format	Part 1
3.1.3 Wrap text in a cell	Part 1
3.1.4 Use Format Painter	Part 1
3.2 Merge or split cells	
3.2.1 Use Merge & Center	Part 1
3.2.2 Merge Across	Part 1
3.2.3 Merge cells	Part 1

Objective Domain	Covered In
3.2.4 Unmerge Cells	Part 1
3.3 Create row and column titles	
3.3.1 Print row and column headings	Part 1
3.3.2 Print rows to repeat with titles	Part 1
3.3.3 Print columns to repeat with titles	Part 1
3.3.4 Configure titles to print only on odd or even pages	Part 1
3.3.5 Configure titles to skip the first worksheet page	Part 1
3.4 Hide and unhide rows and columns	
3.4.1 Hide a column	Part 1
3.4.2 Unhide a column	Part 1
3.4.3 Hide a series of columns	Part 1
3.4.4 Hide a row	Part 1
3.4.5 Unhide a row	Part 1
3.4.6 Hide a series of rows	Part 1
3.5 Manipulate Page Setup options for worksheets	
3.5.1 Configure page orientation	Part 1
3.5.2 Manage page scaling	Part 1
3.5.3 Configure page margins	Part 1
3.5.4 Change header and footer size	Part 1
3.6 Create and apply cell styles	
3.6.1 Apply cell styles	Part 1
3.6.2 Construct new cell styles	Part 1
4. Managing Worksheets and Workbooks	
4.1 Create and format worksheets	
4.1.1 Insert worksheets	Part 1
4.1.2 Delete worksheets	Part 1
4.1.3 Copy worksheets	Part 1
4.1.4 Reposition worksheets	Part 1
4.1.5 Copy and move worksheets	Part 1
4.1.6 Rename worksheets	Part 1
4.1.7 Group worksheets	Part 1
4.1.8 Apply coloring to worksheet tabs	Part 1
4.1.9 Hide worksheet tabs	Part 1
4.1.10 Unhide worksheet tabs	Part 1
4.2 Manipulate window views	
4.2.1 Split window views	Part 1

Objective Domain	Covered In
4.2.2 Arrange window views	Part 1
4.2.3 Open a new window with contents from the current worksheet	Part 1
4.3 Manipulate workbook views	
4.3.1 Use Normal, Page Layout, and Page Break workbook views	Part 1
4.3.2 Create custom views	Part 1
5. Applying Formulas and Functions	
5.1 Create formulas	
5.1.1 Use basic operators	Part 1
5.1.2 Revise formulas	Part 1
5.2 Enforce precedence	
5.2.1 Order of evaluation	Part 1
5.2.2 Precedence using parentheses	Part 1
5.2.3 Precedence of operators for percent vs. exponentiation	Part 1
5.3 Apply cell references in formulas	
5.3.1 Relative references	Part 1
5.3.2 Absolute references	Part 1
5.4 Apply conditional logic in a formula	
5.4.1 Create a formula with values that match your conditions	Part 3
5.4.2 Edit defined conditions in a formula	Part 3
5.4.3 Use a series of conditional logic values in a formula	Part 3
5.5 Apply named ranges in formulas	
5.5.1 Define, edit, and rename a named range	Part 2, Topic 2-A
5.6 Apply cell ranges in formulas	
5.6.1 Enter a cell range definition in the formula bar	Part 1
5.6.2 Define a cell range using the mouse	Part 1
5.6.3 Define a cell range using a keyboard shortcut	Part 1
6. Presenting Data Visually	
6.1 Create charts based on worksheet data	Part 2, Topic 5-A
6.2 Apply and manipulate illustrations	
6.2.1 Clip Art	Part 2, Appendix E
6.2.2 SmartArt	Part 2, Appendix E
6.2.3 Shapes	Part 2, Appendix E
6.2.4 Screenshots	Part 2, Appendix E

Objective Domain	Covered In
6.3 Create and modify images by using the Image Editor	
6.3.1 Making corrections to an image	
6.3.1.1 Sharpen or soften an image	Part 2, Appendix E
6.3.1.2 Changing brightness and contrast	Part 2, Appendix E
6.3.2 Use picture color tools	Part 2, Appendix E
6.3.3 Change artistic effects on an image	Part 2, Appendix E
6.4 Apply Sparklines	
6.4.1 Use Line, Column, and Win/Loss chart types	Part 3
6.4.2 Create a Sparkline chart	Part 3
6.4.3 Customize a Sparkline	Part 3
6.4.4 Format a Sparkline	Part 3
6.4.5 Show or hide data markers	Part 3
7. Sharing Worksheet Data with Other Users	
7.1 Share spreadsheets by using Backstage	
7.1.1 Send a worksheet via email or Skydrive	Part 3
7.1.2 Change the file type to a different version of Excel	Part 1
7.1.3 Save as PDF or XPS	Part 1; Part 3
7.2 Manage comments	
7.2.1 Inserting comments	Part 3
7.2.2 Viewing comments	Part 3
7.2.3 Editing comments	Part 3
7.2.4 Deleting comments	Part 3
8. Analyzing and Organizing Data	
8.1 Filter data	
8.1.1 Define filters	Part 2, Topic 4-C
8.1.2 Apply filters	Part 2, Topic 4-C
8.1.3 Remove filters	Part 2, Topic 4-C
8.1.4 Search filters	Part 2, Topic 4-C
8.1.5 Filter lists using AutoFilter	Part 2, Topic 4-C
8.2 Sort data	
8.2.1 Use sort options	
8.2.1.1 Values	Part 2, Topic 4-B
8.2.1.2 Font color	Part 2, Topic 4-B
8.2.1.3 Cell color	Part 2, Topic 4-B
8.3 Apply conditional formatting	
8.3.1 Apply conditional formatting to cells	Part 1; Part 2, Topic 3-B

Objective Domain	Covered In
8.3.2 Use the Rule Manager to apply conditional formats	Part 2, Topic 3-B
8.3.3 Use the IF function to apply conditional formatting	Part 2, Topic 3-B; Part 3
8.3.4 Icon sets	Part 2, Topic 3-B
8.3.5 Data bars	Part 2, Topic 3-B
8.3.6 Clear rules	Part 2, Topic 3-B

Microsoft Office Excel 2010 Expert Exam 77-888

Selected Logical Operations courseware addresses Microsoft Office Specialist certification skills for Microsoft Office 2010. The following table indicates where Excel 2010 skills that are tested in Exam 77-888 are covered in the Logical Operations Microsoft Office Excel 2010 series of courses.

Objective Domain	Covered In
1. Sharing and Maintaining Workbooks	
1.1. Apply workbook settings, properties, and data options	
1.1.1. Set advanced properties	Part 1
1.1.2. Save a workbook as a template	Part 1
1.1.3. Import and export XML data	Part 3
1.2. Apply protection and sharing properties to workbooks and worksheets	
1.2.1. Protect the current sheet	Part 3
1.2.2. Protect the workbook structure	Part 3
1.2.3. Restrict permissions	Part 3
1.2.4. Require a password to open a workbook	Part 3
1.3. Maintain shared workbooks	
1.3.1. Merge workbooks	Part 3
1.3.2. Set Track Changes options	Part 3
2. Applying Formulas and Functions	
2.1. Audit formulas	
2.1.1. Trace formula precedents, dependents, and errors	Part 3
2.1.2. Locate invalid data or formulas	Part 3
2.1.3 Correct errors in formulas	Part 3
2.2. Manipulate formula options	
2.2.1. Set iterative calculation options	Part 3

Objective Domain	Covered In
2.2.2. Enable or disabling automatic workbook calculation	Part 2, Topic 2-B
2.3. Perform data summary tasks	
2.3.1. Use an array formula	Part 2, Topic 2-C
2.3.2. Use a SUMIFS function	Part 2, Topic 2-B
2.4. Apply functions in formulas	
2.4.1. Find and correct errors in functions	Part 3
2.4.2. Apply arrays to functions	Part 2, Topic 2-C
2.4.3. Use functions	
2.4.3.1 Statistical	Part 1; Part 2, Topic 2B
2.4.3.2 Date and Time	Part 2, Appendix D
2.4.3.4 Financial	Part 2, Appendix C
2.4.3.5 Text	Part 2, Topic 3-A
2.4.3.6 Cube	Part 3
3. Presenting Data Visually	
3.1. Apply advanced chart features	
3.1.1. Use Trend lines	Part 3
3.1.2. Use Dual axes	Part 3
3.1.3. Use chart templates	Part 3
3.1.4. Use Sparklines	Part 3
3.2. Apply data analysis	
3.2.1 Use automated analysis tools	Part 3
3.2.2 Perform What-If analysis	Part 3
3.3. Apply and manipulate PivotTables	
3.3.1 Manipulate PivotTable data	Part 2, Topic 6-B
3.3.2 Use the slicer to filter and segment your PivotTable data in multiple layers	Part 2, Topic 6-D
3.4. Apply and manipulate PivotCharts	
3.4.1. Create PivotChart data	Part 2, Topic 6-C
3.4.2. Manipulate PivotChart data	Part 2, Topic 6-C
3.4.3. Analyze PivotChart data	Part 2, Topic 6-C
3.5. Demonstrate how to use the slicer	
3.5.1. Choose data sets from external data connections	Part 2, Topic 6-A
4. Working with Macros and Forms	
4.1. Create and manipulate macros	
4.1.1. Run a macro	Part 3
4.1.2. Run a macro when a workbook is opened	Part 3
4.1.3. Run a macro when a button is clicked	Part 3

Objective Domain	Covered In
4.1.4. Record an action macro	Part 3
4.1.5. Assign a macro to a command button	Part 3
4.1.6. Create a custom macro button on the Quick Access Toolbar	Part 3
4.1.7. Apply modifications to a macro	Part 3
4.2. Insert and manipulate form controls	
4.2.1. Inserting form controls	Part 3
4.2.2. Set form properties	Part 3

Lesson Labs

Lesson labs are provided for certain lessons as additional learning resources for this course. Lesson labs are developed for selected lessons within a course in cases when they seem most instructionally useful as well as technically feasible. In general, labs are supplemental, optional unguided practice and may or may not be performed as part of the classroom activities. Your instructor will consider setup requirements, classroom timing, and instructional needs to determine which labs are appropriate for you to perform, and at what point during the class. If you do not perform the labs in class, your instructor can tell you if you can perform them independently as self-study, and if there are any special setup requirements.

Lesson Lab 2-1
Creating Advanced Formulas

Activity Time: 10 minutes

Data File

C:\091019Data\Creating Advanced Formulas\annual_sales_summary.xlsx

Scenario

You are the sales manager for your organization. You're preparing a summary of annual sales information for the sales director. Part of your reporting includes providing summary information on sales reps who have reached the year's goal of $250,000 in sales. Specifically, you need to report how many sales reps meet or surpassed the goal and what the average quarterly sales are for these reps. You also need to include a figure for the total commissions paid to all reps for the year. To make entering the associated formulas easier, you decide to define names for the columns in the sales dataset. To save space on the worksheet, you decide to use a single-cell array formula to calculate the total commissions paid.

1. Open Excel 2010, open the **annual_sales_summary.xlsx** workbook file, and then ensure that the **Summary** worksheet tab is selected.

2. Create named ranges for all columns in the main dataset based on the column labels.

3. Change the range names for the quarterly sales figures to *First_Quarter_Sales* and *Second_Quarter_Sales* and *Third_Quarter_Sales* and *Fourth_Quarter_Sales* respectively.

4. Apply the defined name *Sales_Rep_Data* to the range **A2:G70**.

5. Enter a function in cell **K2** by using defined names that calculates the number of sales reps who reached or beat the $250,000 annual goal.

6. Enter a function in cell **K3** by using defined names that calculates the average quarterly sales for sales reps who reached or beat the $250,000 annual goal.

7. Enter a single-cell array formula in cell **K5** by using defined names that calculates the sum of all commissions paid by the company for the year.

    Note: To calculate an individual sales rep's commission, you would multiply his or her total sales by his or her commission rate.

8. Save the workbook to the **C:\091019Data\Creating Advanced Formulas** folder as *my_annual_sales_summary.xlsx* and close the workbook.

Lesson Lab 3–1
Analyzing Data with Functions and Conditional Formatting

Activity Time: 10 minutes

Data File

C:\091019Data\Analyzing Data with Functions and Conditional Formatting
\annual_sales_overview.xlsx

Before You Begin

Excel 2010 is open.

Scenario

You're the director of sales for a large auto parts distributor. Part of your responsibilities involves determining which sales reps will receive a bonus for the year based on performance. One of your regional sales managers has submitted the figures for his team for the past fiscal year. You're going to use that data to determine who is eligible for the annual bonus, which is based on a $20,000 increase in sales from the previous year. You also want to add some conditional formatting to the worksheet so it's easy to tell whose sales increased and whose decreased from the previous year, and so it's easy to see whose 2013 sales were $275,000 or less and whose were $300,000 or more. Because the regional sales manager submitted his data with the sales rep names in the wrong format, you'll need to use text functions to clean up the data first. You have already set up and moved data to a new worksheet to do so.

1. Open the **annual_sales_overview.xlsx** workbook file and ensure that the **Regional Data** worksheet tab is selected.

2. Use text functions to place the sales rep names in the correct format.
    a) On the **Regional Data** worksheet, add a column between columns **B** and **C**.
    b) Use the LEFT function to return only the first letter of the sales rep's first names in the newly added column.
    c) On the **Clean Data** worksheet tab, use the CONCATENATE function to return all sales rep names in the following format: "Last, First Initial. Middle Initial." Example: "Smith, R. J."

3. In the **Bonus** column, enter an IF function that returns the text "Bonus" for all sales reps whose sales increased by $20,000 or more from the previous year and that returns the text "No Bonus" for all other reps.

4. Adjust the width of column **H** to accommodate the new text.

5. Use conditional formatting to add a green, upward-facing arrow to the **Previous Year +/-** column for all sales reps whose sales increased from the year before and a red, downward-facing arrow for all reps whose sales decreased.

6. Use conditional formatting to highlight the values in the FY 2013 column green with dark green text for all values greater than or equal to $300,000 and red with dark red text for all values less than or equal to $275,000.

7. Save the workbook to the **C:\091019Data\Analyzing Data with Functions and Conditional Formatting** folder as *my_annual_sales_overview.xlsx* and then close the workbook.

Lesson Lab 4–1
Organizing and Analyzing Datasets and Tables

Activity Time: 15 minutes

Data File

C:\091019Data\Organizing and Analyzing Datasets and Tables\raw_sales_data.xlsx

Before You Begin

Excel 2010 is open.

Scenario

You are a financial analyst at the distribution center for a mid-sized chain of U.S. department stores. Your supervisor has asked you for some detailed analysis on particular distribution orders to stores around the country for the second half of the fiscal year. Specifically, this is what she would like to know:

- What is the average, pre-tax sale for all transactions in the dataset?
- What is the total pre-tax sales figure for all grocery and electronics orders?
- How many total items did the company sell in orders with more than 20 items per order or in orders with pre-tax sales totals that are greater than or equal to $750?
- What is the average of pre-tax sales for each product department?
- What is the total pre-tax sales figure for each region?

You realize some of these questions would be best answered by converting the dataset to a table, whereas others would be more easily answered by using the dataset as a simple range. You've already made a copy of the dataset on a new tab to keep it as a simple data range.

---

1. Open the **raw_sales_data.xlsx** workbook file and ensure that the **Sales Table** worksheet tab is selected.

2. Convert the dataset to a table, apply a quick style to the table, and add a total row to the table.

3. Use a summary function to calculate the average, pre-tax sales for all transactions in the dataset.

4. What is the average, pre-tax sales for all transactions?

 Note: The solutions section at the back of your course book has the answers to the lesson lab questions.

5. Filter the table and change the summary function to answer this question: What is the total pre-tax sales figure for all grocery and electronics orders?

6. What is the total pre-tax sales figure for all grocery and electronics orders?

7. Clear the previous filter. Use advanced filtering and change the summary function to answer the following question: How many total items did the company sell in orders with more than 20 items per order or in orders with pre-tax sales totals that are greater than or equal to $750?

8. How many total items did the company sell in orders with more than 20 items per order or in orders with pre-tax sales totals that are greater than or equal to $750?

9. Switch to the **Sales Range** worksheet and use the Subtotals feature to answer the following question: What is the average of pre-tax sales for each product department?

10. **What is the average of pre-tax sales for each product department?**

11. Re-sort the dataset and then use the Subtotals feature to answer the following question: What is the total pre-tax sales figure for each region?

12. **What is the total pre-tax sales figure for each region?**

13. Save the workbook to the **C:\091019Data\Organizing and Analyzing Datasets and Tables** folder as *my_raw_sales_data.xlsx* and close the workbook.

Lesson Lab 5-1
Visualizing Data with Basic Charts

Activity Time: 5 minutes

Data File
C:\091019Data\Visualizing Data with Basic Charts\top_sellers.xlsx

Before You Begin
Excel 2010 is open.

Scenario
You have just finished summarizing sales figures for your team for the past year. You have created a summary dataset for your five top-selling sales reps. You want to report on their success at an upcoming meeting and you feel that using a chart would be the best way to do so. You plan to add a 3-D column chart to the worksheet and modify it a bit to make it easier to interpret.

1. Open the **top_sellers.xlsx** workbook file and ensure that the **Summary** worksheet tab is selected.

2. Add a 3-D Clustered Column chart to the worksheet based on the quarterly sales data for the sales reps. Do not include the **Total** column or the **Grand Total** figure in the chart.

3. Position the chart directly to the right of the original dataset near the very top of the worksheet.

4. Resize the chart so that it takes up most of the visible space to the right of the dataset.

5. Apply the **Style 42** chart quick style to the chart.

6. Add a title to the chart title at the top of the chart that reads *Top Sellers*

7. Add an X-axis title below the chart that reads *Sales Reps* and add a vertical title for the Y axis that reads *Quarterly Sales*

8. Save the workbook to the **C:\091019Data\Visualizing Data with Basic Charts** folder as *my_top_sellers.xlsx* and then close the workbook.

Lesson Lab 6–1
Analyzing Data with PivotTables and Slicers

Activity Time: 15 minutes

Data File

C:\091019Data\Analyzing Data with PivotTables, Slicers, and PivotCharts \raw_sales_data2.xlsx

Before You Begin

Excel 2010 is open.

Scenario

You've been asked to analyze your company's sales for the first month of the fiscal year. You supervisor has asked you several questions about your sales data and expects you to report back with your findings before the end of the day. As you will need to analyze the raw data from a number of different perspectives in a short period of time, you decide to create a PivotTable out of the raw data and to add slicers for the key fields you will analyze. These are the questions from your supervisor:

- How many of each item was sold from the housewares department for the month?
- What department sold the most number of items for the month, and what percentage of overall items sold does that represent?
- Which region has the highest pre-tax toy sales for the month and what was the sales total?
- Which three markets had the highest pre-tax sales in the electronics department and what are the sales totals?
- Which market has the highest average of clothing items sold per sale and how many items does it average?

---

1. Open the **raw_sales_data2.xlsx** workbook file and ensure that the **Jan Sales Data** worksheet tab is selected.

2. Create a PivotTable out of the entire dataset that appears on the same worksheet as the data.

3. Insert slicers for the **Region**, **Department**, and **Item Number** columns.

4. Use the PivotTable to answer this question: How many of each item did the company sell from the housewares department for the month?

5. **How many of each item did the company sell from the housewares department for the month?**

6. Use the PivotTable to answer the following question: What department sold the most number of items for the month and what percentage of overall items sold does that represent?

7. What department sold the most number of items for the month and what percentage of overall items sold does that represent?

8. Use the PivotTable to answer the following question: Which region has the highest pre-tax toy sales for the month and what was the sales total?

9. **Which region has the highest pre-tax toy sales for the month and what was the sales total?**

10. Use the PivotTable to answer this question: Which three markets had the highest pre-tax sales in the electronics department and what are the sales totals?

11. **Which three markets had the highest pre-tax sales in the electronics department and what are the sales totals?**

12. Use the PivotTable to answer this question: Which market has the highest average of clothing items sold per sale and how many items does it average?

13. **Which market has the highest average of clothing items sold per sale and how many items does it average?**

14. Save the workbook to the **C:\091019Data\Analyzing Data with PivotTables, Slicers, and PivotCharts** folder as ***my_raw_sales_data2.xlsx*** close the workbook and close Excel 2010.

Solutions

ACTIVITY 2–3: Locating and Using Specialized Functions

2. Which of these functions would best answer the question: How many authors have been with the company for five or fewer years?

    A: COUNTIF

ACTIVITY 4–3: Filtering Data

2. How many titles sell at the highest price?

    A: 43

6. Does the COUNT function result in the Sell Price column answer the question "How many authors have been with the company for one year or less?"

    A: Yes, the COUNT function in any of the total row cells would give the correct answer. A total of 48 authors have been with the company one year or less.
    Let the students know that the built-in functions in the Total row of tables reflect the currently filtered state of the table. So, in this case, for any filter performed, the COUNT function would accurately count the unfiltered entries.

ACTIVITY 4–5: Using Summary Functions in Tables

5. How many authors signed their initial contracts in 2012?

    A: 64

6. How much income did those authors produce?

    A: $197,351,621.43

ACTIVITY 4–6: Using Database Functions

3. What is the average number of books sold for these authors?
   A: 427,179

5. What is the total income earned by these authors?
   A: $550,441,558

LAB 4–1: Organizing and Analyzing Datasets and Tables

4. What is the average, pre-tax sales for all transactions?
   A: $526.99
   The solutions section at the back of your course book has the answers to the lesson lab questions.

6. What is the total pre-tax sales figure for all grocery and electronics orders?
   A: $36,575.83

8. How many total items did the company sell in orders with more than 20 items per order or in orders with pre-tax sales totals that are greater than or equal to $750?
   A: 3,255

10. What is the average of pre-tax sales for each product department?
    A: Athletics: $64.93; Auto: $547.62; Clothing: $523.14; Electronics: $530.49; Grocery: $486.72; Health/Beauty: $514.74; Housewares: $515.63; and Toys: $541.03.

12. What is the total pre-tax sales figure for each region?
    A: MW: $33,115.11; NE: $31,003.65; SE: $32,033.91; SW: $28,644.77; and West: $32,773.09.

ACTIVITY 6–2: Analyzing PivotTable Data

4. Which genre is the biggest overall seller?
   A: Romance with 110,272,958 copies sold

6. What is the total number of units of fantasy and romance books sold in the APAC and EMEA markets?
   A: 64,309,243

8. What percentage of total sales is made up of fantasy sales in the LA market?
   A: 2.91 percent

10. Which market has the highest percentage of science fiction sales?
    A: The NA market with 26.84 percent.

14. Which author has the lowest total sales?

    A: Author 1017 with $5,454,183.55

16. Which book for author 1017 has generated the most sales?

    A: BookTitle0135 with $2,390,754.44 in sales

18. What percentage of author 1048's total sales are electronic book sales?

    A: 15.21 percent

ACTIVITY 6-3: Presenting Data with PivotCharts

3. Which genre/market pair is the most successful in terms of number of units sold?

    A: The romance genre in the NA market.

ACTIVITY 6-4: Filtering Data by Using Slicers

5. How many romance print books has author 1029 sold in the APAC market?

    A: 1,935,355

8. Of author 1056's electronic fantasy and science fiction book sales in the NA market, what percentage is represented by science fiction sales?

    A: 31.42 percent

LAB 6-1: Analyzing Data with PivotTables and Slicers

5. How many of each item did the company sell from the housewares department for the month?

    A: Item 7001: 205; item 7002: 108; item 7003: 223; item 7004: 198; and item 7005: 102.

7. What department sold the most number of items for the month and what percentage of overall items sold does that represent?

    A: Housewares: 14.3 percent

9. Which region has the highest pre-tax toy sales for the month and what was the sales total?

    A: The Midwest (MW) region with $4,940.81 in toy sales.

11. Which three markets had the highest pre-tax sales in the electronics department and what are the sales totals?

    A: Midwest (MW): $4,834.58; Southwest (SW): $4,183.65; and West: $3,265.67.

13. Which market has the highest average of clothing items sold per sale and how many items does it average?

    A: The Northeast (NE) region with an average of 21.14 clothing items sold per sale.

Glossary

add-ins
Supplemental programs for Microsoft Office applications that provide additional features and functionality not available in a standard installation.

array
A range of data that can be entered into a computer's memory and accessed by Excel for data analysis that does not necessarily have to exist within worksheet cells.

array constants
Series of values, logical values, or text entries that are stored in memory or entered directly into array formulas, as opposed to being entered in cells.

array formulas
Type of Excel formula that allows users to perform multiple calculations on cells in an array simultaneously.

AutoFilters
Preconfigured, common filtering options that enable Excel users to quickly remove from view all data that does not meet some specified criteria.

cell names
Meaningful names users can assign to particular cells to make it easier to both understand what specific calculations are being performed in a formula and reuse the references for a number of purposes.

chart elements
The individual objects that can appear on charts and that convey some level of information to a viewer about the chart's data.

charts
Graphical representations of the numeric values and relationships in a dataset.

color scales
Various shades of color used as graphical representation of the relative values of cell data. Color scales are a type of conditional formatting.

comparison operators
Another term for logical operators.

criteria range
In terms of Excel advanced filtering and database functions, the worksheet range that contains the user-defined criteria to perform a particular operation.

Ctrl+Shift+Enter formulas
Also known as CSE formulas. Alternate name for Excel array formulas, as users must press **Ctrl+Shift+Enter** to enter an array formula.

custom AutoFilters
User-defined Excel AutoFilters.

custom sort
A user-defined sort that can be applied to either rows or columns, can be applied to

multiple rows or columns simultaneously, and that can be highly customized.

data bars
Graphical representations of the relative value of data in a range of cells compared to the rest of the data in the same range. Data bars are a type of conditional formatting.

database functions
Set of Excel functions that enable users to perform calculations on ranges of data based on specific criteria.

entry
An individual row of data in a transactional dataset. An entry represents one single transaction, such as a sale.

fields
The columns in a transactional dataset.

filtering
The process of removing from view any data entries that do not match some specified criteria.

icon sets
Collections of images used as graphical representations of the relative values of cell data. Icon sets are a type of conditional formatting.

level
In terms of Excel custom sorting, an independent, specific criterion by which a dataset is sorted. Users can specify multiple levels for a custom sort.

logical operators
Type of Excel operator used to compare particular values to determine whether or not they meet some specified criteria.

logical values
Excel data type that expresses whether or not particular data meets some specified criteria. There are only two logical values in Excel, TRUE and FALSE.

multi-cell array formula
Array formula that performs multiple calculations on arrays and display the results in multiple cells.

outline
Excel feature that enables users to organize datasets into hierarchical groups of varying levels of detail that they can expand or collapse depending on how much detail they want to see.

PivotCharts
Similar to standard Excel charts, these are graphical representations of numeric values and relationships among those values. The key difference between charts and PivotCharts is that PivotCharts are linked to the data in PivotTables.

pivoting
In Excel, a form of data manipulation that can take a column of data and pivot it into a row and vice versa.

PivotTable
A dynamic Excel data object that enables users to perform data analysis by pivoting columns and rows of raw data without altering the raw data.

quick sorts
Preconfigured sorting options that enable workbook users to quickly sort data based on common criteria.

quick styles
Preconfigured table styles.

range names
Meaningful names users can assign to particular ranges to make it easier to both understand what specific calculations are being performed in a formula and reuse the references for a number of purposes.

rule precedence
The order in which Excel evaluates and applies conditional formatting rules to cells.

separators
Vertical boundaries users can insert into the Quick Access Toolbar to organize commands into related groups.

shared slicers
Slicers that are connected to and that filter multiple PivotTables simultaneously. Any PivotTables based on a common dataset can share slicers.

single-cell array formula
Array formula that performs multiple calculations on arrays and display the result in a single cell.

slicers
Individual Excel objects used to filter the data in PivotTables.

sorting
The process of reordering worksheet data based on some defined criteria, such as alphabetically or from highest value to lowest value.

SUBTOTAL functions
A specific set of Excel functions that perform calculations on subsets of data.

subtotals feature
Excel feature that enables users to automatically perform SUBTOTAL function calculations on subsets of data within a particular dataset.

summary functions
Excel feature that automatically performs SUBTOTAL function calculations in tables. Users can access this functionality from the total row down arrows in each column.

table
A dataset comprised of contiguous rows and columns that Excel treats as a single, independent object.

table styles
Particular configurations of formatting options users can apply to worksheet tables.

text pane
Element of the Excel user interface that enables users to add and edit text on SmartArt graphics.

transactional data
Data that represents each individual transaction, or event, in a series of transactions, and that is not summarized in any way shape or form. Transactional data does not typically contain row labels, only column labels.

Index

091019S rev 1.0
ISBN-13 978-1-4246-2250-4
ISBN-10 1-4246-2250-6

90000

9 781424 622504